In the Wake of Suicide

*Stories of the People
Left Behind*

by

Victoria Alexander

Jossey-Bass Publishers • San Francisco

FIRST PAPERBACK EDITION PUBLISHED IN 1998.
THIS BOOK WAS ORIGINALLY PUBLISHED BY LEXINGTON BOOKS.

Substantial discounts on bulk quantities of Jossey-Bass books are
available to corporations, professional associations, and other
organizations. For details and discount information, contact the
special sales department at Jossey-Bass Inc., Publishers
(415) 433-1740; Fax (800) 605-2665.

For sales outside the United States, please contact your local
Simon & Schuster International office.

Jossey-Bass Web address: http://www.josseybass.com

Printed in the United States of America on acid-free paper.

Excerpts from "Little Gidding" in FOUR QUARTETS, copyright 1943 by
T. S. Eliot and renewed 1971 by Esme V. Eliot, reprinted by permission
of Harcourt Brace Jovanovich, Inc.

Library of Congress Cataloging-in-Publication Data

Alexander, Victoria.
In the wake of suicide: stories of the people left behind / Victoria Alexander
p. cm.
Updated ed. of: Words I never thought to speak. 1991.
Includes bibliographical references.
ISBN 0-7879-4052-6 (pbk.)
1. Suicide—United States—Psychological aspects—Case studies.
2. Bereavement—Psychological aspects—Case studies.
3. Suicide victims—United States—Family relationships—Case studies.
I. Alexander, Victoria. Words I never thought to speak. II. Title.
HV6548.U5A42   1998   362.28'3—dc21   97-37016
CIP

HB Printing
1 2 3 4 5 6 7 8 9 10
PB Printing
1 2 3 4 5 6 7 8 9 10

In memory of my mother,
Lois Roskam Goodman,
and in celebration of my daughter,
Kimberley Anne Alexander

Contents

Acknowledgments

Many people have contributed to this book. First and foremost, I am deeply grateful to all the people who shared their stories with me. Only some of those stories are included here, but all of them have gone into the making of this book and have contributed to its substance and form.

My gratitude goes out to many other quarters as well:

To Judi Gibian, Mauricia Alvarez, and Martha Cutler, my "witnesses and anchors." When I first sought the words to put to my loss, they were there, in the fullest sense I could ever imagine, and I will always be grateful for that gift.

To Elizabeth Merica, Steve Edelheit, Lorraine Loviglio, and Jim Goldberg—my very dear friends who are as passionate and persnickety about language as I am. They listened, read, spurred me on, read some more, and kept me honest.

To Mimi Elmer, Dorothy Koerner, Archie Brodsky, Karen Dunne-Maxim, and Dale Young, for their invaluable help in bringing this book to fruition.

To Margaret Zusky, at Lexington Books, for bringing it to print.

To Matthew Sperber, for his patience and innumerable tours of duty on the Massachusetts Turnpike.

To my Massachusetts and Vermont family, for their love, support, and relentless enthusiasm.

And to my Monday evening family, for always holding me to the possibilities within.

So I find words I never thought to speak
    —T.S. Eliot, "Little Gidding"

Introduction

This is a book of stories told by people whose lives have been touched by the suicide of someone close to them. Beyond that, it is a book about storytelling: finding the words for an unimaginable loss, speaking them out loud, and knowing that they are heard. The stories in this book are also, in a sense, encompassed by the story *of* the book. And that, in turn, is part of the spiraling story of my explorations over the past ten years.

On October 27, 1980, my mother killed herself. Before that day, suicide was simply a word to me, a rather abstract word that hovered on the outskirts of my mind, barely perceivable. It named something that happened in other, unknown families, certainly not in mine. But when my mother killed herself, a reality that had once been safely remote thundered through every corner of my life. What I was left with felt strange and bare, a lunar landscape. On that October day, suicide took up a permanent place in my consciousness.

After my mother died, I was hungry for information and for reassurance. I wanted to know what suicide *was* and what it was for my mother. I was searching for some way to make sense of the incomprehensible thing that she had done. And I wanted to know whether I would ever again have a life that felt whole, whether other people had survived this kind of loss and been able to put their lives back together again.

I combed the literature on suicide, trying to find something that spoke to me about my mother. Searching for answers to the questions rioting in my mind, I sifted through statistics, risk factors, case reports, and theoretical discussions. Even small bits of information, I thought, might point the way toward an explanation of what she had done, one that would put all the questions to rest. But I found nothing of what I was looking for.

And I found nothing that seemed to touch on the aftermath of suicide, with the exception of a few clinical articles on the "pathological" effects of parental loss in early childhood. I began to wonder why there was so much attention to preventing suicide and so little to the repercussions in other lives when it occurs. The silence on the subject was unsettling; it somehow seemed to confirm the freakishness of my loss and my fear that I would always be alone with it.

Three weeks after my mother's death, I started seeing a therapist. I told her the details of that day in October, voiced the questions, and searched, over and over, through my memories of my mother. I did the same with my close friends. I needed to speak these things in the company of people I felt I could trust. And as I did, I found that the telling made me feel less alone, less overwhelmed. I was also hungry to talk with others who, like me, had survived the suicide of someone close to them. I asked my therapist whether she could recommend a support group, but neither she nor her colleagues knew of any groups for survivors of suicide. They knew of bereavement groups, but none that dealt specifically with bereavement after suicide. I had the sense that there was something so shameful here that no one wanted to touch it, least of all those in mental health. To recognize that a population of people might need some help in dealing with the aftermath of suicide in their lives would be to acknowledge that efforts at prevention too often fail, and that acknowledgment comes hard. The instinct to preserve a life is much stronger than the desire to address a death, especially one that is intentional.

Frustrated, I finally decided to start a group myself, and did so a year after my mother's death. An important thing happened for me in that small gathering, and it was apparent from the very first evening, when we introduced ourselves and said whom we had lost and how. Telling my story and listening to those told by the others in the group, I found that my experience of loss resonated with theirs in many ways, despite differences in circumstances, relationships, and so forth. We were strangers to one another, and we were talking about secret, horrific things, yet I felt a strong connection with these people, as if I had found some familiar faces in a faraway place.

During this time, I continued to look for books or articles that would speak to my experience, and eventually I came across two. Neither concerned suicide, yet both touched on feelings that I knew well. The first was *Children of the Holocaust*, by Helen Epstein, an exploration of the emotional heritage of the Holocaust for the children of the survivors. The second, an article by Barbara Kaplan titled "A Survivor's Story," was an account of an attack by a patient at a mental health clinic that had seriously injured the author and killed two of her close colleagues. Both authors described their struggle to make some sense of an overwhelming loss and to understand what it meant in their lives. I was transfixed. These stories covered a terrain that was familiar to me: the barriers of silence, the isolation, the need to tell and to be heard, and the powerful connection with other survivors who had experienced similar losses.

Gradually, as I felt my life becoming whole again, I started to think about writing a book on the aftermath of suicide, drawing on my own experience and on the stories of other survivors. I began by interviewing five people about their experiences of loss in the wake of suicide. I decided to transcribe the tapes of these interviews and then plan the structure of the book before going on to do more interviewing. As I transcribed, I was struck both by the power of the stories that these people had told me and by the force of their telling. Until then, I had assumed that the book would be in my words and that I would use portions of the interviews to illustrate the points I wanted to make. But as I listened and transcribed, it became clear to me that I did not want to carve up these stories. Their power seemed to lie in the very act and language of the telling. I began to envision a book of spoken stories, grouped in a way that would give the reader a sense of the evolution of grief after suicide.

As I sat alone in my office at home, transcribing the tapes, I also began to feel overwhelmed. The pain that I heard on those tapes swelled my own, and I realized that, though it had been three years since my mother's death, it was too soon for me to be undertaking this outward exploration; the one within was still too immediate. I shelved my plan to write a book, not knowing whether it would ever come to fruition.

Three years later, in 1986, I was invited to write a chapter for a book titled *Suicide and Its Aftermath: Understanding and Counseling the Survivors* (edited by Edward Dunne, John McIntosh, and Karen Dunne-Maxim). Intended primarily for an audience of mental health professionals, the book was to include a section of personal accounts by survivors. I was asked to write about my experience of my mother's suicide. Having still not returned to my earlier plan to write a book, I welcomed this opportunity, thinking that a chapter about my own experience, although not what I had originally intended, might at least satisfy my urge to write something that could be helpful to other survivors.

I had a hard time writing that chapter; every phrase seemed to bear so much personal weight and history. But I felt a sense of completion when I finished it and later saw it in print. Instead of putting to rest my earlier desire to write a book, however, the experience rekindled it. Now, looking back, I realize that I needed to tell my own story fully, not only orally but in writing, before I could undertake a book of other people's stories. The process of writing about my mother's suicide helped clear the way, and I came to a juncture in my own personal exploration where I could resume the work that I had put aside earlier.

In the past two years, I have interviewed forty people about their experiences in the wake of suicide; two of the forty I had first interviewed several years earlier. To find people who would be willing to talk with me about their loss, I put the word out through friends and colleagues, posted a sign-up sheet at a regional conference for survivors, and sent letters to the leaders of support groups in several New England states.

Of the forty people I interviewed, thirty-one are women and nine are men—an imbalance that probably reflects the relatively greater ease with which women seem to be able to voice their grief and seek help in doing so. Many more women than men attend support groups for survivors, although the number of men is increasing.

Twelve of the people I interviewed (including two siblings) had lost a parent, nine a spouse or lover, five a sibling, five a child, three a close friend, and three (siblings) a stepparent. I also talked with three therapists (two social workers and a psychiatrist) whose patients had killed themselves. The suicides had occurred from seven months to more than twenty years earlier. At the time of their loss, the survivors ranged in age from eleven to more than seventy years, but the majority were in their late twenties to early forties.

Ten of the people I interviewed work in the field of mental health. This high proportion is probably not surprising, given my own work as a writer and editor in that field. Some of these people were already working in mental health at the time of their loss; others entered the field later in their lives. Three have led support groups for survivors, and many others have attended such a group. Many have also sought help in the form of individual counseling.

I talked with many people in their homes; some came to mine. Two of the people I interviewed who lived in another state generously offered to put me up for the night. In two homes, I was shown the room where the suicide had occurred. I was also shown photographs of those who had died, suicide notes, and other writings. One woman read to me from a journal that she had kept before and after her sister's suicide. I interviewed a man whose lover had killed himself after a long battle with acquired immunodeficiency syndrome (AIDS); later, I saw the panel in the AIDS quilt that commemorated his life.

Time after time, I was struck by the generosity and the courage of the people I interviewed. They knew little about me, yet they opened up the most painful parts of their lives to me. Many of them said that they hoped, by doing so, to be able to offer something of value to other survivors. Many also wanted to know about my story, and sometimes that led to a dialogue about similarities and differences in our experiences of loss. In fact, these were really not interviews at all in the sense of question-and-answer sessions. I would ask a preliminary, open-ended question just to get people started, and they would take it from there; the stories simply unfolded. For the most part, I listened rather than questioned, occasionally mentioning something from my own story or asking a question for clarification.

The experience of going to people's homes (or having them in my home) and listening to their stories was powerful for me. I often felt the same quick, deep connection with these people—strangers to me, and I to them—that I had in the support group.

I came away from the interviews enriched by the wisdom of the stories I had been told and honored to have been entrusted with them.

Each interview lasted from two to three hours. I tape-recorded it and then transcribed the tapes. I asked people to read the transcripts of their interviews and make any corrections or deletions that they wished but not to add extensive written material, since I wanted to preserve the spoken words. I also asked them to decide whether they wanted me to change names or other identifying details of their stories. (This was a question I had struggled over several years earlier. On the one hand, I wanted to honor each person's right to decide what felt comfortable. On the other hand, one purpose in doing the book was to address the problem of secrecy, and a book of stories with concealed identities, I had thought at the time, would undercut that purpose. Now I see it quite differently: a question of privacy rather than secrecy.)

After the transcripts had been reviewed, I assembled a story from each interview. In spoken speech, the narrative line often digresses and jumps back and forth in time or from one substory to another. A transcript can be difficult to read because of these shifts and, more important, because the physical context of the telling (gesture, intonation, facial expression, and so forth) is missing. The challenge I faced was to assemble a spoken story that would also read well. To do this, I omitted certain portions of the transcript and saved others for a later part of the story. Passages were rearranged to preserve the chronology of the account and of the journey through grief. I edited the language as little as possible, only correcting grammatical errors, omitting extraneous words or phrases, and clarifying certain references. I allowed my own words to enter into the stories only to the extent that I felt the need to clarify by adding or substituting a word or phrase (for example, substituting a person's name for the pronoun *she*). Otherwise, the words are entirely those that were spoken to me.

Thirteen stories (some in two parts) are included in this book, yet all forty told to me over the past two years have left their imprint on these pages and are thus an integral part of the book. I hope the stories in the chapters that follow will speak to people who have survived the suicide of someone close to them. Just as I felt a strong connection to those who told me their stories, reading them may help others feel less alone with their pain and more hopeful for their own lives. The stories in chapter 4 tell how people, over time, have not simply survived a loss from suicide but grown from their experience of that loss and moved on to lead full lives.

Although I have written this book primarily for survivors of suicide, it may also speak to people in the mental health professions, some of whom are themselves survivors of suicide in their personal or professional lives. Others not directly touched may find that they gain a greater understanding of the emotional repercussions that suicide leaves in its wake, so that they can be helpful to survivors who seek counseling.

Finally, I hope that this book will be of interest to people who are neither survivors of suicide nor therapists but who simply want to know more about this kind of loss, perhaps to be able to listen—or to listen more easily—to someone else's story. To listen fully is perhaps the greatest gift one can give to those who are trying to find a voice and a language for their grief.

PART ONE

We tell ourselves stories in order to live.
> —*Joan Didion*, The White Album

Suicide, Grief, and Storytelling

Death brings an end to one life but is only the prelude to loss in other lives. This is true of any death, whether it is sudden or expected, the result of physical illness or an accident. After a prolonged illness from cancer or AIDS, a sudden heart attack, or a car crash, death leaves the survivors to struggle with their loss and its meaning in their lives. Like a fatal heart attack, suicide is sudden, and like an automobile accident, it is violent; like death from cancer or AIDS, it marks the end of a long battle with pain. Suicide is all these things, and the suffering of the survivors is as intense, complex, and paradoxical as the act of self-destruction itself.

In one respect, suicide is unlike other deaths: it is a deliberate severance—the most profound act of disconnection that a human being can undertake—from one's own self and life, from others who have been part of that life, and from the human community. Suicide is an untimely chosen death, carried out alone and most often secretly. The isolation, secrecy, and discon- nection of suicide become the survivors' legacy.

Over the past decade, suicide has been brought out of the shadows into the light of public concern. Until recently, how- ever, our focus has been entirely on prevention: how to prevent people from taking their own lives. There has been little atten- tion to the fact that our efforts at prevention sometimes fail and that, when they do, the repercussions in other lives are profound. Suicide is the end of one person's struggle, but it is just the beginning for many others—the survivors of suicide.

To survive, says *Webster's Ninth New Collegiate Dictionary*, is to "live on . . . to remain alive after the death of [someone else] . . . to continue to . . . live after [a catastrophe] . . . to continue to function or prosper despite [a loss or catastrophe]." The term *survivor* has become a prominent part of our current language, reflecting our concern with the problems of rape, sexual and physical abuse of children and women, and alcoholism in families. The people who live through and beyond these experiences of violence and disruption are often identified—and identify themselves—as survivors. Those who, against all odds, have survived catastrophe are also called survivors: the Jews who lived through the Holocaust, the surviving residents of a town wiped out by an earthquake, the few passengers who somehow escaped death when their airplane plunged to earth. These are people who, largely or entirely by chance, have survived wholesale violence and destruction.

Yet when used in the context of suicide, the term *survivor* has caused some confusion. In clinical parlance, it may refer to someone who has attempted suicide and survived that attempt. Despite its ambiguity and the confusion that it sometimes causes, the term has persisted as a way of identifying a person who has experienced the loss of someone close through suicide. This use of the word is fully in keeping with the other uses that speak to the sense of living through an overwhelming personal or collective loss.

Who are the survivors of a suicide? They are all the people who experience that death as a loss in their own lives. Survivors are family members, friends, lovers, colleagues, neighbors, schoolmates, therapists, and even whole communities. Ultimately, we are all survivors, in the sense that when one individual ends his or her life, that death is a loss for human society, for all of us collectively, as well as for some of us individually.

The statistics on suicide only hint at the magnitude of its repercussions. The eighth leading cause of death in the United States, suicide claims some 30,000 lives each year. But those are only the deaths reported as suicide. Many suicidal deaths are attributed to other causes, either to avoid the stigma associated with suicide or because the intentionality of the death is ambiguous or masked. For example, a drug overdose may be reported as an accidental death even though it was, in whole or in part, an intentional act of self-destruction. A fatal automobile collision may well be the result of suicidal behavior. Substance abuse and various forms of risk taking represent indirectly self-destructive behavior. Some researchers believe that the actual number of suicides is double or triple the reported number, accounting for 60,000 to 90,000 deaths each year.

Whatever the actual number, each of those suicides has enormous repercussions in the lives of other people. Assuming, as a conservative estimate, that at least five people are profoundly affected by one suicide, some 150,000 to 450,000 people become survivors of suicide each year. These large numbers are startling, because we tend to think of suicide—and the loss of someone close to that kind of death—as unusual. In fact, loss from suicide is all too frequent, but because it is so often veiled in secrecy and silence, we think of it as an uncommon experience.

Language and Taboo

Suicide is a word that is often whispered or avoided; it is the stuff of rumor and speculation. Obituary notices tiptoe around the word, using evasive phrases such as "died suddenly." Survivors may avoid public use of the word, instead referring to a "sudden illness" or "heart attack" when questioned about the cause of their loss, or they may simply change the subject entirely.

It isn't easy to find the language to talk about suicide or about its aftermath for the survivors. The words are few, and they come hard. They don't fit well with the other words we use to clothe our lives in familiar ways of thinking, feeling, and seeing. The few words we can find for suicide are harsh when spoken aloud; they put an end to innocent conversation: "She killed herself"; "He committed suicide"; "She took her own life." These are brutal words for brutal losses. We have no way to gentle them. Language is a good barometer of our cultural aversions, and the poverty of our language for suicide and its repercussions says much about our discomfort with the subject. Suicide, after all, is one of our most powerful taboos; it threatens both our individual connections with other people and our collective connections as a social community. Individually and collectively, our instinct is to avoid the term as a way of retreating from the reality that it names.

The secrecy and silence that surround suicide have a long history in Western culture. Over the centuries, the act of suicide has been considered a sin against God and a crime against the state, with punishments meted out accordingly. The bodies of people who killed themselves were denied burial rites and publicly desecrated, sometimes in particularly gruesome ways, and their property was confiscated. The problem, of course, is that death brings immunity to punishment, as it does to all else in life. The pain of these harsh sanctions was felt not by the person who had died but by the surviving family members. They suffered the consequences of the forbidden act, as if by proxy. To protect themselves, they learned to cover up the true cause of death, to remain silent. Fortunately, our sanctions against suicide are no longer so severe, but the legacy of shame, secrecy, and silence is still, in large measure, with us.

Grief After Suicide

Grief is a universal human experience and one that is unique to each person. Both our mortality and our need to connect with others make all of us vulnerable to loss. Yet it is also true that the way in which a person experiences a loss—whether from suicide or another kind of death—is shaped and colored by the particular combination of personality, physiology, family, and culture that makes that person an individual. Just as people have idiosyncratic styles of expression and gesture, they also have characteristic styles of thinking and feeling that influence their response to loss.

The self-help movement has done much to reassure us of the universality of trauma and loss. Through support groups and the media, people have found solace in the knowledge that others have gone through similarly painful experiences—rape, childhood incest and violence, substance abuse—and have struggled in similar ways to give them meaning and integrate them into their lives in an affirmative rather than a destructive way. This need to be reminded that we are not alone is especially strong when it comes to experiences that are linked with taboos and are therefore stigmatizing, engendering feelings of shame and aloneness. Even more basic is our need to categorize individual experiences and generalize from them as a way of affirming our humanity. But in considering the similarities among individual experiences of loss and grief, it is important that we balance a generalized view with an equivalent appreciation of differences.

Much has been written in recent years about the stages of grief that people experience after the death of someone close. Elisabeth Kübler-Ross's writings on the terminally ill have helped many people struggling to come to terms with their own impending death. Her books have also helped surviving family and friends find a path through their grief in the aftermath of death. Kübler-Ross traces that path through a series of stages: shock and denial at first, then guilt and anger, bargaining, depression, and finally acceptance.

The landscape of grief after suicide has similar features, yet the path through it is not nearly as straight as these stages might suggest. It starts at the same place—shock and denial—and eventually arrives at the same destination—acceptance—but in between those two points, the path turns and twists, at times so sharply that it almost seems to be doubling back on itself. Grief after suicide is often unpredictable, erratic, even terrifying, leaving the survivors to wonder whether there is really any path at all. There is, and in many ways it is the same as the path through grief after other kinds of loss, but in the aftermath of suicide, it may be longer and more difficult to follow.

A sudden death is almost always greeted by shock on the part of the survivors, because they have had no opportunity to prepare for the loss or to anticipate its repercussions, both practical and emotional. Suicide is no exception. It is a sudden death that is almost always unanticipated. Even if preceded by earlier attempts or a long history of self-destructive behavior, suicide takes the survivors by surprise. No matter how well acquainted one might be with the self-destructive thoughts and actions of another person, there is something that keeps one from fully accepting the possibility that the line between life and death, however narrow, will really be crossed. When that line is crossed, the mind simply cannot take in the reality. Shock intermittently numbs the mind and the heart, as well as the body, providing a kind of respite as the survivor experiences the suddenness of the loss.

Suicide is not only a sudden death but a violent one. It is, after all, self-murder. Moreover, the means of suicide may be particularly violent—a gunshot blast to the head, a leap from a tall building, asphyxiation by hanging. Many suicides happen at home, and the person who discovers the body is often a family member. For these survivors, the shock of discovering the body, which may be badly disfigured, is added to the shock of the loss itself.

Denial is a close partner to shock. Confronted with the news of a sudden death, the mind instinctively recoils and refuses it. A common first response is "No, it's not true!" After a suicide, the denial may be fed by feelings of shame, prompting the surviving family members, when passing along the news to relatives and friends, to explain the death as the result of an accident or sudden illness. Sometimes the survivors themselves become convinced that the death was not a suicide but a murder or an accident. Any measure of ambiguity surrounding the suicide may also feed the inclination to deny it, especially if the police are investigating the death for any signs of foul play. Even murder, at some level, might be easier to take in and accept than the realization that the death was intentional.

The rites of death provide an important structure in the initial period of loss, a time when all the usual habits and expectations that dress our daily lives fall away, leaving the survivors feeling bare and helpless. Attending a funeral service, sitting shiva, holding a wake—these and other rituals provide a framework for the first expressions of grief, while the survivors are still in shock and have not yet assimilated the full reality of their loss.

After a suicide, however, some survivors retreat from public exposure, feeling that the death is too shameful to be acknowledged publicly and that they, just by virtue of being the survivors, are somehow tainted by it: "What kind of person would do this, and what kind of person am I that my brother or wife or child would leave me in this way?" As a result, they may decide to bypass the usual rituals, choosing a private burial, for example, with no formal period of condolence. Behind closed doors, the feeling of shame is augmented as the survivors cut themselves off from the usual social networks of support and comfort—friends, relatives, neighbors, co-workers. This tendency toward isolation may be prompted by actual public judgment or by anticipation of it. And sometimes the survivors' own judgment—whether of themselves or of the person who has left them in this way—is confused with their experience of being judged by others.

Shame is a social emotion in the sense that it is linked to social definitions of unacceptable behavior, and suicide is clearly defined as unacceptable in our society. When someone dies by suicide, the response to that act is visited upon those who were closely connected with that person. The public reaction may range from condemnation to sympathy, but even at the latter end of the spectrum, there tends to be an element of uneasy questioning: What went on in that family to drive that person to suicide? As suicide is brought out of the shadows, there is wider recognition that it is the act of a desperate person experiencing excruciating psychic pain. This has tempered, to some extent, the whispers and rumors that violations of taboo behavior so often spawn, but the tendency to judge is still there in many instances. The survivors are attuned to those whispers, so much so that sometimes they are imagined rather than real. Either way, the sense of shame can loom large over the landscape of grief after suicide, making it difficult for the survivors to find—and perhaps to accept—comfort and support as they struggle with their loss.

Suicide seems to engender blame. We feel compelled to find someone at fault for an act that we consider unacceptable. We may call the person who has chosen to exit in this way a coward, or we may implicate the surviving family, speculating about what would drive a husband or wife or child to such a desperate end. Like shame, blame tends to be contagious, and even when it is placed squarely on the person who has died, the survivors, in their very proximity to that person, may feel the brunt of it. Indeed, the survivors may blame themselves for the suicide of this person with whom they were so closely connected, or they may blame someone else—another family member, perhaps, or a therapist. Sometimes the need to find an external locus of blame blankets a deeper sense of self-blame that is too frightening to acknowledge.

Much has been written recently about the clues that people

provide, however covert or subtle, when they are feeling suicidal: giving away favorite possessions, for example, saying such things as "Maybe you'd be better off without me," demonstrating abrupt changes in mood and behavior, or even speaking directly about their wish to die. Public education about these and other signs of suicidal behavior is, of course, an essential part of the effort to prevent suicide. In its aftermath, however, the survivors may blame themselves for having overlooked these clues or not taken the signs seriously enough. Hindsight can exercise a relentless tyranny, as the survivors struggle with their own role in the suicide: "If only I hadn't fought with him that night, he'd still be alive today"; "If only I had stayed home that day, I might have been able to talk her out of it"; "If only I'd kept that gun locked up, he wouldn't have shot himself." Revisiting the events leading up to the suicide over and over again, the survivors castigate themselves for what they did or did not do. Grief after suicide is made all the more painful by these feelings of guilt and self-blame.

Anger is another feature of the landscape of grief that may be particularly prominent in the wake of a suicide. Not all survivors feel anger, just as not all survivors feel shame or guilt, but it often arises as people struggle with their loss. For some, anger is a prominent part of the landscape from the very start. For others, it emerges later in their grief, either abruptly or gradually. It is difficult to be angry at someone who is no longer alive, and it may feel safer or easier to direct that anger elsewhere—at oneself or at some other person who, just by virtue of being alive, is present to receive it. As the survivors struggle with their sense of responsibility, they may focus their anger on themselves for not having foreseen or prevented the suicide. As they begin to experience the full force of their abandonment, the anger may be redirected toward the person who has left them: "How could you leave me like this? How could you leave me *with* this?"

Suicide is such an incomprehensible act that we are driven to find some explanation for it, one that will reassure us that there is meaning in our individual and collective lives. Grief after suicide is punctuated by a litany of recurring questions: "Why did he do it? Why that night? Why that way? Why, why?" The survivors search frantically for answers to these and other questions, fearful or even convinced that they cannot resume their own lives as long as those answers elude them. Sifting through the minute details of the days and weeks that preceded the suicide, turning over and over in their minds the intonation, shade of meaning, and accompanying glance of every word in every remembered conversation, they try to find clues to an explanation that will give their loss a context of sense and meaning. This compelling need to reconstruct the person and the act is a response to the void in which the survivors find themselves. The answers they seek, however incomplete, have been taken away; they are as unreachable as the person who died.

At a deeper level, the questioning and the search for answers are an attempt to bridge the gulf that suicide creates between those of us who choose to live and those who choose to die. Ironically, most of us do not even realize that we make that choice each day of our lives, but suicide teaches us that we do. It takes us to the farthest regions of our lives and dares us to look over the edge. Grief after suicide is largely experienced in these remote regions, and it can be terrifying to the survivors. A "tiny giant step," as one survivor has put it, separates those of us who continue to live from those who choose to cross the boundary. In the wake of suicide, some survivors may feel suicidal themselves, as Catherine did after her lover's suicide (see the first part of her story in chapter 2). Others may simply wish to know what it feels like to want to cross that boundary, as a way of trying to reconnect with the person who died. Chris, for example, whose story appears in chapter 3, tells of her fantasies about taking that tiny giant step as she holds a kitchen knife or stands in the shower and thinks about drowning. These thoughts are a way of feeling closer to her brother, who, by killing himself, "has done something that no one here has done [and is] distant because of that."

Perhaps the hardest and lowest point of grief that survivors experience in the wake of suicide is the feeling of powerlessness. Having struggled with questions of their own role in the death—how they failed and what they might have done to keep that person alive—they must finally come face to face with the limitations of their responsibility. In the end, we cannot keep another person alive; we cannot exercise that kind of power over another life, no matter how closely connected with it we are. And yet, at the same time, we are responsible for our part in that connection. There is always something we might have done differently, but it might not have made a difference. We do and do not make a difference in other people's lives; we are both powerful and powerless. That is the paradox that suicide teaches us. It is a painful lesson but one that is also in some sense freeing.

As the survivors find their way along the path that leads through grief after suicide, most eventually come to the point where they are ready to put aside their search for answers and acknowledge the limitations of their responsibility for, and power over, other lives. Having arrived at this point, they are finally able to accept their loss and regain a sense of power in their own lives. In a sense, the entire journey has been a struggle to find a way to say a full good-bye after the door has been shut. Perhaps this, more than anything else, is what characterizes the landscape of grief after suicide.

Giving Voice to the Loss

Storytelling is as fundamental to human life as language. By telling stories, we bear witness to our own lives and to our connections with others. Memory and metaphor, the tools of our telling, give substance, shape, and continuity to our experiences so that we can link past and present, self and other. In the face of events that threaten to overwhelm our lives, storytelling gives us a way of reclaiming ourselves and reaffirming our connections with other people—those who listen to our stories and, by doing so, bear witness with us.

The stories that survivors tell in the wake of suicide start with an end and work toward a beginning. They are powerful stories, and their power lies not simply in their content but in the very act of telling them. Why should telling the story of a loss by suicide be so powerful? The answer goes back, once again, to the legacy of suicide: the secrecy, silence, and disconnection that frame the act and are passed along to the survivors. Taboos and secrets go hand in hand. In a society where the word *suicide* is whispered more often than spoken out loud, the act and its repercussions tend to be shrouded in secrecy. By giving voice to their loss, by speaking of it out loud and being heard by others, the survivors break the secrecy and put an end to the silence. Perhaps most important, in the telling they begin to find a way of reconnecting—with both themselves and others.

Many survivors feel compelled to tell of their loss; to retrace the years, days, and hours preceding the death; to reconstruct the life and person they have lost; to give full voice to the hundreds of questions that suicide leaves in its wake. As people find their way through their grief, the stories they tell begin to change. At first they are stories of lost lives; eventually, they become stories of lives that have experienced loss. The storytelling mirrors a change in the survivor's sense of self—from a person whose life has become defined by the suicide of someone close—father, wife, child, lover, friend—to a person with his or her own life and own story. By telling of their loss and knowing that they are heard, the survivors can gradually claim it as part of their own history and move on in their lives.

In the immediate aftermath of suicide, the survivors struggle to find words for their loss, to frame it and make it real. Just the feel of the words as one forms them and their sound as one speaks them help let in the reality, bit by bit. Suicide is unspeakable, and to speak it is somehow to bring it into a human, imaginable sphere, even if only in the moment of speaking.

The need to tell is both a need to tell oneself and a need to be heard. If one can speak the unspeakable to another person, the burden is somehow shared. One is not alone, and the secret no longer has the power that it did when unspoken. By giving voice to their grief in the company of other people whom they trust, the survivors begin to find a way through it, however obscure the path may seem at first. Telling and being heard are the first steps toward reconnection. Here is how Natalie (who tells the first part of her story in chapter 2) explains why she needed to tell other people about her mother's suicide, which was particularly violent:

The first day I sat by the phone and called up all the friends I felt fairly close to. My way of dealing with the shock, the unbelievableness of it, was to tell each person. I didn't want other people to make the phone calls for me, because if I did it twenty times, maybe I'd start believing what I was saying. Each time it was a relief to me. Each time, if I could allow myself to break down while telling people what had happened, it gave me an enormous amount of comfort. . . .

I think the thing that healed me the most was that I was able to talk to people about what happened. I told people the gory details. I would go through, step by step, what happened. And all of that was necessary for me to repeat and repeat and repeat. This is what happened, then I did this, and then this is what happened. Telling people how she killed herself became enormously important to me. Each time I would tell someone how, in my mind I would imagine it, and the horror of it would somehow be worked out for me. I could imagine this horrible thing, and I didn't feel so alone. I brought people with me so that I didn't have to go through imagining it alone.

As they are able to take in the reality of the loss, the survivors become more fully engaged with the questions that suicide leaves in its wake. Giving voice to all the if onlys and the whys, over and over as they arise, people can begin to move through them, however long it may take, and eventually be able to put them aside.

By finding their way through their grief and giving it full voice, most survivors are gradually able to accept their loss. Where the suicide once swamped any sense of self or hope for a full life of one's own, it now assumes a smaller place within that life. The need to tell subsides, and at the same time, the telling becomes more comfortable, the story a more integral part of one's life history. Natalie (whose story is continued in chapter 4) explains the change she experienced in her need to tell:

When people ask me about my parents, I say that they're both dead, and I don't have trouble saying how my mother died. There might be circumstances in which I wouldn't tell, but if they're people I like and I'm getting to know, I want them to know who I am and what my life has been. There was a time when it felt pressing to tell people about my mother's suicide. I almost couldn't be with someone unless that person knew. Now it really surprises me to think that in the group of people I've met more recently, there are some who didn't know for a long time. I didn't have to tell them. I could be with these people and feel that they actually knew me without my having to say, "There is something terribly important that you should know about me."

Storytelling not only reflects but also aids the process of grief and healing after suicide. Naming it, speaking the words of loss, one gradually claims it as part of one's own life story, an experience through which one can move and grow rather than remain a silent hostage to it.

Although the stories that survivors tell all start with an end and work toward a beginning, they are not all the same. Each is unique, just as each experience of loss and grief is unique. Yet the stories, like the experience, have much in common. They are all stories of the struggle to take in, understand, live with, and accept another person's suicide, then move on with one's own life—to say a full good-bye.

Finding a Way to Tell the Story

Storytelling requires a listener as well as a teller, and a time, place, and context for the telling. After a suicide, the listeners and the opportunities for telling may seem few, particularly if the survivors are inclined to retreat from public exposure and seek refuge in silence. Ingrained in all of us is the instinct to turn away from suicide. By naming it and telling about it, one risks losing the listener. Again, there are no gentle words for the story of a suicide and its aftermath. It takes courage to find the words that need to be said and to speak them. They are brutal and harsh, perhaps too frightening for some people to be able to hear them and continue to listen.

Moreover, the path through grief after suicide is long and arduous. Opportunities for giving voice to the grief may be ample at the beginning of that path but diminish over time, while the survivors are still trying to find their way along it. Natalie says:

I worried that people would eventually tire of hearing about it, that I would wear out my welcome. Mostly, that didn't happen. But after about six months to a year, they needed to have it behind me. It wasn't uniform, and I wouldn't say it was all the time, but even with people I think are very sensitive, there was a real aversion to staying with it for that long. They didn't have to stay with it, and I could understand that they wouldn't want to. I had to stay with it, because it wasn't gone yet. . . . There was a certain amount of tolerance beyond which people could not deal with the magnitude of the loss that I had experienced. Their wanting it to be over was their way of containing the horror of it for themselves. That's the way I came to understand it. At a certain point, they really reached a limit. . . . I had the sense that there wouldn't be someone who could listen long enough and hard enough to what I had to say for me to feel that I had really been heard, to the end.

Survivors need to feel that they have the time to tell and retell their stories and that their listeners will really hear the words they speak, to the end. But, like Natalie, they may find that the story is too frightening for some listeners to stay with as long as is necessary for the full story to be told.

Many people find it easier to voice their grief in the company of other survivors. Support groups provide a valuable opportunity for storytelling and for listening. Survivors often find comfort in knowing that the stories told in these groups partake of one another, describing the same essential experience of loss. Telling one's own story to other survivors and bearing witness to their stories can be enormously healing. Teller and listener realize that they are traveling the same path, which makes the journey more bearable and helps counteract the feelings of shame and isolation that are so common in the wake of suicide.

Individual counseling can also be helpful in giving survivors an opportunity to tell their stories as they make their way through their grief. Some survivors seek pastoral counseling, others psychotherapy. In each case, the healing comes in having a trusted listener bear witness to one's story and hear it through—as it is told and retold, as it changes and evolves—to the end. The purpose of all these resources is to provide a safe setting in which survivors can voice their grief in the aftermath of suicide, speaking that which seems unspeakable and telling stories of loss that eventually grow into stories of their own lives.

As more and more people tell their stories, and as we bear witness to the dimensions of suicide, its impact on individual lives and on our collective life as a society, we will find—and voice—the words for the loss that we all suffer as survivors.

PART TWO

Every phrase and every sentence is an end and a beginning,
Every poem an epitaph. And any action
Is a step to the block, to the fire, down the sea's throat
Or to an illegible stone: and that is where we start.
                              —T.S. Eliot, "Little Gidding"

The stories that follow are of and by survivors trying to find a meaning and a context in their own lives for the loss by suicide of someone close to them. Divided into three sections, the stories reflect the process of storytelling as survivors gradually make their way through their grief, first trying to find the words to put to such a loss, then struggling to live with and understand the import of those words, and gradually finding a place for them within a larger and continuing life story. Chapter 2, "At the End / At the Beginning," contains stories about suicide and its early aftermath. Chapter 3, "In the Midland," describes the long pathway through grief, as the survivors experience the deeper repercussions of suicide in their lives. In chapter 4, "Then and Now," survivors look at how their experience of loss has changed over time. Where names have been changed, I note that fact in the introduction to the story. I have also included a small part of my own story as a prologue to each section. Although these three chapters reflect an approximate chronology of grief after suicide, it is important to bear in mind that the duration and timing of each part in the process varies from person to person.

Every story is one and many, a story within a larger story within an even larger story. And even though the stories that follow are divided into three chapters, as the tellers make their way along the pathway of grief over time, the later stories contain earlier ones within them. For example, although the stories in chapter 4 speak primarily to the experience of loss years after the suicide, some contain within them stories from the beginning and the midland of grief. The story of now in some measure always encompasses the story of then. Where these stories within stories are more easily separable, I have placed them in different chapters. For example, Natalie's account of the beginning of her grief (although told years later) is in chapter 2. Her story about her life now is included in chapter 4. Both are part of the larger story that she tells about her loss.

The six stories in chapter 2 are the most difficult to read, because the pain they describe is raw, not tempered by time or change, as in subsequent stories. But I have arranged the book in such a way that it need not be read from chapter to chapter. Since five of the stories in chapter 2 and one in chapter 3 are continued in later chapters, some readers may want to follow a particular story from one chapter to another rather than reading all the stories in a chapter before moving on to the next. The chapters can also be read independently of one another; it is not necessary to read the stories in chapter 2 before reading those in chapter 3 or chapter 4. Read a chapter at a time, the book gives a sense of the regions of grief; read a chapter at a time in sequence, it gives a sense of the overall movement through those regions; read a story at a time, it tells of individual journeys through grief.

Every story is unique not only to the teller but also to the time and place of the telling. If each person whose story appears in this book were asked to tell it again, it would be a somewhat different story, because time changes the telling. If told to a different listener in a different place, the story would also change. In some sense, then, these stories are like photographs: they reflect a perspective bounded by time, place, and context. That perspective inevitably changes and grows over time and over the course of one's life. Yet there is something lasting about these stories as well. They provide an important personal and collective documentation of life after suicide.

2

At the End / At the Beginning

Each of the six stories in this chapter is about the end of a life and the beginning of grief in the life of the survivor. Some of these stories, told years after the suicide, are continued in chapter 4. Catherine's story, told a year and a half later, is continued in chapter 3. One story, Joan's, was told just nine months after her son's suicide; it is entirely about the end and the beginning and is therefore told in full here.

Prologue

OCTOBER 27, 1980. Monday, a late-afternoon hour of sudden darkness—clocks having just been turned back—that is etched deep within me. This is the day my mother chose to end her life. I don't know the time of her death; I never asked the medical examiner or saw the death certificate. But I know well the moment of her death in my life: it was the very moment that my father said to me, as I pulled into the driveway, "She's dead; she killed herself." And yet it took many moments—many days, weeks, and months—for those words to fight their way through the thickened layers of a life built on thirty-one years of expectations about my mother. She might be taken from me by illness or accident (even that was unthinkable), but she would never abandon me.

She did. She cut a length of garden hose, attached one end to the exhaust pipe of the car, and ran the other end into the window at the driver's side. My mother had no sense of smell, for some reason, although she had said that, once in a great while, she could smell gasoline fumes. She died from the carbon monoxide that filled the car. I've wondered whether she lived long enough to smell the exhaust fumes.

I couldn't take any of it in on that Monday afternoon. I ran up the stairs of my parents' apartment, first into the kitchen. I was looking for some sign from her, a sign that this was anything but what my ears had heard and my mind refused to let in. I could not bring myself to look at my mother in the car; instead, I looked for her in the apartment. And I found her everywhere: in the coffeepot on the kitchen counter (a cup's worth left over from breakfast—so unlike her to leave it there), in her handwriting on a shopping list next to the phone and on a calendar hanging on the wall, in every corner of the bedroom, but especially on the bedside table, where she had left a note for each member of her family. I found signs and notes but no sense. She was everywhere and she was gone, the door slammed shut.

The notes were written on envelopes, with something of hers inside each. My note said, "This—and all my other jewelry. And all my love—and hope that you will forgive— I know that someday there will be happiness for you." Inside was the opal ring she always wore. Just the evening before, she had asked me to try it on. That memory froze me in my tracks. The night before— Why wasn't I paying attention? I could not wear that ring any more than I could have bent a razor blade around my finger, but I also could not be without it. I put it on a chain and wore it around my neck.

Beginning that night, a host of fears took up residence within me. I was afraid of the dark; it seemed bottomless. I was afraid to sleep; if I closed my eyes and let go, my mother's ghost might visit me in the night, disfigured and full of accusations. In the daylight hours, I braced myself for the next disaster—my daughter struck by a car, the house in flames. This one had overtaken me while I was looking the other way. I hadn't been paying attention. From now on, I would keep watch and be prepared. It seemed the only way to ward off all the losses that I sensed waiting in the shadows.

My life as I knew it fell away from me on that Monday. Only remnants were left, reminders of how comfortably, unquestioningly, I had clothed myself in the assumption that those people who were most important to me would still be there when I awoke in the morning.

✱

Natalie: Dreams of Catching Her

Natalie (not her real name) is a social worker in her late thirties who lives with her husband and young son. In January 1981, sometime during the early hours of the new year, her mother jumped from the roof of an eighteen-story building. Natalie, single at the time, was visiting from out of state. I interviewed her eight years after her mother's death.

Natalie's story tells of the struggle to come to grips with an extremely violent form of death and with all the contradictions surrounding suicide, which can be haunting. One person may choose a relatively nonviolent means of dying—a drug overdose or carbon monoxide poisoning—and leave an angry note behind. Another may choose a violent end—a fall from a tall building or a bullet shot at the head—after writing a gentle good-bye. Some people take great care, as Natalie's mother did, to make sure that the family members will not be the ones who find the body. Others kill themselves at home. One might assume that the more violent suicides are also more impulsive, less carefully planned, but this is often not the case. Natalie's mother made intricate plans for the jump to her death. Such contradictions are left for the survivors, part of the aftermath of suicide.

My mother killed herself on one of the coldest days of the year, during a period of subzero temperatures. It was not just winter; it was like hell. I mean, it was unbelievably cold. She went out in the middle of the night and jumped off an eighteen-story building. The violent aspect of her death is something I can barely keep in my consciousness for more than a second at a time.

For the longest time, I obsessed about her being cold. I guess you attach yourself to these stupid little things. The thought of her being out in the cold just drove me crazy. I found her boots in the car, and I got very freaked. What was she wearing? Did she go out barefoot? I asked the police what they'd found on her feet. I wanted to know what she was wearing, and basically the coroner's report was a list of every bone in her body being broken. They said, "There's nothing left of what she was wearing. It was all shredded." That was one of the things I obsessed about—her shoes and whether she was cold.

I went through garbage pails, looking, trying to put together pieces of paper that she had torn apart, so I could figure out what was going on. It was just pure hell going through that, having your world fall out and trying to put the pieces together, trying to figure out what could have happened.

I had been visiting her that week, and I thought, "How could I have not known? How could I have not figured it out?" She had hidden everything. She had gone to the point of trying to rent an apartment so that she could jump out of it. Later, we found all these ads that she'd clipped. And in fact, she'd put a deposit down on an apartment. I don't know whether it was so that she could get inside the building and see what it was like and how she could do this. It was like a James Bond thing. My mother was a schoolteacher who never did anything; I don't think she ever had a traffic violation. Yet she had worked out this elaborate scheme. She had made all these calls about apartments and had gone through the process of putting a security deposit on one of them. She had rented a car and hidden it somewhere, because it was nowhere near the house. She must have parked it far away.

The night my mother killed herself, my sister got a phone call, at around 4 A.M. My sister said she heard a kind of whispering sound at the other end. At the time, she thought it was a crank call. Afterward, we were pretty sure it was my mother, that she wanted to hear my sister's voice. She may have been in a psychotic state by that point, or she was just trying to keep my sister on the phone so that she could hear her voice before. . . It's hard to imagine someone being that tortured. It's not hard to imagine, it's hard to let in that she could have been that tortured. And that was always the hardest thing for me with my mother: she was in a lot of pain, and I just couldn't do anything to help her. I tried. I feel that most of my growing up had to do with realizing that I couldn't. And it just rips me apart, because it's so sad.

My mother and I had seen the movie *Elephant Man* the

night that she killed herself. It's about a person who was so physically deformed he felt he had no place in the world and was totally a misfit. At the end of the movie, he lies down to sleep, which because of his deformity essentially kills him. I was holding my mother's hand in the movie theater, and when that happened, I squeezed her hand. I don't know what was going on, whether she thought I knew she was going to do it, and she felt that was my way of saying it's okay. I was just feeling that I knew how alone and awful she felt.

It blew me away that that's what we saw that night. I think maybe if we had seen something else, if we hadn't seen that movie, maybe she could have changed her mind at the last minute. People have gone over this with me a million times. She had planned this—she had rented a car, looked for apartments. She had been doing this for weeks. It's not something she thought of that night. But I just think, how could we have seen *that* movie *that* night? It was one of the saddest movies I've ever seen in my life. And to me it encapsulates that experience, the whole time. My mother's deformity was totally internal—it was her experience of herself—but I don't think she felt any less of an elephant person.

Sometime late that night she drove to the apartment building in the rented car. She went up to the roof and jumped. I can't imagine what she was thinking as she looked over. She left her purse and a stepladder. There must have been a ledge, and she needed the stepladder to get over it. I don't know whether she brought the ladder with her or found one when she got there, whether she got there and all of a sudden realized she couldn't do it without a stepladder—I don't know.

She left a note in her purse saying that the person to contact was my sister's boyfriend. She made sure that neither my sister nor I would be contacted by the police, that we would be told by someone else. She didn't want either of us to be alone when we found out, and I think the way she thought it out was by starting it off with the first contact not being either of us but my sister's boyfriend. Then he would tell my sister, and my sister would tell me. I think she chose not to be in the house so that neither of us would find her body. I don't think she thought that we'd still have to identify her body.

The next morning I woke up and noticed that the front door was ajar. I didn't understand that. I never could understand why she didn't close the door after she left. She didn't have any keys on her, and I guess my fantasy was that she wanted to get back in the house. That was my wish, somehow, that she was allowing herself to get back in.

Her bedroom door was also slightly ajar, and it looked like she was in bed. My mother was an early riser, and it was unusual for me to get up before her, but I figured she was sleeping late. Finally, it was about 10 A.M., and I thought it was really odd, so I opened her door, and I realized that the bed was stuffed with pillows. I think at that point I knew that something was terribly wrong, but my denial kicked in. I started looking around for her. I called my sister, who said to call her back in an hour if I hadn't heard from my mother. Her car was still there, and I couldn't imagine where she'd gone. That was the thing that really threw me off: her car was there. It never occurred to me that she had rented a car.

I started driving around, thinking maybe she had walked somewhere. Maybe she'd gone crazy, and she had just all of a sudden done some lunatic thing. Not that my mother had ever done anything like that, but I was thinking of these possibilities more than thinking that she could have done something like kill herself. But I know that was in the back of my head, because eventually I drove over to my aunt's house. My aunt had died six weeks earlier. I looked in the window. I was terrified, because I thought I'd see my mother lying there, dead. That's where I thought she would have gone. I thought of death and my aunt and her going back to my aunt. And she had gone back to my aunt, in a sense; she'd killed herself. There are times when I get into otherworldly kinds of thoughts . . . that somehow my mother was with everybody she had always wanted to be with all these years and had been separated from through death: my father and her father and mother and my aunt.

We didn't realize that she'd rented a car until we got a call from the rental place a few days later. We ended up having to go to the building where she'd jumped, because we had to find the car and return it. That was awful. My sister and I were both terrified to go there. It was as though we thought we'd see her lying there, although by that time we had buried her. But I had to get out and look. A newspaper story had said something about a broken tree limb, and I wanted to see which tree was broken.

For the longest time, whenever I passed a tall building, I'd start counting—one, two, three—trying to figure out whether it was as tall as the building my mother had jumped from. Most of them were not eighteen stories. I'd count the stories, and it would be fourteen, and I'd think, "Bigger than that?" I'd seen the actual building, but it was just this unconscious thing where I'd pass a building and start counting stories.

Another thing I got very stuck on was my mother's letter to my sister and me, which she'd left in her purse. At the police station, after we'd identified her, they wouldn't give us the letter. I guess they wanted to keep it because there had to be some kind of investigation to make it official that it was suicide. Someone could have pushed her, I suppose, which of course entered my mind. You know, it's so unbelievable that a lot of unbelievable thoughts come into your mind. Suicide seemed as bizarre as the idea that she might have been having an affair with some person and he pushed her. What's more bizarre? They're all bizarre!

At first, the police were only going to let us read the letter. They wanted us to leave without it, but I would not leave. I said, "This is all I have left." They'd seen the body of my mother, which was in a bag essentially, and that they could even imagine keeping that letter from us seemed like more of an injury than we should have to bear. They finally gave us a copy.

I wanted the letter read at the funeral. That was the other part—not wanting to hide that it was a suicide. My uncle asked me what I wanted to say to people, and I said, "What do you mean? I'm not ashamed. That's what she did, and that's who my mother is, and I'm not ashamed of it."

The funeral, in a way, is a blur to me. There were so many people there, and I was fixated on wanting the letter read and not hiding the suicide. My sister and I had gone back to the temple we had belonged to when we were kids and asked the rabbi there to do the ceremony. The only thing I insisted on was that the letter be read. Other than that, I said, "Do a funeral." The rabbi did read the letter, but he left off the last line, which was, "I can't go on."

One thing that was really bizarre was that the rabbi's name was the same as my mother's maiden name. There was a way that I attached myself to these kinds of things and drew great comfort from them. I felt they were signs of something.

It was amazing how many things like that happened. When

we sold my mother's house, the lawyer representing the bank was the same lawyer who had been there when my mother and father had bought the house thirty years before! He had done the closings for the developer. The same person who'd sat with my mother and father thirty years before, when they'd bought the house, sat with me and my sister when we sold it. And my mother killed herself after making the last payment on that house. The last payment had been made, the house was finally hers, and she killed herself.

I was very attached to that house. After my mother died, I felt that I needed to soak it up as much as I could before it was gone, because I knew that part of my life had been irrevocably changed and taken away from me. I felt comfort in the house. I wanted to be close to my mother. I wanted somehow to get whatever it was that she was trying to say. I was desperate for answers, desperate to know, desperate to feel connected to her.

I don't think I could have made it without my sister. We had different ways of coping and different ways of wanting to deal with the situations that arose, but we had always been very tight, and through the initial period after my mother's death, we were incredibly close. We went through a rough time shortly after that, which I think had to do with the anger that was bouncing off the walls at that point. Just the basic stress of what we were dealing with could make any two people go at each other. But also my mother was removed as a buffer between us. In some ways, we'd been able to put a lot of the tension in our relationship—the competitiveness or whatever—onto my mother, and now we were left with each other. We were dealing with this trauma together, and we desperately needed each other, yet sometimes we drove each other up the wall.

My sister and I have very different styles. I'm more of a talker, more of an emoter. This is all relative. When I'm in a group of people, I realize that I'm pretty shy, but my view of myself is so shaped by how I was in my family. In that microcosm of the world, I was the emoter and my sister was the quiet one.

We were like Siamese twins for the first twenty-four hours after my mother died, and for the next two weeks we were like Siamese twins attached by a string. The first night we didn't let each other out of sight. The thought of losing each other, even if only by sight, was unbearable, so we stayed together.

Someone had told me, at some point, that spirits don't leave the earth for twenty-four hours. I said to my sister, "We've got to talk to her, because if she's still around, it's our only chance to clean up our act with her." We cried and we laughed and we half-jokingly tried to talk to her. We were trying to reach her or reach ourselves or something. Basically, I think we wanted forgiveness from her. And what we were probably saying was that we forgave her, that we loved her and wanted her to be at peace, finally. But I think we were also terrified that she was around and would grab us up. It's a wish and a fear at the same time. It's the wish to have the person still be there and the denial that the person is gone. The fear is that what's happened is horrific; it's murder. When people kill themselves, there's violence. Will they come and get you? Will they take you with them? To me, that's part of the stuff of survivors—being scared that we'll kill ourselves, too.

I had many dreams about my mother. They were all nightmares to me. Often, they were dreams of me trying to catch her. I had awful dreams, so awful that I couldn't stand them. But I'd also been terrified after my father's death, when I was a child. I remember being scared to take showers. So in a way it's not only the suicide aspect; it's the death itself that's scary. Death is such a hard thing to comprehend. When someone dies, it brings death closer to you, so you fear you'll be taken. Maybe the fear comes from beginning to deal with your own mortality.

After my father's death, when I was so scared of ghosts, my mother said to me, "If your father did come back, you know he would never hurt you, because he loved you very much." She didn't say, "There's no such thing as ghosts." She said, "Your father's ghost would never hurt you." That helped me when my mother died, because I believe in my heart that she truly loved me and didn't want to hurt me. There are ways that she did things that were hurtful to me but never intentionally, always almost against her will. So I think that I let her statement come back to me and comfort me.

Other than finding out about the suicide itself, closing out my mother's house was the hardest thing I ever had to do. It was the house that I had grown up in. It had every piece of that life in it, and it was also the only place that I had known my father. So letting go of that house was really saying that I didn't have any parents anymore and that I didn't have a family, in a sense. There was no way that I could ever again feel like a child in this world. I was an adult, like it or not, for the rest of my life. I had no cushion. I was really dealing with the rock bottom of it, the realization of how completely and drastically my life had been altered, how it would never be the same, and how my parents were never to be in my life alive.

And then there was the whole issue of possessions, the classic who's going to get what. God help me, I never thought I'd get into that, never in a million years! I was from the nonmaterial era—you know, give me a sleeping bag and an orange, and I'll survive. And here we were, my sister and I, fighting over my father's desk, the only thing that we knew was my father's possession in the house. We both wanted it, and we each felt the other wasn't willing to make compromises. I know this is how she felt, and I felt the same way. In the end, I said, "You can have the desk," because I felt that my dead father's desk was not as important as my living sister. I'm sure she would not see it as generously as that, because she thought I got everything else! And I felt that I gave her the only thing I really cared about. We were each in our own camp. When I look back on it now, I think I felt that I wasn't getting what I wanted. I didn't want this whole situation, and the fact that I didn't get the desk was just part of the picture—things were not going my way. And maybe I allowed those feelings to surface around the possessions. At the time, some of those things stayed with me and became important.

My sister and I healed over a period of time; it took a while. We were really angry but not disconnected; we never gave up on each other. This was the first time in our lives that we were really angry with each other, other than when we were children. But there was always such unconditional love and support between us.

I was so devastated and needy when my mother died. I was like a dry sponge; any little bit of moisture I made into more than it was. If someone said anything nice to me, I could take that small amount of support and stretch it into a much bigger thing, because I was just needing so much at that point.

I contacted my mother's former therapist, and the things that she said that were comforting to me I held on to and really milked for all they were worth. [I felt as though] my mother had somehow said, "You're not okay enough for me even to stay alive for." When her therapist saw me afterward, she didn't say, "You're the daughter? You're the cause of this. You were terrible!" She still treated me like an okay person. And for my mother's therapist to be doing that meant that maybe I didn't have to think I was as awful as I could have thought I was.

As much as I was struggling internally with all these things, to the external world I was coping remarkably well. People were just amazed that I seemed to be handling it so well emotionally. Plus I was dealing with the police, the funeral arrangements, lawyers, and closing the house. And in all my dealings, I think I was coming across as appropriately sad. No extremes—I wasn't falling apart, and I wasn't pretending that it hadn't happened. I was the perfect bereaved survivor. That people perceived me this way helped me feel that I could keep on keeping on.

I did allow myself to depend on people in a way I hadn't ever before. The first day I sat by the phone and called up all the friends I felt fairly close to. My way of dealing with the shock, the unbelievableness of it, was to tell each person. I didn't want other people to make the phone calls for me, because if I did it twenty times, maybe I'd start believing what I was saying. Each time it was a relief to me. Each time, if I could allow myself to break down while telling people what had happened, it gave me an enormous amount of comfort. And people's responses to me were incredibly genuine and wonderful. I didn't feel stigmatized at all.

I think the thing that healed me the most was that I was able to talk to people about what had happened. I told people the gory details. I would go through, step by step, what happened. And all of that was necessary for me to repeat and repeat and repeat. This is what happened, then I did this, and then this is what happened. Telling people how she killed herself became enormously important to me. Each time I would tell someone how, in my mind I would imagine it, and the horror of it would somehow be worked out for me. I could imagine this horrible thing, and I didn't feel so alone. I brought people with me so that I didn't have to go through imagining it alone.

I worried that people would eventually tire of hearing about it, that I would wear out my welcome. Mostly, that didn't happen. But after about six months to a year, they needed to have it behind me. It wasn't uniform, and I wouldn't say it was all the time, but even with people I think are very sensitive, there was a real aversion to staying with it for that long. They didn't have to stay with it, and I could understand that they wouldn't want to. I had to stay with it, because it wasn't gone yet. I remember saying to one friend, "I'm worried that you'll think there's something wrong with me because I'm still so upset." And she said, "Oh, no, I don't think that. If you were still like this in a year, then I would worry about you." I made a mental note of that, and I said to myself, "Okay, in a year I'll never say another word about it to this person." There was a certain amount of tolerance beyond which people could not deal with the magnitude of the loss that I had experienced. Their wanting it to be over was their way of containing the horror of it for themselves. That's the way I came to understand it. At a certain point, they really reached a limit.

I was always in a race against time. I was trying desperately to make sure that I could push everything back in and get it all back together in the time frame that I thought people expected of me. I had the sense that there wouldn't be someone who could listen long enough and hard enough to what I had to say for me to feel that I had really been heard, to the end.

[Natalie's story is continued in chapter 4, page 180.]

Laura: Right at the Core of Life

Laura's husband killed himself in June 1984, shortly after their separation. She was twenty-eight at the time. She met her husband's family and visited his homeland for the first time when she flew to Britain to attend his funeral service. I interviewed Laura almost five years later, in March 1989. The names in her story have been changed.

The abrupt disconnection of her husband's suicide was also the occasion of a series of unexpected, and equally abrupt, new connections for Laura. Her story suggests how the very sense of loss and dislocation that survivors feel in the wake of suicide may hold a surprisingly intense experience of the immediacy of life. Dreams also are important to Laura's story. They tell a parallel story of her evolving understanding of the part she played—and the part she did not play—in her husband's life and death.

I sometimes think of this whole experience as something that gets thrown up into the air and lands in a million different places and then gets put together in a new way.

When I met Stuart, I was twenty-five and he was twenty-three. He was just shy of his twenty-sixth birthday when he died. He was from Wales. He was extraordinarily brilliant and funny and gifted but kind of failed, in a lot of ways, in his life. He was very much the defeated existentialist. We fell into a relationship, and within a very short period of time, it became clear to me that it was not right and that what he needed from me I couldn't give him.

Eventually, we broke up, and Stuart got into therapy and was put on antidepressants. We were somewhat bitterly estranged for several months and then had a dramatic reconciliation. We decided to go for broke and were married in December of 1982.

It was a really pathological relationship in a lot of ways. We got into couples counseling, and I began to understand that what

I was doing with Stuart was my story, my history with my family. When my brother, who's six years older than I, was born, he had a cerebral hemorrhage and almost died; [it left him with] minimal brain damage. My sister was killed in a car accident the day that my mom found out she was pregnant with me. I came into this really broken family, and I was the "perfect child." I thought it was my role to heal everybody. So I spent my life being smart and funny and cute and capable and relational. And then Stuart came along.

I carried a secret around with me after Stuart died. I was in therapy for some time before I finally put it out, because it felt weird and shameful. When I was seven or eight or so, I had this play fantasy that I was in love with Paul McCartney or Chad Mitchell of the Chad Mitchell Trio—it varied. I used to listen to these records all the time. And in the play, we were in love and he wanted me to marry him. I wouldn't marry him, and he would try to commit suicide. Then I would be at his bedside saying, "I'll never leave you again. I'll love you, and we'll be happy." And then we would live happily ever after. I went home shortly after telling this story to my therapist and talked it over with my mom. I learned that when I was about six, my father, who's a filmmaker, was making a training film for police about how to intervene in suicides. The director was at our house all the time and apparently had a number of friends who had committed suicide, so there were these discussions about how to keep people from committing suicide.

In September of 1983, Stuart tried to commit suicide and I intervened. We had had a horrible fight. It was the middle of the night, and I was sick with the flu. He wound up going into the bathroom and was there for a long time. I finally came out and called his name, and he didn't answer me. I looked under the door and saw his feet on the floor with what looked like a phone cord dangling. I looked and saw that the phone cord was off the phone, and I realized that he was trying to hang himself in the bathroom with the cord. So I banged on the door, and I screamed, "Stuart, if you don't open the door right now, I'm going to throw on my clothes and run into the hall and scream and wake up all the neighbors. They're going to come and break down the door!" And then he came out with this horrible mark around his neck. It was really a dreadful experience.

A few months later, we decided we would end the marriage.

Stuart got increasingly depressed. At first he decided to go to St. Croix, where we had gone on our honeymoon. It sounded like he wanted a geographic cure, and there was something frightening to me about his being so isolated. I think I was afraid that he might kill himself there, and I'm sure that he would have. I talked him into going back to Britain. There was a part of me that wanted to get rid of him and wanted to send him home to his family, although he had absolutely no relationship with them. But I was tired, and I think I needed to stop taking responsibility for his life.

We had a very sad last few weeks together. The last few days, I started to backpedal and said, "This should be a separation, and then in December let's talk, and maybe. . ." I just couldn't let go. He sort of went along with that. And I remember saying to him that if he decided to kill himself, I promised to forgive him and to accept that as his choice. I was really trying to let him have responsibility for his own life. And I said, "But promise me one thing. Promise me that you'll say good-bye first." And he promised me that. Since then, I've come to understand a lot about the role that I played in sort of entrapping him in promises that he couldn't keep. I thought I was giving him responsibility for his life, but I was really trying to control him.

About a week later, on Monday, I was at work, and I got the news. I had had a profound experience over the weekend. I'm not one who believes in paranormal events particularly, although I'm also a true agnostic, and I don't say they can't happen. I had a dream that I was in the apartment, where there was a closet that we had never really used. In the dream, the closet door was quite small, and it led to a series of tunnels, like a catacombs or an Egyptian tomb, with spiderwebs and secret chambers, dark and cold. Stuart and some others—I don't know who those others were—had gone into this tomb and had disappeared. They were either dead or about to die, or perhaps they would come out at the other end of the tunnel. There was some sense that there was another end, that you could come out into the world. It was *really* frightening. I felt that I had to go in there to rescue them, and I was scared to death. I didn't want to do it, because I was afraid of dying in there. There was some hope that they might be okay anyway, or it might be too late, and I couldn't know that. It didn't even feel like a choice. I *had* to go in there.

I was trying to get prepared to go in and was almost pro-
crastinating, thinking that the longer it took me to get stuff
together, the greater the chance that they would emerge through
the other end and be okay. I remember that I found some dental
floss, and I thought, "Dental floss will be good, because it's long
and sturdy and I can tie it to the beginning and leave a trail for
myself so that I can find my way back." Then, all of a sudden, I
lost the dental floss. I had just had it in my hand, but it was
gone. My mother had given me keys to the front door of my
apartment, in case I came out of the tunnel much later and
everybody had gone to bed. I could let myself back into the
apartment if I had these keys. But I wanted to have as little to
encumber me as possible. And I kept thinking, "Oh, God, I
don't want to go in there."

That was the dream. It left me with this profound sense that
Stuart was going off to this place of death and that I was trying
to save him by following him, at my peril. And I didn't want to
do that.

That was Saturday night. Sunday I was watching TV, and on
comes this movie called *The Slender Thread*, about a psychology
student who does volunteer work at a suicide hot line and a
woman committing suicide. He's talking to her, and she's telling
her story. And part of the story is about a bird. She finds a
dying bird on the beach, and she's trying to save it. It took me
back to a time when I had found a dying bird and had taken it
home and tried to keep it alive. I mean, things just kept on
entering the picture that felt so symbolic.

Monday I went to work, and I was called out of a meeting
for a phone call. It was my mother. We had talked about the
possibility that Stuart might someday—*some day*—kill himself.
And she just said, "It happened sooner than we thought. Stuart
overdosed." In the split second of hearing that, I thought he had
overdosed on drugs of some kind, but I didn't think he was
dead. In this half second, before the rest of the sentence, I
thought he was in a hospital somewhere. Then she said, "And
the funeral is Wednesday." And I just said, "Oh, my God!" in
this sort of high-pitched voice. While waiting for me to come to
the phone, Mom had told the person who answered what had
happened, and the word had gotten to my coworkers. I was in
my office, sitting on the floor and talking to my mom, and I
absolutely couldn't believe it. My office door opened into a big

room. I looked out into the room, and all these women, my coworkers and friends, were there. It was like an eerie tableau of women holding each other in pairs, crying. And then somebody came into my office and sat behind me and just put her hands on my shoulders.

At that time, I was smoking these clove cigarettes—not a lot, but I would take a couple of hits maybe once or twice a day. It was sort of like a legal high. And I started chain-smoking these things. I still had a cold, and every time I inhaled, it was like getting kicked in the chest by a horse. It was almost as if I needed that to remind myself I was alive, you know? Because everything was changed—my body was changed and the way I saw the world and felt the world and heard the world. It was like being in Jell-O. And there was something about inhaling and feeling the pain in my lungs that brought me back to reality, just kept bringing me back.

I flew to Britain Wednesday morning, and Stuart's family met me at the airport—his mother, the man she later married, and Stuart's sister. I had never been to Britain, and I'd never met my in-laws. We just fell into each other's arms crying. They are the most loving, caring, decent people, and we formed a very intense bond. That was one of the real benefits. I mean, suddenly we didn't have Stuart, but we had each other. And I learned more about him in three days than I had known in three years. It convinced me of the importance of really getting to know your man's family and history.

I was there for about a week and a half. It's hard to describe, but it was a strange mix of the deepest sadness and loss and the highest. . . The words that I search for are words like ecstasy. It was like being right at the core of life. My husband had just committed suicide, and here I was confronting this very existential reality of aloneness and despair and meaning or lack of meaning. Here I was trying to make sense of it, and I think I was connecting in a very deep way to my sense of life and of meaning—how Stuart had made a choice to die, and getting up every single day is a choice to live. I was suddenly so aware of life and death and everything in between. So I want to say there was a way in which my experience felt good—that's really a very inadequate word. Part of me also needed to have that experience. That's what I did to keep myself from just collapsing into a little puddle in the corner and never emerging again.

The times alone, when I'd go to bed at night, were horrible. I did keep a journal, which was very useful to me and very interesting to look back on. At times, I misremember what my experience was; I think of it as all one way or not enough of this way. And I look back in the journal and see that I wasn't as helpless as I remember, which is nice to know.

It was summer [when I was in Britain]. I can remember going to bed at ten thirty at night, and it was still light outside. I'd never been in an environment where it's still light at ten thirty. It just contributed to the sense of surreality. It was so beautiful and eerie and different. Everything was different. I remember reading an article several years ago called "Why Men Love War." It was a very well-written, powerful article. There was one line in particular where the author described the experience of being at war by saying, "It's like you've lifted up a corner of the universe and peered underneath." That's what this felt like to me, like I had suddenly been beamed into another kind of existence.

I saw Stuart's body at the funeral home. I was ushered into a little room that was all candlelight and chapel and a casket. Stuart was in the casket, wearing this white, synthetic satin. He looked like the nutcracker, from *The Nutcracker Suite*. He had this gauzy thing over his face, and I pulled it back. It didn't look like him. I remember checking his hand. Stuart had a wart on his hand, which was very distinguishing. His hands were folded, and I remember checking. The wart was there, and then I knew that it was Stuart, that he really was dead. If I hadn't seen him dead, I think I would have had active fantasies about him coming back. I *still* had fantasies about him coming back, even though I saw his body. What would I do if he just appeared around the door? I would be so mad at him.

The casket was closed for the funeral. And I can remember the pallbearers, these red-faced men grunting and carrying the casket. They were strangers, hired hands. The organist was a woman about 110 years old. She had blue hair and was wearing a hat that looked like an inverted bird's nest. And she had glasses with these clip-on sunglasses that were flipped up! In the midst of all the pain, she was playing the organ. It was almost as if Stuart was [looking] over my shoulder. I could hear him making some funny, biting remark.

What was hard about the funeral was that there was a lot of religion, and Stuart was an atheist. I really felt there had to be one person there who didn't betray him at the end by praying or going through the religious rituals. I spent a lot of energy being loyal to Stuart in whatever ways I could.

There was a nice point in the service when the vicar said, "Take a moment to remember Stuart in a way that you want to remember him." And I flashed on this: Stuart had found a rug—his boss was throwing it away. It was a fake Oriental rug. And we had been talking about wanting to get some kind of rug. I remember Stuart said, "Oh, oh, I got something!" And I said, "Is it a rug?" And he went, "Da, daaaa!" He was cute. Stuart didn't often do cute. He was far too sophisticated to do cute. But in some ways that was the essential Stuart, that was the Stuart I really loved. So I had a chance to remember him in that way.

I sat through the whole service and cried. There was a hymn that I wanted to sing, but my throat just wouldn't sing. And then it was over. At the end, these little doors opened, and the casket disappeared. But the machinery that moved the casket groaned. I remember thinking it was amazing the way life kept getting in the way of death. We just could not send him off as flawlessly as he had sent himself off. That was very reassuring to me.

Afterward, we went out to a cement patio around which there were little wire stakes that you could put cards and flowers on. And there was an area set aside for flowers for Stuart, including a wreath of roses sent over by my staff in the States. I think I knew that they were sending something, and I remember looking for flowers from them. I had this mounting fear that they wouldn't be there and that I would be alone. And then I saw the wreath. It was so important to me. I really felt I was not alone. I took a rose from the wreath and saved it.

We stood around a bit, and then we went out to the parking lot. I was aware of an odor, a very distinctive odor of burning flesh. This was a crematorium. I turned around and saw a chimney out of which was rising a huge, wide, black column of smoke. I couldn't believe that was Stuart. I couldn't believe that they didn't wait until we had left, that they would allow him to be so . . . huge and black and . . . I remember I was holding my sister-in-law and looking over her shoulder, and she was weeping. I just stared at the smoke, and I could smell it. Even though I was appalled, I was breathing it in so greedily, as if I were taking him in for the last time. I didn't say, "Hey, look up there, that's Stuart." It was a secret. It was this thing that I was experiencing, and I was just taking it in.

And then I spoke with the woman who had found him [at the Y in Britain where he had killed himself], and she was lovely. She didn't even know him, but she came to the funeral. I asked her questions. She said he had looked peaceful, and that was good to hear, because he didn't have a lot of peace in his life. I really took whatever I could as comfort.

When I was on my way back to the airport, we stopped to pick up the ashes. We had them put in two boxes, one for Stuart's family and one for me. On the way back, I kept that box with me the whole time. I didn't want to lose it; I didn't want it to get lost. I mean, this was half my husband.

I think possibly the worst part of the whole experience for me—it's so painful even to remember this—was when my friend Judy, who had picked me up at the airport, dropped me off at my apartment. I had to come back to my apartment alone. Another friend had been looking after my cats, Phoebe and Murphy. They are not outdoor cats. When I got back, Murphy was there but Phoebe was not, and the window was open. We were on the fourth floor, and the window was open. I literally tore the house apart. I opened closets, I opened drawers—everything was turned around. That's when I lost it. I just walked around in circles, almost hysterical. I went outside and walked around the neighborhood crying and calling, "Phoebe! Phoebe!" I wanted to go look for her by the reservoir, but it was dark out. And it was just like the dream: I needed to go and rescue Phoebe—I thought she might be there—but I was scared to death. I didn't go. I thought, "God, if this is a result of Stuart's suicide, it would have been the one thing that would have kept him from killing himself." He loved the cats; he loved them so much. And I could not bear the idea of losing Phoebe, too. Finally, when I came back to the apartment, I went out the back and called one more time and heard this meow, and she was there.

A couple of days later, I opened the box that had the ashes in it. They were in two lots, in bags. I got one of them to my parents somehow—I don't even remember if I sent it or how it happened. But they spread some of the ashes in the backyard. My father was going down to St. Croix, and he spread some in the ocean there. I scattered my lot in a beautiful place in the countryside where Stuart and I had lived together briefly. You always hear about how people cast the ashes out of an airplane or out of a boat, but they never tell you what they do about the Baggie. The Baggie somehow seemed important, because little bits of ash were still on it. I had boots on, and some of the ashes were just slightly blown onto my boots. Stuart was on these boots. And I had this Baggie. I had a friend with me, and we laughed about that. You know, in the midst of all the sadness and the grief and the death and the ashes, you've got a Baggie with a twist tie! There was a bin of rubbish and plant stuff, and I put the Baggie in there.

Stuart had left a letter, and there were pictures that he had had and his journal—all this stuff that his family and I couldn't see. They wouldn't let the family have access to it. He died in June, and the inquest wasn't held until August or September. All we wanted was to get our hands on this stuff. Waiting for the inquest and getting the report and reading it—doing all of that was very, very hard. It went on for a long time. It's still going on emotionally, but there were concrete things that were drawn out. On the other hand, how could one really take it all in at once?

The letter he left was hurtful in some ways, and in some ways, eventually, it was helpful. He said that he really feared a failed attempt. He wanted to do it right, and he had researched it. He died by taking an overdose of his antidepressants. He knew that it would be a heart attack that would kill him. And he was drinking rum and orange juice—I think to help him through it. He said, "I'm going to write my way through this death for the purpose of medical research," or something like that. Stuart had a way of being quite grand at times. The letter was addressed to a variety of people. He thanked some of his friends and was very tender and loving. And then he got to me and said something like "Good-bye. I have nothing more to say to you." That was like a knife. But he got looser, clearly, as things started to kick in. I think he was also getting drunker. He came back to me later. He talked about the cats and was much softer. And he said, "Perhaps we'll meet again, if that's the way of the world." That was very uncharacteristic of him. With Stuart it was always "This is what it is, and it's not much." But in the moment before death, he was entertaining thoughts about an afterlife.

He said one thing that was very hard for me, and eventually it was partly the key toward a better understanding and maybe a liberation. He said something like "I can't help but harbor some resentment at the deceit and the entrapment and the treachery." I heard that as an indictment of me. I heard Stuart blaming me for deceiving him. Stuart believed that I'd somehow lured him into thinking he might be happy and that he should take a chance on life with me, and that I held the responsibility for that.

He also said, "I'm glad to go. It's been hell." That was *so* . . . from the heart. And I think that was his last way of saying, "I'm going to have some peace."

I tried to work for the first three months after Stuart's death. I kept on going to work and being a superwoman. I was crying, but it was only one level down. It wasn't all the way through. And then I fell apart. I couldn't do it. I lost my self-esteem, and I lost my base of support. I felt absolutely abandoned by those same people I had felt held by at first. I remember going to get coffee down the street with somebody I worked with. I said something about Stuart, and she said to me, "Gee, that seems so long ago now." And I said, "Feels like yesterday to me." What I inferred from her statement was the sense that I should be over this by now. My clock was saying, "It's been a month; I shouldn't be crying every night now." Or, "Okay, I had a day when I didn't cry—good, good, good. I'm almost over it now." Or, "It's been three months, I should be back to normal." Or, "It's been a year." Or, "It's been *five* years." I still slip into that belief that I couldn't even grieve right. Not that anyone was there telling me how to grieve or modeling for me how to do it. I didn't know anything about support groups for survivors. I didn't know . . . anything.

I remember talking to a coworker in a different part of the state who was in for a meeting. She said, "How are you doing?" I said, "Well, what do you hear?" And she said, "I hear you're not coping very well." I wanted to say, "How the hell do you think I should be coping? I mean, what do people expect? How do you know that this isn't exactly what I should be doing?"

There was a level at which I knew that I had experienced something outside the realm of most people's experiences. My connection to my in-laws was almost— There should be a secret handshake or something. I had been ushered into this very secret society that only a privileged few understood. I wanted to be understood, but I just couldn't explain—I couldn't even explain it to myself.

And there were rumors. For example, I remember learning at one point that someone had suggested I was now having an affair with my friend who had picked me up at the airport when I returned from Britain. People were really curious about my life and just how deviant it might be. I had a sense that I was like a freak show and that people were these curious onlookers. They wanted to know, but they didn't want to get *too* close. There was another rumor—this was very peculiar. A girl I went to high school with, who never knew Stuart and hadn't seen me since high school, told her mother that she had heard that Stuart was a victim of incest. I mean, it was wild stuff, some of the fantasies that were stirred up by this titillating event of suicide.

Part of me wanted to open myself up to the world and say, "This is it; this is what's going on," because I felt I was containing so much. And then there was part of me that really desperately needed to hide because of the shame that I was carrying and the sense of failure. For me it was about having failed. I had raised the stakes to the highest level I could, and I had failed.

I lost a lot of weight in those first few months, and I was thin. I was hunched over a bit and took small steps and just felt shamed. I wasn't wearing makeup because I was crying all the time, so there was no point. I think part of me wanted the world to see how damaged I was.

I finally made a decision to stop working. My parents really got me through that year financially. And there was a very small cadre of friends who stayed with me. One was Sam, who lived across the street and also had worked with me, so we knew each other quite well. Sam's two best friends had committed suicide within a week of each other while he was out of town. This had happened some time before Stuart's suicide. Sam thought that if he had stayed in Denver, where he was living at the time, he might have gone the way of his friends, because as he put it, "A precedent had been set." Suddenly, suicide was some kind of an option that it hadn't been before. And while I wasn't thinking consciously about suicide as an option for me, there was a way in which I think I was vulnerable. I mean, suddenly, I didn't have a clear conviction anymore that I would never commit suicide under any circumstances. We didn't talk about suicide all the time, but Sam was there.

My friend Jane was going through her own sense of shame and failure at the time. We were sort of buddies on the phone, helping each other through it. I would say, "I can't even grieve right." And she would say, "You're doing this just right." And she would talk about my inner wisdom, things that just didn't make sense to me at the time. But it was very important to have witnesses and anchors and people who would accept me for hiding out in my apartment. People came to me. I didn't go out. They came over, and we would cook feasts. I had moved to an apartment in another part of the city. I can't really go back to that part of town now without getting filled with sadness, because that time was all about ruminating about death and Stuart and just obsessing over it.

I have no contact with most of the people from my work at that time. I don't want to know them now. It's too much of a reminder. Also, I've changed so profoundly that it's very difficult to think about even being with them. I really feel betrayed and abandoned by them.

I had a lot of dreams about Stuart. In the beginning I would just have a sense that I had dreamed about him, and it felt comforting. There was one time I knew that I had dreamed about him, but I didn't remember the dream. Later on in the day, I remembered it. It was a terrible dream, a sad dream. But there was something about knowing that he had been there, that he had come to me in the night. I welcomed the dreams, even when they were painful. Sometimes they were lovely and soothing, and sometimes they were so sad. I've sort of measured my progress through my grief by noting the pain or the anger that's come through the dreams. I've had dreams in which something horrible happened, but he was there. I've had a number of dreams in which we were getting married again. Over time, the fact of the suicide has come into the dreams more. Eventually, I had a dream in which he was being as cruel to me as he ever was, and I was furious with him. I miss the dreams sometimes. I miss them less now, because I feel I need him around less and

I'm not betraying him by giving him up. I still periodically have dreams about him, but the first year was the most intense.

[Laura's story is continued in chapter 4, page 183.]

Susan and Philip

Susan and Philip are sister and brother. I first interviewed Susan in 1983, almost two years after her father's suicide. She was in her mid-twenties at the time, pursuing a graduate degree in psychology. In 1989, I revisited her and also interviewed Philip, a writer, who was twenty-three when his father died. Names and certain details have been changed in their stories.

Susan and Philip have a similar understanding of their father's suicide. Both see it as the end of many years of depression and a debilitating physical illness, multiple sclerosis (MS). And both feel that it reflected a decision, on their father's part, that was in some measure rational. Yet their roles at the time of his death and their subsequent responses to it differed, reflecting two very different relationships with their father. Susan's had been raw and painful, and as an adult she preserved a certain distance from her father. She feels that she started mourning his loss in her life years before his death. Philip, always closer to his father, became his confidant as a teenager, a role thrust on him when his father first began to tell his son about his wish to die.

The stories that Susan and Philip tell are also quite different, even though they are both stories of their father's loss and share a similar perspective on what led up to it. No two people respond to a death in exactly the same way, and family members often have strikingly different experiences of loss, reflecting the different qualities of each relationship with the person who has died.

The most striking contrast between these two stories is the difference between knowing and not knowing. Unlike his sister, Philip knew about his father's plans to kill himself and in a very real sense, though not literally, was a witness to those plans and their execution. Much of his story is an exploration of what it means to know, the weight of that knowledge. Suicide takes most survivors by surprise; they come to know only after the fact. Few ever know as immediately and directly as Philip did. (Richard, whose story appears in chapter 3, is the one exception in this book.) Not knowing leaves people feeling cut out and cut off, yet the burden of knowing can be enormous.

Susan: Grieving Long Before He Died

My father would really get irrational with me sometimes. To him, I think I represented my mother, perhaps, or his mother and a lot of anger about stuff that happened with my mom and her decision, finally, to get out of the marriage because it was going to destroy her. I look back and realize it wasn't me, but at the time, I felt like I must be bad, I must be an awful person. I used to think that he was just totally evil. I really couldn't understand why he would get so enraged. He wasn't all evil, and he loved me a lot, and he loved my brother a lot, but at the time I didn't understand, so I grew up thinking he hated me.

He would do things. He had some money, and when I wanted to go to camp, he decided he wouldn't give his permission so my stepfather would have to pay. It was a lot harder for my stepfather to pay for me and my brother, as well as his own kids, but my stepfather would do it. He wanted us to have those things. My father just wanted to get back at Mom, so he didn't send us to camp. But there was some letter saying that he had made a contribution to a special needs camp to make it possible for ten handicapped children to go to camp. Things like that.

One thing he did do, he saw us consistently, and he did care. We saw him every Sunday. But he was so rigid that when I had high school performances or some kind of social thing on Sunday, he would be really angry and demand that I see him rather than try to be flexible and agree that maybe I could see him another time. No, no, no, no.

So I grew up with a lot of anger. There were times when I really wanted my stepfather to adopt me and I wished my father were dead. I know that if I hadn't worked a lot of this out in therapy, when my father died I would have been burdened with an unbelievable amount of guilt.

Sometimes he would call me up and be very upset. He would have loved it if right after college I'd gone back to St. Louis and become nurse-mother-wife-therapist. Thank God I didn't. I could have—I felt guilty enough—but I knew that it wouldn't have been that helpful for him, and it would have been very destructive, given our relationship, which had been thorny from a long time ago. So I'm really glad that I was able to maintain some distance and then try to be as supportive as I could long distance. I'd call him all the time and go out there and visit more frequently than I would have if he hadn't been ill. But he would be very demanding—you know, "Why aren't you coming?"—and get very upset.

The February before he died, he had overdosed. It wasn't a bad overdose, but he had taken some pills. I found out more and more, during that year, about the extent of his drug use. I had had no idea. He got prescriptions from different doctors and mixed medications. So some of the symptoms that I attributed to the MS were toxic effects of the medications, I'm sure. I was becoming increasingly concerned, and I was in touch with some of his doctors just to say, "What's going on?" I told him that I was going to call; I always asked my father's permission before I did.

I went back there in the spring, after he had had some difficulties with the medications, and tried to sort things out. I urged him to go see a therapist. He finally agreed, but he did it for me; he didn't do it for himself. I went with him the first time. He didn't continue. Then I brought him to see one of his doctors, one of his regular appointments. At one point, I was in the hall—Dad was somewhere else—and the doctor was asking me some questions about the psychological difficulties. I said, "Well, he's had problems. He's a mess." Somehow, the doctor told him I'd said that. Later, my father called me up and said he was going to disown me because of what I had told the doctor. I just felt helpless, and I was mad. You know, I try to help, and then what does it get me? He could be really irrational. A few days later, he called up and acted as if it hadn't happened. That kind of thing was common. We used to get into long, difficult arguments on the phone. I finally learned to say, "Wait a second, Dad! Talk to me in a different way. I can't deal with this right now. Call me back." If you tried a rational argument about something, he wouldn't hear it, so it didn't help. That was something I had to learn over a long period of time, and it was painful.

The last day of my visit that spring, he was in bed, and he was really upset about something. He said, "I want you to release me from my promise." I said, "What promise, Dad?" He said, "The promise that I wouldn't ever kill myself." I think he had once said, "I would never do it." But I had never said, "Pa, I want you to promise me." How do you respond to that? I mean, I didn't want to say, "Sure, no problem, go right ahead!" And I also didn't want to say, "Forget it, you have no right." What I said was that I felt that wasn't within my rights or my domain and that I really wished he would not break that promise to himself, that it had to be for him to decide. I was just so torn up about that. I felt that, as the years went by, things were more and more difficult for him.

After that visit, late in the spring, he kept asking when I would be coming home next. I had a job for the summer, after finishing my first year of graduate school, and I had a new boyfriend I wanted to go away with for a week or so. We had talked about going camping. So I said, "Sometime this summer I will be home, but I don't know when." He was insistent. He wanted me to come home for Father's Day. He was really upset about it, but I guess, by the time that I left for the camping trip, he'd grown used to it. He asked me to call him while I was away, and I called a few times. The conversations were really warm.

When I got back from the camping trip, there was a package. He had sent me a stuffed animal with a card, which said something like, "I love you, puddycat." He used to call me that when I was very, very young. I was astounded. It was kind of an ugly stuffed animal. On the other hand, I was really touched and pleased. I called him, and I called him one more time, or he called me. It was on a Saturday. I remember talking to him. That last conversation was just really good and peaceful; he seemed at peace. And he seemed loving, not that that part of him wasn't there other times, but I was surprised by how calm he was, how undisturbed.

I also talked with Philip on the phone, and we were saying how bad things were for our father. My brother was the good boy, because he had made it home on Father's Day. He was doing a [story] in the West and stopped on his way back. There was a lot of stuff that went on at the time that I didn't know about, that Philip really didn't tell me. My father had him talking with a lawyer. I mean, this was no impulsive act. My father was saying his good-byes.

The night I talked with my brother, I had a dream. In the dream, the phone rang and someone told me that my father was dead. Two days later, the phone rang at 6:30 in the morning; it was my brother. All he said was, "Susan," and I knew, I just knew. It was awful. He told me that he'd been up all night. He'd even made plane reservations.

Dad had tried to kill himself twice that week. He had told my brother that he had gotten really, really scared. Philip had said, "Well, Dad, if this is something you're determined to do, why don't you take a drink, why don't you calm down, so it won't be so awful." So he really helped him. I had not known this. My brother had not told me. And in some ways I'm really glad, because I don't know what I would have done. I might have been moved to intervene, which might not have been a good idea. I had really mixed feelings. Basically, rationally, I felt that, given my father's situation, it was the right thing to do. However, I don't think I could have done it. I also was resentful for a while that I had not known and that my brother had kept things from me.

A lot of people came to the funeral. We had a ceremony at the graveyard. It was hard. We had put a few things in the casket. One was a baseball, another was Beethoven's Ninth, and some other things he really loved.

After the funeral we had some people back to the house. By the time they had all cleared out, it was evening or late afternoon. I didn't want to be in the house, but we'd decided that someone should be there. When there's a funeral, you know, an announcement . . . so one of us had to be there all the time. My brother said he'd stay there later, but he didn't want to be there then. My father had had a part-time nurse whom my brother liked, and they went out to a movie. I was in that huge house alone, and it was awful. I really didn't want to be there. I just sat in the family room, thinking about all the times I'd sat there with my dad. The clock was ticking, and it was isolated and scary and dark. I'd never felt comfortable in that house.

I called a few people that night and talked to them. This guy I was seeing at the time was going off to Europe for ten days with his parents. He was someone I'd been closer to than any boyfriend in the past. Even though it hadn't been a long relationship, I felt that it was the best one so far. He had driven me to the airport, and I'd given him my father's number, but he hadn't called. I called him on Tuesday. He knew the funeral was on Thursday. He didn't call. He was leaving for Europe early Friday morning, and he didn't call. I was so upset, and I was angry at my brother for leaving. I felt very abandoned.

I didn't see my boyfriend for two weeks, because he was in Europe and I was away. We had a big showdown when he came back. We talked all day about it. He was scared. It wasn't maliciousness. He was just immature and scared, and he felt like he didn't want to encourage my being dependent on him, so he had kind of withdrawn. I was severely disappointed, because he'd been a huge source of support to me. That was really hard.

Everybody else, all my friends, were so much there for me, Mom and my stepfather, and people were just wonderful. I felt very good about that. My friendships were really deepened. It was the first time that I felt I needed my friends badly. They had called on me many times, and they felt that this was something they could do for me, so I was very glad of that. It really helped me a lot. Philip handled things very well and efficiently and really did a lot of business. He was the executor and I wasn't, which at first I felt was unfair. But it was also just a plunge into all this business stuff, which I had no idea about. The whole estate—it was complicated. It was a whole new world, and it was coming really fast.

I felt very sad, very angry, like, God, I'm so young, why do I have to deal with all this now? It affected me in many ways. I felt very grateful that I wouldn't have to worry so much, that there would be some money. It made me feel lucky. But it was just too soon. I was also feeling that there was really no one to help. There were some people, one man in particular who was very helpful in terms of the business side of things. But I didn't grow up learning about a lot of this stuff. I had this distaste for business, maybe because I associated it with my father. It was stuff I had to learn fast.

My mother was really angry and upset. She was very worried for us, how we would respond, very condemning of my father. It took a long time, I think, before she came to realize that this was something that was long in coming. But she finally came around and realized how we felt. In many ways, it was a relief to all of us. There were a lot of ways in which my father's death was a tremendous relief to me. The psychological burden of his illness and the kind of nasty dance that we would sometimes get into were really hard and painful. Sometimes I felt guilty about how freed I felt. But it was like this huge burden and worry lifted. He didn't do it in a horrible way but in a very loving way. He left a note that someone else had written because he could barely write anymore. It was very loving. It wasn't done out of anger. He made it known that he wasn't angry at us and that he really cared about us and that, of everything in his life, my brother and I meant the most to him, which was very consoling. I'm glad about that. The way he did it was very humane in a lot of ways.

I think my grieving and my mourning, dealing with the anger and sadness, started way before my father died. I mourned the fact that he wasn't really emotionally available to me most of my life. I'd already done it for the most part. But there was something really significant about getting through that first year after his death. My therapist left the next spring. I had been in intensive therapy, and his leaving was really difficult. It was the only time that I felt like I was going to fall apart. I functioned fine, and I did well in school. But personally I felt like I was going through the dregs. His leaving was incredibly difficult but also really important. It dredged up so much old stuff about my parents' divorce and about my father and about all these other losses. Afterward, I realized, hey, I'm okay, I can do this on my own, and I felt much better. I had felt a lot, and I knew that

that had to be and that I would be okay. The world goes on.

On the first anniversary of my father's suicide, I remembered stuff about Dad and I was sad, but it wasn't as significant as I'd expected. I think because I was expecting it to be significant, it wasn't. During the whole previous month I had done a lot of grieving, so the date, in and of itself, wasn't so heavy. A lot of the memories and thoughts and feelings that I have don't necessarily come out around anniversaries. Little things touch them off. Like seeing the movie *Sophie's Choice*—the horrible choice that she had to make—and my father saying, "I want you to release me from my promise." That was my choice, and I couldn't choose. Little things that I read or see or hear—memories come back.

Right after my father's death I felt like I aged about five years. I got a little cynical, perhaps. I've changed quite a bit, but I don't feel like a different person now. I don't feel that the core of me is any different. I think I can handle things differently now, or I may be less scared about certain things or more willing to take risks. I may have a more existential viewpoint. I think the experience has freed me in a certain way to be easier on myself. But I can't separate the suicide per se from the kind of organic developing relationship I had with my father and the other things in my life, other difficult things I've gone through. I don't feel like this event, in and of itself, has changed me totally, but it's part of a process of growing and developing. It speeded up that process, but I don't think it's essentially changed who I am.

[Susan's story is continued in chapter 4, page 189.]

Philip: A Loss of Innocence

My father's suicide came out of years, and probably a lifetime, of frustration, difficulty, and pain. His life condition led up to it, both his problems with relationships, which led to two divorces, and a very serious physical ailment. I don't see any particular thing that triggered the crisis. It was a much more incremental, gradual thing. It was sort of a wearing down, till he got to the point where he didn't want to live. He first mentioned suicide to me when I was sixteen, a sophomore in high school, and he did it when I was twenty-three, just twenty-three. So there were seven years there, certainly, when it was something that occurred to him.

As far as the actual incident, I probably had a fairly unusual experience, compared to most people, and a very different one than my sister had. He had spoken to me about suicide more directly than he had to my sister. I was more involved with his uncertainty about whether he wanted to continue his life. He would call me at two in the morning sometimes, when I was in college, and be in a bad way, that sort of thing. Susan and I would talk about it, and I think she appreciated what was going on, but I don't think, for whatever reasons, she and my dad talked about it very much. She was never as actively involved in his life. There was a structural difference in the relationship, which I don't think was just father-son, father-daughter. For instance, there was one summer during college when I worked in the family business, and I worked in his office a couple of different times during high school. So when it came to the actual time when the feelings that he would do it started to take prominence over the feelings that it would be a stupid thing to do, he shared those feelings with me. I know Susan knew what was going on in some way intuitively and because I talked about it with her, but not so much from the horse's mouth.

So you cut to 1981, the summer. I was out West in a godforsaken place, doing a story, and I talked to him. I won't forget it. I was at a convenience store, standing at the pay phone. I was facing north out of the store, and I can remember exactly the way the road went. He was very down. He said he wasn't sure he could last as long as he needed to last to see me again. And I said I was sure that he could. I talked to him fairly frequently over the next couple of weeks. We made plans—I don't remember whether they were made when I was out West or whether the plans were set before I went out there—that I would stop in St. Louis for a day on my way back home.

[During that visit] he introduced me to his lawyer and his accountant. I mean, I would have had to have been a real dunce not to know what was going on. And I did know what was going on. We talked about it some more. I remember that he went upstairs and was lying in bed, and I was sitting in the chair by his bed. We had something like the *Great Treasury of Western Thought,* a big compendium of things. There would be times we'd look at what Camus said about suicide or what X, Y, or Z said about suicide, and we'd talk about it. We had talked, too, about Exit and Death with Dignity [organizations providing information about euthanasia and suicide for the terminally ill] and stuff like that. I knew for a long time he was scared away, because he was worried that we'd be ashamed of him and it would reflect badly on him. I told him that wasn't the case. I don't think I ever encouraged him, but I told him that I'd support what he did, that to me it wasn't a completely irrational thing, and that I understood and I'd still love him.

As I'm sure my sister told you, there was a lot of suicidal ideation. There had been a number of what might have been called very soft attempts. I don't think there was ever a really honest-to-goodness, serious attempt. I mean, there was a lot of pill taking and that kind of thing. He'd go to the hospital and have his stomach pumped. But he was taking so much medication, he would have had to take the pharmacy to kill himself. So we'd talked about that. I don't remember if I knew how he was going to do it or not, but I knew that the means weren't going to be violent.

So we had that meeting, and I left him there in bed. I remember looking at him, and I said, "I won't say good-bye. I'll just say so long for now. I'm sure we'll hook up on some other cosmos," or something like that. I don't believe in life after death, but it's the sort of thing you say at that time. And that was the last time I saw him.

Susan and I had both told him that if he was going to do it, we wanted to know, so we could prepare ourselves. And at that point, or possibly a bit before that, he told me he had changed his mind and he wouldn't tell us when it was, because he just didn't want to put us through that. He didn't think it was right. We'd have a general idea, but he wasn't going to tell us. When I last saw him, I think he wanted to do it relatively quickly, but Susan was on a camping trip, and my dad thought that would be a horrible time to do it. It's not the kind of thing that he thought she'd want to come home to, so I guess he decided to put it off. He'd been putting it off for years.

About a week after I left, a woman came to live with him, a friend of his. I can't remember her name, but I know she was a friend from way back, someone he must have felt comfortable with. There was some link they had that was significant and not to be doubted or questioned. She was essentially there to support him in carrying out what he wanted to do. And I knew that. It didn't endear her to me. She was not a Svengali. I never felt that she had a great deal of selfish gain in doing what she did. I mean, I think there was something for her in his will, but it wasn't a king's ransom, especially compared to what she might have gotten, because my dad had a lot of money.

We talked a couple of times after I left, and it got quite specific. He'd say things to me, sort of joking about it. That was the summer of the baseball strike. He was a big baseball fan, and he couldn't stand the summer without baseball. He told me to tell the rabbi, when he addressed people, to make sure they knew it wasn't the MS that did it. It was the baseball strike. And he said, "Make sure that I'm not cremated, because you know how bad excessive heat is for us MS patients." You know, things like that. Or, "I want to be buried standing up, because I'm worried about the environmental crisis."

So I knew that he was close to at least making a real attempt. And I didn't stand in his way. I didn't want to stand in his way. He called me on a Sunday afternoon. (We often talked on Sunday—typical divorced dad. You know, Sundays were for my father until I went to college. That was the first time I really realized there were seven days in the week and not six—six days and then a day for Dad.) He was very weepy. And he was saying that Thursday night or Friday night he had gone down to the garage and gotten in the car—I don't remember what he related to me and what his friend related to me—and he had turned on the engine. After a minute or two, he panicked and turned it off and started honking the horn. And she came down and got him.

I said, "What was wrong?" And he said he had been very scared. I said, "What were you scared of?" He said he didn't know, but it was just that the whole thing was very frightening.

I asked him if his decision to honk the horn meant he wanted to live. And he said, "No, it just meant that I was scared of dying. It didn't mean that I wanted to live. I've really been having a miserable time." I guess part of me was hoping that maybe it was going to be a turning point. If it meant that he came to some realization over the next couple of days that this was not really what he wanted, and, okay, maybe he was going to try— then you're talking. But it wasn't that. I think I gave myself that possibility, the idea of the possibility that it might be that. But it wasn't that.

So I talked to him, and he said he was going to try to do it again. I asked, "When?" He said he didn't want to tell me. And I said, "That's okay." His friend had been trying to help him. She had some relaxation technique where you imagine that you're someplace that you love more than any other thing. It's like concrete visualization and all that. I remember my dad talking to me about it and saying he wanted to think that he was in Disneyland. My father loved Disneyland. He always thought it was for adults and not for kids, and in some ways, I think he was right.

He said he just was jittery; he was nervous. My father was never a drinker. I don't think I ever saw him have a beer— maybe a mixed drink once. And I knew he had vodka there and could tolerate the taste of it, because there wasn't much taste. And I said, "Well, if that's the problem, that you just can't calm down, maybe you should have a drink so that you can." I mean, the man was in agony. If he were an animal, you'd say, "Take him out behind the barn and shoot him," because he was just in agony. I didn't think I was pronouncing a death sentence on him or anything like that. And I've thought many times over the years about whether I should have recommended that he take a drink—was I facilitating in a way that was wrong. I thought I was being, at the time, charitable, almost charitable. I mean, I was sort of the parent, and he wanted to be put out of his misery. He would have done it anyway. So I made that suggestion, and we talked a while. He was very weepy, and he said good-bye again on the phone, and that was it. And I thought maybe a week later, five days later, two days later. . .

I got a call that night from his friend. She said, in words that I think I can remember fairly well, "Your father's in the garage with the engine running. He's been in there for ten minutes." Here I am on the phone, long distance, and I didn't know what that meant. I didn't know how long it took. She called me because she was panicking. It was a hard night. I must have talked to her a couple more times, as far as how she was going to handle things and all that. And I said, "Don't tell anyone until I get home." That was one of the things that pissed me off, because she ended up telling some people. Maybe it was her way of unburdening herself of the information and the guilt and her sort of privileged position, when she was the only person who knew. If she could tell other people, then they would know, and they would be as guilty as she was.

That night I remember putting on a record by a saxaphone player I really liked, someone who had done the sound track for *Last Tango in Paris*. That had been one of my father's favorite movies. I thought it was an extraordinary movie and that my father in some way identified with the Brando character's embittered man. And I love the music to that movie. It was by a saxophonist named Gato Barbieri, and I put on one of his records, although not that. And I remember building a table that night—I couldn't get to sleep—and I watched Mary Tyler Moore, you know, like two-in-the-morning repeats.

I also made plane reservations for myself and for my sister so that her flight would arrive in St. Louis at almost exactly the same time as my flight. But I didn't call her to tell her about it. I figured, why should I make both of us miserable tonight? And not knowing— For all I knew, in the morning he would be asleep in the car, with the engine turned off, and he'd have an upset stomach. I didn't know that; I didn't know if he'd be in a vegetable state; I didn't know if he was dead; I didn't know if he was back upstairs sleeping, although I doubted that—I figured I would have gotten a call. I had no idea. So I figured, why call my sister? I thought I was protecting her, but upon reflection, maybe I didn't call my sister because I was almost feeling possessive of the horrible experience in some way. I'm the one who's gone through all this stuff with Dad, and this is something that's really happening or not happening, and it's *my* thing, you know? I'll make sure that she gets there when I do, but it's not her thing. I wouldn't have ever thought that at the moment, and I'm not sure I think that now, but for whatever reasons—and I don't know all the complex psychological reasons—it didn't seem to me to make any sense to call her and say, "Dad might almost be dead."

I did get to sleep for an hour or two. I don't know how I did it, but I did. And his friend called at five forty-five or six forty-five in the morning and said, "I discovered the body this morning, and your father's been pronounced dead by the paramedics." And, boom, you just go into a survival mode. I called Susan—it was very early in the morning, which would have been unusual for me—and I said, "Susan, I've got to tell you something." And she knew right away, as I'm sure she told you. She said that before I even said it, she knew what it was about. I told her what her flight was and where I'd meet her. And I told my roommate. Actually, I had told him that after-noon what was going on with my dad, and he had chosen not to be home that night, to go spend the night with his girlfriend, which was really shitty, but that's the way a lot of people are, as you know. People run from the very idea of suicide like they do from fire and high places. He later apologized for that.

I met my sister at the airport, and we went to the house. And then I had to drive his car around. I mean, I didn't *have* to drive his car. I could have rented or borrowed a car, but I was driving his car. It's crazy! I was hating it, really hating it. I never liked the car anyway. It was a Cadillac. It's not me, and it wasn't me when I was twenty-three either. I called it the deathmobile. That was my defense—humor—and I needed a lot of it and gave myself a lot of it at that point. One of the first things I wanted to do was sell the goddamned car. And I accomplished it, I don't know, maybe a couple of weeks later. But it was really weird. Now I look back, and I can't *believe* I was driving around in this car. You know, you get anesthetized.

Susan probably related to you the scene at the funeral parlor. My father had said he wanted a very simple Scandinavian type of casket—as he said, "Nothing with dual exhaust and chrome headlights." A Jewish funeral is pegged to the price of the casket for some bizarre reason. And I said, "This is what we'd like to get." I remember there'd been a flood, and the room where all the caskets were on display had indoor-outdoor carpeting, which was squishing under my feet. And the guy says, "Well, I took the liberty of looking up what your father spent on his father's funeral. And he certainly didn't follow that advice." People are just so astoundingly insensitive. That was the most brutal thing anyone said. And actually, to me, the idea of $15,000, $20,000, seemed like an extraordinary sum of money, because I wasn't used to it, even though I knew my father was worth millions of dollars.

I was the one who had to be responsible in terms of financial dealings and selling the house and his estate. I was the executor. It created a lot of problems, learning about all this financial stuff. I don't think I have a predilection for it, although people say I'm a lot better at it than I think I am, but I don't really like it. He left a very messy estate behind. He had made a lot of bad decisions and irrational decisions at the end. It was very complicated, and it took a lot of time. I mean, he died in 1981, but his estate didn't get closed until 1985, something like that. It was a long time, and there was a lot of stuff that had to be done. What happened is that I went about taking care of all the things that had to be done and taking care of the business. I essentially became the managing general partner for the benefit of the other partners.

I was up to my knees in stuff. I did have feelings, and I was cognizant of them, but sometimes you've got to deal with them and still function. That was one of the fallouts that accentuated in death what had already been there in life, in terms of how I related to my father and how my sister related to my father. If anything, his death brought me closer to him and furthered the divergence between my sister's level of relation to my father and mine, intensified it.

My father had had opportunities to sell his business, and he never had, and I wasn't going to either. It was something I liked to preserve. There was a sentimental attachment to it, though not particularly related to my father, more related to my grandfather. But it was a very long and tortuous process. We did end up selling it and actually changing it into a different, less labor-intensive business, less work for me. And as of last year, I take a very small percentage of the income in return for my labors.

Being left-wing and democratic socialist—that's sort of my background—I always felt guilty about the money to begin with, so why should I get compensated for this work? But it was work, and it is work, and damn right I should get compensated for that.

I didn't cry for a long time. I'm pretty emotional. The tears don't come hard for me—for a boy, at least, growing up in this country. I was encouraged, I think, by my mother to show emotion. And I didn't cry for a couple of years. There might have been one or two instances when I got angry and probably misdirected it at some people. The lawyers were my favorites. It was so easy to get angry at the lawyers. But it wasn't until I saw that sort of pathetic movie, *Terms of Endearment,* the scene where she's dying, at the end. I remember coming back here to this apartment with my girlfriend and just exploding into tears in the cab. And it really felt like it was the first time I was crying about my father. But it took two or three years. There was just so much of a mess to deal with, I probably couldn't afford to do it.

[Philip's story is continued in chapter 4, page 196.]

Joan: How Can a Mother Not Know?

When her son Jim killed himself in March 1988, Joan was at home and heard the sound of the gunshot coming from his bedroom. The seventh of Joan's eight children, Jim was twenty years old when he died. I interviewed his mother nine months later, on January 1, 1989. She was fifty-two at the time.

Joan's story is about many things: the compounded horror of a violent death that occurs at home, the help-lessness and guilt of a mother whose son never let her know the depth of his turmoil, and the ruptures in family relationships that suicide may leave in its wake.

A suicide that occurs at home, especially one so violent that it mutilates the body, augments the horror of the loss. For the survivor who discovers the body, the impact is enormous. Yet if there is no opportunity to see the body, the reality of the loss may be much more difficult to accept. In addition, the survivor's presence in the home when the suicide occurs can intensify the feeling that he or she should have been able to prevent it.

The death of a child—even if that child is an adult—shatters the parents' assumption that their children will outlive them. If the death is a suicide, the parents' sense of responsibility and self-blame may be profound. They have given life to that child, and the child has renounced it.

Joan's story is all the more painful because of her family's conflicting responses to her son's death. Suicide can have different meanings for the individual members of a family, and those differences may leave them feeling estranged from one another rather than drawn closer together in their grief. Moreover, in the aftermath of suicide, relationships that were already strained by conflict may be entirely ruptured.

My son Jim was twenty years old when he died last March. That night has devastated me. I still have difficulty living with it. The thing that bothers me the most is that I was here, and I couldn't prevent his death. I was sitting right here watching TV. I often wonder if I had gone upstairs and tried to talk to him, whether I could have talked him out of it. That is something I will never know.

That day I had felt that something was going to happen. All day long I had an awful feeling. I was taking care of my parents that day, and I got very upset with my mother and actually yelled at her. And when I got home, everything went wrong.

Jim had had an argument with his sister and her boyfriend. When he came in that night, he looked very upset. He went upstairs and screamed, "I'm sick of people blowing me off. I'm sick of it, I'm sick of it." He went up to his room. I was sitting right there watching TV, thinking no more of it, never dreaming he'd commit suicide. When he used to get that upset, he'd play his Nintendo game. I figured he'd go up and play the tapes. Rosie, my youngest daughter, came in and said, "He's pissed off at me." And then we heard the shot. He was a hunter. He had a lot of guns.

Rosie found him. The look on her face I have to live with. She came out of the room. She slammed the door and said, "Don't go in there, Mom, don't go in there. He has no head. Oh, my God, Momma, he has no head!" She just screeched. She doesn't remember saying it. She doesn't remember slamming that door. I wanted to go in the room and see, but I couldn't. I went in partway. The door was ajar, and I saw his arm. I didn't see all of him. My husband went in. I don't know how he could have gone in. I couldn't. I wanted to, and yet I couldn't. I went downstairs and called the police. First, I called an ambulance and said, "My son got hurt."

That night was a nightmare forever. First, the ambulance driver came in. They were going to give us tranquilizers, and I said, "No, I don't want you here. I don't want you to touch me." The whole yard was full of cruisers. I kept asking them, "Are you sure he's dead? Are you sure he's dead?" Well, of course he was, but I kept hoping that he was just wounded really badly and Rose didn't realize it. I just prayed he was alive. But I knew. I knew the minute the shot went off that he was dead.

The police drove me crazy that night. They wouldn't let me use the phone. They kept getting calls. I got hold of most of my kids. But I wanted to call my friend, and every time I would go to do it, they'd be on the phone. And the questions they ask you: Why was I here? Did I know he had been drinking? Was he on drugs? I said, "No, he didn't do drugs." And they said, "Are you positive?" And I said, "Of him, I am." "Are you sure?" They kept asking me, to the point where I just said, "I don't want to answer your questions. Leave me alone." In fact, I asked them to get out of my house, but of course, they couldn't. This happened after midnight, and the coroner didn't come until three in the morning, so it was a long night of cops. Every time I turned around, there was a detective or a cop, and the DA's office came down, somebody from the state police came down.

I remember saying, "I'm going up and seeing him," and one of the cops said, "You're not going upstairs." I said, "Don't you tell me what to do in my house. I'll go upstairs." He said, "You're not going up." Then one of the kids came in and said, "Mum, please." I said, "I want to see Jim." And he said, "No, you don't want to see what's up there. Don't let her up there, please." I never got to say good-bye to him. Of course, I wouldn't want to have seen him like that. I probably wouldn't have survived it, but it's just that when something like that happens . . .

He killed himself Saturday night, they took him out of here about three, and they didn't release his body until that Wednesday. The day we went to see the undertaker, I couldn't even pick out a casket. I wanted to see him, and the undertaker said, "No, you don't." I wanted to see him, and everybody kept saying, "No, you don't." It's not saying good-bye that's hard.

I only had the wake one night, because I couldn't take any more of it. I wasn't going to have anything. I couldn't see any purpose to it. He was dead. Having a wake or a funeral could not change things; it only hurt more. So we had the wake one day and one night. So many people came. It started in the afternoon, but that night, from seven to nine, there seemed to be no end of people. If he had only known the number of people who really cared for him—there were a lot of people. I couldn't even tell you who came and who left. I was just so numb.

The next day, his funeral was held here. I thought that day would never end. He was cremated and buried here. He had always said he wanted to be cremated. That was the only decision I made about anything, that he would be cremated. He was born and brought up a Catholic, but the last few years he did not believe at all. He used to say to me, "If there was a God, Mum, people wouldn't suffer." He would not go to church, yet we found rosary beads in his room, and that baffles me. He had them hidden in a cup.

The day he was buried was warm. The sun stayed out all day. There was a woman with a balloon that she let go, and it went right up to his window. It was strange, it really was.

He's up on the hill. He always wanted to stay here. He said he'd live here till he was an old man. Well, he got his wish. He will never leave here. Most of the people I've talked to who have lost a child can't go to the grave, but I find going up to Jim's grave and talking to him very comforting. Many a day I just end up crying and asking him, "Why, Jim, why? There had to be a better way for you."

I noticed a change in him from Thanksgiving until this happened [in March]. He became very agitated with people; his temper was terrible. He and his father weren't getting along at all. It's a terrible thing to go out with that much anger and hatred in you, to leave the world that way. Nobody should ever leave that angry.

His sisters say, "Mom, he was depressed." I couldn't see it. Maybe I was never looking for it, and maybe I just blanked it out. But the week before he died, he and I had a lot of long talks. I'd wait up for him to come home from work. He was a cook. He was planning his future, his life. His idea was that he'd work, get a cabin in the woods, and hunt. That was all he was going to do.

He did have a drinking problem, but that night he wasn't drunk. I never realized that alcohol was a depressant till this happened. I never realized alcohol was like drugs till this happened, because I don't drink. My husband has a brother who's an alcoholic, and my brother was an alcoholic, but he hasn't touched a drink in fifteen years. My mother had brothers who were alcoholics. They drank themselves to death. My husband's grandfather and his mother's brothers—all of them drank heavily. At parties and on holidays, there was alcohol. So my kids grew up with alcohol in the house, but neither my husband nor I drink it. I used to have cases of beer in here, because Jimmy always had beer. I thought nothing of it. I've learned from this. I hope I've learned for the best. I now look for signs in my kids.

You know how every family has one member who always feels like an outsider? That's my oldest son. After Jimmy died, his friends stayed with him for months, for fear he'd do the same thing. And to this day, he says, "Mum, it should have been me and not Jimmy, because everybody loved Jimmy. I'm always in trouble." I said, "That's got nothing to do with it. Nobody decides which person lives or dies. Because Jimmy died, it doesn't mean I want you to die. I love you equally." But the kids always used to accuse me of liking Jimmy best.

For Rose it's doubly hard, because she lost her brother and a friend. She and Jim were always together. If you saw one of them, you knew the other one was not far behind. It's going to be very difficult for Rosie, because she found him and she has to live with more than I do, a lot more. The look on her face that night—I still have nightmares of that night with her. I couldn't go in when she shut the door. It was like I put the whole burden of it on her, because she went in first. When she went upstairs, I followed her. I should have insisted, "No, Rose, you let me go in there first," but I thought she was going to talk to him. And she has to live the rest of her life with what she saw.

In the beginning, she was very, very bitter, to the point where she became very demanding of all of us, like we owed her something. She seems to be a lot better now, but there are moments when you look at her and she's off in thought. She has talked about it every now and then, but then she stops and up and leaves. I think she's blocked a lot of it out because it's too painful to remember. One day she's going to have to face what she saw.

My daughter Trisha is very angry at Jim. She thought it was a selfish act. She has said he was very cruel and that what he did to us was totally unfair. Yes, it was, but what he did to himself . . . I mean, he never actually lived, and now he's dead. So to be angry, no, I can't get angry at him. He hurt himself as much as he hurt me. Maybe he is finally at peace—I don't know—maybe he isn't. That's something I'll never know. I don't think anybody really knows that answer. He's not here. He doesn't have to suffer anymore. He doesn't have to live with the everyday problems anymore. They're over for him, but for me they go on.

My oldest daughter blamed me for Jim's death. She said that if I had made the right choices, made their lives different, none of this would have happened. She said, "You've destroyed us all." That hurt, that really hurt.

My son Johnny, who was very close to Jim, has such an attitude now. It's like he's built up a hard shell so that nothing, nobody, will hurt him. Nobody can reason with him or even talk to him. It's awful.

You'd think that something like this would have brought the kids closer together or tied the family tighter. I have a daughter who won't come down to the house unless I can guarantee that I'm not going to be depressed. I can't guarantee that. I get up, and if the day's fine, the day goes fine. If the day isn't, I can't help it.

Christmas Day [nine months after Jim's death] was good. Nobody was depressed until that night. The next day, I got up and started to undecorate the whole house. I took the tree down Thursday. It's the first time in all these years since I've had kids that the tree has come down before New Year's. On New Year's Day, we'd watch the parade, we'd have dinner, and then we'd all take the tree down. This year I could not wait to get that tree out of here.

It's so hard dealing with reality. Sometimes I'd just like to think I'm asleep and I'm going to wake up and this will be all over. Or he's on vacation. It's just a nightmare. Just something I dreamt one night, and he's going to drive in the yard. Every time a red car comes down the road, I think, "Oh, it's not true." But it is. The car goes by, and he's not coming home.

I think when I finally could accept it a little better was one night when I was sitting here all alone—I hate being alone anymore—and I kept thinking of that night and thinking of Rose and thinking of the circumstances and seeing that I honestly didn't know he was going to kill himself. He knew the dangers of guns, and he knew what they were to be used for.

I just can't understand why anybody would not want to even discuss it and say, "Look, I'm afraid I'm going to kill myself. Can you get me help?" I would have gotten help—if I had had to work two jobs to get him counseling. Plus he had medical insurance. He could have gone and gotten help. There is help there. Why they don't seek an alternative, I don't know. I wish he had. I wish I had been smart enough to realize he needed help.

How can a mother not know? I just accepted him as shy and withdrawn. I did everything for him in a way. I made sure his car payment was sent in on time. He'd give me his check. He'd sign it, and I'd fill it in and mail it. I paid his bills. If he wanted to go somewhere and he wanted me to take him, I took him. If he was having a problem at school with a subject, I helped him through it, or at work, if he was having problems. And to have known him, you would have understood. I made everything easy for him so that he wouldn't have to feel different, even though I knew he was. I always said he was just extremely shy, but I don't know now. Maybe he was depressed and I just never noticed it. I don't know.

He was twenty years old, and he never really had the experience of dating or falling in love or someday maybe getting married and having a home. He never went from boyhood to manhood, and that's sad. At twenty years old, his life was just beginning, and then it was ended, very violently. One moment of anger, and I lost a whole world. I think if I could have gotten him through that moment, I would have him today. I really do believe I could have gotten him through that moment. If I had realized what he was going to do that night, I would have him today, because I don't think anybody honestly wants to die.

There are so many unanswered questions for me. I don't know if they'll ever get answered. They probably never will. Him of all people, knowing he had started to talk to me, why he couldn't let me know. Why he couldn't say, "Mum, I'm having a problem. I'm having a hard time dealing with things. Can you help me?" There's too much unsaid and too much undone, too many avenues that had not been traveled yet. I would like to know why, but I never will. Why he chose such a violent way, especially when he knew I don't like violence. Why he chose to do it here. Why he chose that particular night, the night his brother went off on a cruise. Was he afraid of going into a new job? He was starting a new job on Monday. They were going to teach him management. Whether he was afraid of that step forward I don't know.

I feel the most guilt because I was the one who said that guns could come into the house. My husband did not want them in the house. I went against everything I believed in, letting him have the guns. If they hadn't been here, maybe it would have been something else, I don't know, but it wouldn't have been that night. I might still have him; then again, I might not. But if I had not let the guns in the house, this never would have happened. I feel more guilt about that than anything.

I have yet to feel angry. I just feel very hurt and very rejected. To think he didn't have enough faith in me to want to talk to me or let me know he was hurting. We all hurt at points in our lives; we all have things that make us hurt. But I do feel upset that he didn't come to me and say he was hurting or that something was bothering him.

I can't get angry yet. I've been angry at the other kids. I can't get angry at him, because he hurt himself more. It makes you wonder though. I know I've been very angry at my husband, very bitter. I still am to a degree. I don't think I've ever admitted that till now, but I am very bitter. I resent the fact that he's still here and Jim isn't. Yet my husband didn't do it. I imagine he's hurt in his own way.

My mother is so afraid of telling people what happened. It's like I've sinned and she's saying, "I'm ashamed of you, Joan. I don't want you to say anything to people. You've done something wrong." I was up at my parents' place yesterday, and a friend of my mother's was there. She said, "You've lost a lot of weight." And I said, "Yeah, after my son died, I lost a lot." And she said, "Oh, which son?" And I said, "My second. He committed suicide in March." She said, "Oh, your mother never told me." My mother just looked at me as if to say, "Why did you say that, Joan?" She cannot put Jimmy at rest. She cannot let me put him at rest.

Some people don't want to talk to you; they avoid you. It makes you feel like you've done something. Did I do something wrong? I walk around with a lot of guilt feelings. I have days when it won't bother me at all. I think, "He's finally at peace." And other days I'll find myself, even at work, out of nowhere, crying. My voice breaks up, or I'll find tears rolling down my face. Something, even a person's voice, will start it.

A lot of nights I just don't sleep. I'll wake up many a night and hear his voice. I wake up at about one, because he used to get home from work then, and we used to sit and talk till maybe two in the morning. So from one to two most nights, I don't sleep. I'm wide awake, because that was our time together.

If I sit and watch TV—especially at night when I don't sleep, if I get up and sit in that chair—I can feel him there. I feel like he's sitting on the couch watching TV with me. When I go up into his room, I know he's there. And if I go into the kitchen to cook, it's just like he's standing there, teasing me, like he used to, about my cooking.

For the longest time, I could not go into his room, even after they had painted it. We hired somebody to clean it up. A lot of the clothes that were in his drawers I've gotten rid of, but the kids asked me to keep the jackets and sweaters, so I said, "All right, for now I will. The rest of it I'm not keeping." A friend of ours is selling the guns.

I've made the room totally opposite what he would have liked, so it's not his room anymore, it's just a room. It's all done in blues and pink. I put curtains up I knew he wouldn't have liked. Yet he's still there. I can't change that. He's filled this whole house. That's why, eventually, I would like to get out of here, start all over somewhere else.

He's been dead nine months, and for nine months I haven't done housework. Now I've got to try to catch up on things. I've let everything go, even bills. Magazines keep sending me demand notices. I don't remember ordering them. Everything I did that whole day is a blank. I mean, I ordered subscriptions to magazines that I don't even remember sending out. And then the next week or so, I sent out checks for our car payments, insurance payments, everything, and I never signed one of them. So that made our payments late. They sent our checks back to the bank, and we had to reissue all new checks. I find I do that a lot lately, and I never did that before. I'm very careful with things.

I finally went through all Jim's papers. He was just like me. We're like packrats in many ways. He saved advertisements, little things that really served no purpose. He had a membership in the National Rifle Association, and they kept writing letters asking him to renew it. So I finally wrote them and said he'd killed himself and that I would appreciate it if they would not send any more mail. I'm still getting his magazines. I called, and they said, "There's nothing you can do. His subscriptions will have to run their course."

The bank harassed us about his car payments from May on. They told us he knew what he was going to do, that we must have had a warning and we just didn't pay attention. One of the collectors came and said, "You can't tell me you didn't know he was going to do this. Everybody knows." A woman called us up and said, "He knew what he was doing. We're going to give you twenty-four hours to give us an answer. Take over the payments, or we are going to repossess the car." We had to pay a lawyer to get the bank off our backs. We made arrangements for them to take the car out between 8 A.M. and 4 P.M. At nine forty-five that night, they came for the car. I was really upset to see it go. He'd polished it, vacuumed it. That was his world. And to watch somebody just hoist it up and take it out— Then we got another letter from them demanding that we pay them the difference between what Jim owed and what the car was auctioned off for. Again I had to get a lawyer. Now they're not bothering us. But I thought the way they handled it was very tactless, very cruel.

Since Jim died, our whole way has changed. Our eating habits are all gone. We don't even sit down and eat anymore. Everybody eats and runs. Of course, there's only two of us here most of the time. And certain foods that I've always eaten, all of a sudden I won't eat. Jim made spaghetti. He made the best spagetti sauce going. I can't stand spaghetti anymore.

I've found that all our attitudes have changed, our dispositions. I hope we don't stay this way. I'd like to go back to the way it was when the kids were little. It was good then, because I controlled everything really. I could protect them. They stayed in the house with me most of the time, because we lived on a busy street. They knew they weren't allowed out in front of the house. Jimmy was in most of the time anyway. He stayed in a lot. If he went out to play, he'd only play for a short time and then he'd come in. He was with me. But the others knew they couldn't play in front of the house. They stayed in the backyard, and they were good. I could control it. If I knew they were going somewhere and they were going to get hurt, I wouldn't let them go. My kids were my world, each and every one of them in their way. I had no life beyond that, so having him do this really took a big part of me with him.

The support group I go to is helpful, because I don't feel as though I've done something drastically wrong. I'm not alone, and I'm not the only one who's lost a child. There have been a lot of people in the group who have lost children to suicide. One woman lost two children, years apart. Some of them have lost an only child. Some of the kids had been treated for depression, and some had not. One woman said her son was depressed, but they didn't realize how severely. Most kids go through a state of depression going from adolescence to adulthood. They don't want to become adults yet, but they can't stay children forever, although we would like to keep them that way.

You don't expect to grieve for your children. Your parents, yes. Eventually, they get old, and time ends for them. But not a child, not this way, not by his own doing. I'm a firm believer that God put us here for a purpose, and only He has the right to take us back. We can't do it ourselves. We can't wish it to happen, although since Jim died, there have been many times I wished I could go, too. But I would never put my kids through that. I used to pray sometimes, "Why can't you take me back, God? Just let me find out why. Did I do something wrong in this lifetime?" I mean, at twenty years old, his life was just started, and he ended it. It just doesn't seem right, it really doesn't.

I know I'm not alone in this, and I know I'm not the first mother who's lost a child, and I know I won't be the last. I wish I could be. I wish each one of us who has lost a child in this past year could be the last parent to lose a child to suicide, but we know we won't be. I wish they could find some way to prevent it—either educate the kids better or educate parents better on looking for signs. There has to be an alternative to this so nobody has to suffer this way and no child has to feel that there are no other alternatives when there are. I don't know if they'll ever find the answer, but, God, I pray they do.

After Jim died, I asked people to make donations to the Samaritans [a suicide hot line] or to Safe Place [a support group for survivors] instead of sending flowers. Every year on Jim's birthday and on the anniversary of his death, I will send something to them. If it helps keep some young kid from doing the same thing my son did, or if it saves some parent from this agony, maybe then it will make what I'm going through easier.

I seem to have moments when I can feel so good about everything, and then, out of nowhere, this awful feeling comes over me. I keep saying, "Next year will be better. Next year will be better." But I still don't have him. I still can't change that fact.

Catherine: A White-Knuckle Ride

Catherine and her lover, Marion, shared their lives for eight years before Marion's suicide in July 1988. Marion was fifty-two at the time, Catherine thirty-five. Since most people did not know the nature of the relationship between the two women or the true circumstances of Marion's death, they could not appreciate the depth or the complexity of Catherine's grief. I interviewed Catherine in March 1990.

When suicide occurs in the context of a nontraditional relationship, the survivor often experiences a double dose of stigma. If that relationship has been concealed, the survivor may feel unrecognized and therefore unsupported in her or his grief. The additional decision not to reveal the true circumstances of the death can augment the sense of isolation.

Catherine's story also tells of a family's need to reconstruct itself after the suicide of one member. Marion's two sons, Andrew and Samuel, were twenty and eighteen, respectively, at the time of their mother's death. Catherine's relationship with them had been framed by her connection, and theirs, with Marion. Once she was gone, the three survivors had to find new ways to feel connected with one another. This kind of "realignment," as Catherine calls it, may be necessary not only in nontraditional families but also in nuclear families.

I guess my experience after Marion's death was very similar in some ways to what a married person goes through. All of a sudden, I was isolated. The world travels in couples, and I didn't have the other part of what I needed to function in the groups of people we had been comfortable with.

Shortly after Marion and I met, which was eight years before she died, she told me that she had had a serious depression and tried to kill herself when she was in graduate school. She left graduate school and lived in Europe for a couple of years and then came back to the States and spent probably eight or ten years under the care of a psychiatrist, with medications and therapy and that kind of thing, through her twenties. She was not finding that her mood was getting any better or that she was feeling any more positive about life. So she had shock treatments on an outpatient basis for, I guess, a six-week period. And then after that, she just decided that she had to do something. Her boyfriend was very supportive through this whole thing. They'd been going together for about five years. So she decided that what she needed to do was get married. She got married and had two boys, Andrew and Samuel.

About eight years later, her sister committed suicide. Following her sister's suicide, Marion began addressing the issues in her life in a more direct way. That's when she came out sexually. She left her husband in 1980. It was a very painful and difficult time for her. There was a lot of stress and acclimation. She was always talking about how depressed she was and about not wanting to live anymore. And my response was always, "How could you consider doing something like that to me or to the boys, knowing what it does, having experienced losing your sister?"

Then she developed fibromyalgia, which is a joint and muscle disorder that is chronic but not debilitating in the same way that arthritis is. She was in constant pain from irritable bowel syndrome, which she had developed shortly after her sister committed suicide. So we were dealing with a woman who had a very restricted diet, was in constant physical pain, and was still struggling with depression. She would have periods of being able to cope and then periods of not being able to cope and function. Six or eight months before she died, we started doing a major renovation on the house. She would periodically say to me, "I can't live anymore. You'd be better off without me." And I would say, "How can you possibly say that?" I tried all the usual reasoning tactics to make her understand and appreciate how much the boys and I cared for her and how much we needed her in our lives.

In the spring, around April or May, I got a phone call from her at work, and she was hysterical. She said, "I'm losing my grip. I can't function." I said, "Well, I'll meet you. Where do you want me to meet you?" I left work and picked up some flowers and met her at a park and basically chased her around the pond while she was just hysterical. She ended up sitting in the middle of the path at the pond, sobbing. I didn't understand what was happening. I had no idea. I was very affectionate and tried to be supportive. We went home and had dinner, and she seemed to feel better.

We decided that the way we were going to address this was for me to go to therapy with her and give her support. We went in to see her psychiatrist, and that was the first time that I heard that she was clinically diagnosed as having a mood disorder. I'd never been aware of that before. I just thought that this was a cyclical thing, and some times were better than others. I hadn't really understood, and she had never really told me. The doctor was explaining this whole thing to both of us and what the future was going to be like. I'm sitting there saying, "That's fine, that's fine, as long as I can understand it, as long as we can educate ourselves about it and Marion understands that I'm here for her and that, by my coming, we can break the isolation that she feels with the illness." We had also decided that once I became comfortable with understanding and being able to support her, we would include the boys, so that the family could understand, because we were always very affected by the ups and downs.

Before she died, she was missing a lot of work. I would get very impatient—"You have to get up. You have to go. You can't stay here. It's just going to get worse." When we went to see the psychiatrist about it, the last thing she said to Marion as we were walking out the door was, "Do you feel suicidal? Are you okay?" That was a relief to me, because it made me understand that Marion had talked about killing herself in a clinical setting, as well as talking about it at home. It wasn't a secret. And Marion said, "No, I'm fine." When we left, I was feeling very positive, although I was physically exhausted and drained. This was the most difficult period we'd been through. For a month before she died, she was eating baby food. She could not digest food anymore and was losing a tremendous amount of weight and had been missing a lot of work and complaining about pain.

We went to the movies with Andrew, her older son, that Friday night. Samuel, the younger one, was going on a canoeing trip in Maine and had called us when he arrived there. So everyone was connected. Everyone knew what was happening, where everyone else was.

The next day, Andrew and I were working outdoors. Marion was out doing grocery shopping. I came inside later, and she was sobbing. I said, "What's wrong?" She said she wasn't feeling well and didn't know what to do. I called Andrew in, and both of us were comforting her. Then I left the two of them alone. When he came outdoors, I went back into the house. I said, "I think it's important that Andrew be able to comfort you and be part of your illness and understand it." And I asked her if that was okay. Later, Marion was upstairs, and I had to do some errands. I was walking out the front door, and I said, "I'm going to the store. You going to come down and say good-bye to me?" She came down and gave me a kiss and said, "I love you." And I said, "Just hang in there. We're both tired. We have two weeks off. We'll just relax." I was trying to be very reassuring.

When I came back, there was a note from Andrew saying that she had been in a car accident and the police were looking for her. The police had come and picked him up at the house. The accident had occurred just a quarter of a mile from the house, down at the end of the street, around this back country road. So I got in the car and drove down there. Her car was not there, but the police were. Apparently, she had gone into three trees with the car, was injured, bleeding from her face, and ran from the scene. Someone who had been traveling behind her chased her and said, "Are you okay?" And she said, "I'm fine. I live around the corner. Leave me alone," and ran from him. After I had driven back to the house and the police had driven Andrew back, I said to him, "Andrew, there's something you have to know. Your mother is suicidal. We've got to find her." I got in the car and went screaming into the woods, looking for her. We couldn't find her.

There were search parties out all night long. They kept grilling me: Did she drink? Did she do this? Did she do that? No, no, no, no. Around three or four in the morning, I remembered that when we came back from the movie the night before, she wouldn't come to bed. She was out in the kitchen, working from her briefcase. I remembered her preoccupation with her briefcase. So I went out to the closet in the kitchen and found it. Inside there was a note, a suicide note, addressed to me and written to the boys and myself. And there were manila folders for every aspect of her life—her insurance, her personal effects, bank accounts, everything. I didn't tell the police that I'd found a suicide note.

At dawn, they called in the state police dogs and searched the woods for her. They didn't find anything. Then they called the troops from the air base and sent search parties out. Around ten in the morning, they sent state police helicopters out and were scanning the whole area. And the whole time I had this note. I kept thinking, "If we could just find her, maybe she's unconscious from the injury to the head."

Around ten thirty in the morning, the lieutenant came down the street in the patrol car and said, "I think we've found her." So I jumped in the car, and he said, "I think everything's okay." We started heading toward a recreational pond down the street from the house. All of a sudden, he shut the radio off and said, "I don't think it's good news." We arrived at the pond, and they were putting her into a body bag. They'd found her under the float on the far side of the pond. I had been at that pond three or four times, all of us had, during the night. But there's a town side, which is the beach part, and then the other side, where nobody goes. That's where she was. The policeman came back and said to me, "Someone has to identify the body." And I said, "I can't do that." So I described some jewelry I'd given her. And he went back and said, "It's her." Then a female police officer came over, got in the car, and couldn't get it started. She was hysterical. She said, "Are you a family member?" And I said, "Yes." She said, "Well, you're going to find out anyway." I said, "What am I going to find out?" She said, "Her wrists were slashed."

The boys and I made all the arrangements for the memorial service ourselves, as a family, which I think was essential, and we were together through the whole thing. We selected poetry and other readings. Each piece would be identified, and the final words would be, "With the reading of this piece, Catherine says good-bye. . .Andrew says good-bye. . .Samuel says good-bye." And we selected the music that would follow. I'll never understand how the three of us made that happen, how we were ever able to come together and go through that process. I have no idea where the thoughts came from, I have no idea where the music came from, I have no idea where the energy came from.

The day of the service, the three of us went upstairs, and the boys ironed my dress while I showered. We came down the stairs together and went to the service after everyone was already in the church. There was a real feeling of connectedness among the three of us. There were people from all aspects of Marion's life at the service: from her professional life, her personal life, her family life. I don't think people knew all the facets of her, because we all shared so many different connections with her. We really made an effort in the service to take all the fragments and make them whole again and share with people our view of who Marion was. And I know that we were successful in doing that.

People were very vigilant the first week and following that. They were at the house. But it was bizarre. It was as though people couldn't accept the truth, not only the truth about her death and the fact that she had really died but also the truth about how it happened. A few very close friends knew the truth and couldn't accept it. The majority of people did not know—and to this day do not know—what really happened. I know it was very painful for people. Marion's pictures were around the house. But I don't understand why they couldn't cope. Some friends made a real effort to continue to stay connected, and other people ran like hell. They just couldn't connect anymore, didn't know what to say and didn't know what to do.

I couldn't focus on anything for probably six or eight months. I could listen to music, but I couldn't listen to voices. It was as though there was too much noise in voices, and I'd just block it out. So I'd watch Windham Hill videos. The stereo system had been disconnected because of the construction in the house, and that's the first thing we put together after Marion's death. We played things we thought would be comforting or soothing to listen to.

I went through a period of real trauma thinking that what had happened to Marion was going to happen to me. Fortunately, I was seeing a therapist who was able to say, "Listen, you're thirty-five years old. You have shown no signs of any kind of clinical mental disorder. You're not schizophrenic; you're not depressed. You're situationally depressed because of what's happened, but you've been able to function. I can say with a reasonable amount of certainty that you're probably going to be okay." That was a relief to me. I didn't have to worry that I was somehow going to get to a place where I wouldn't be able to manage my life anymore and that the only alternative I would think I had was to kill myself.

The day after we found Marion, the boys and I were sitting in her psychiatrist's office. We went to see her psychiatrist again the day after the memorial service and then saw a family therapist for the rest of the summer together and basically tried to work through the issues and the realities of what had happened. Her younger son, Samuel, was going off to college as a freshman in September—this was July—so I got him ready and took him to school. He was fine for the first week or two, and then he started to crash. He saw a counselor at school, and that seemed to be better. Probably on a daily basis he was calling me. We were all very needy at that time. Marion's older son, Andrew, tried very hard just to go on. Samuel and I were the basket cases, and Andrew was trying to be strong. He said to us, "I feel as though I said good-bye to Mom the day of the service." I had some real concerns about him, because two summers before that, he had been anorexic and was in therapy for almost a year, working through this eating disorder, which is a form of suicidal behavior. I felt that he was really repressing and didn't quite know what to do. I did what I could. I stayed in constant communication with the kids, let them know that I was there, and made sure that we had time together.

I was completely blown away and didn't want to live anymore myself and had gotten the message from every clinical person I had spoken to, "You can't kill yourself. That's not an option for you. You've got to stay alive for these kids. They cannot deal with that kind of loss." I'd get angry and say, "Why do I?" And I kept struggling along and verbalizing my frustration with therapists and with the boys and trying to understand why I was left in this situation. I was a coparent, but I wasn't the primary parent.

I tried to talk to the boys' father after Marion died. I said to him, "We have to think about what's important for these boys. It's obvious that we are going to have a relationship, and you and I need to work out the logistics of doing that, because I don't want the boys to feel as if they have to choose. We should be able to coexist." He said, "Those boys are fine. They're strong." He had no idea that his son was anorexic, no idea that his son was seeing a therapist at school. These were all things that Marion and I had assumed responsibility for, and now I'm assuming it, on my own, for the boys. Every time there was a crisis or a decision to be made, Marion and I dealt with it, and I've continued to deal with it since Marion's death.

I joined a suicide survivors' group and met a woman whose husband had killed himself seven years earlier. I found that I had a lot in common with her. She has two children who are the same ages as Samuel and Andrew. We were both struggling with the same issues and having a tremendous amount of difficulty understanding how someone could kill herself or himself. The other people in the group had lost blood relatives—father, brother—and they seemed to have an easier time understanding and expressed some insight into that kind of depression. And Sam and Andrew have said that they can understand a little bit that kind of desperation and depression. That's something that I still go over and over again in my mind: I don't understand it. I can't get around it and accept that it's a possibility.

I remember meeting a man at a restaurant about five or six months after Marion died. We somehow ended up sitting on the same side of the table and started chatting. He asked me what I was doing, and I mentioned having lost Marion. This man had never seen me before. He put his arm around me and said, "I want you to know that it's not your fault." He was a retired college professor and had tried to kill himself a year before that. He said, "You don't understand. Marion didn't even know you existed when she was at that place. She wasn't thinking about you, she wasn't thinking about the children, she wasn't thinking about anything other than escape." He gave me, just in that encounter, something else to try to hold on to, to keep going with.

The five months from Marion's death until Christmas were like a white-knuckle ride of terror, but once we made it through that period, we started somehow to have some faith that we could make it through other things—her birthday, the anniversary of her death, our birthdays.

The boys and I have tried to stay connected with one another—to find a way of letting go and making Marion a part of our lives in a positive way, not in a way that feels like a burden and a shame that will never go away. We're trying very hard to make her death something that we can live with. All three of us—and we've said this to one another—have made the decision to live and go on. It may be shitty at times, but we're going to do it. And I think that's a really important decision to have made, because Marion certainly showed us that there are other alternatives.

[Catherine's story is continued in chapter 3, page 93.]

*

Epilogue: Finding the Words

A sense of disconnection echoes through the stories that survivors tell. Suicide leaves them hanging, their own lives suddenly fragmented, like "something that gets thrown up into the air and lands in a million different pieces."

The loss is a blow to every fiber of one's being, an assault so great that at first the mind and heart and psyche recoil from the reality of it. That is why so many survivors recall initially feeling numb. "I was on automatic pilot," says one person. "It was like being in Jell-O," says another. Memories of the first few moments, hours, days, and weeks after the suicide are often spotty. One may recall a small circumstance in minute detail but be unable to remember who attended the funeral or how the burial arrangements were made.

The initial shock is physical as well as psychic. "Your stomach just drops," says Chris (whose story appears in chapter 3), describing her reaction to the news of her brother's suicide. Laura recalls that, despite having a cold at the time, she started chain-smoking clove cigarettes, because "every time I inhaled, it was like getting kicked in the chest by a horse. It was almost as if I needed that to remind myself I was alive. . . ." Not only feelings but physical sensations seem to be temporarily or intermittently numbed.

It Can't Be True

An almost universal response to suicide is disbelief—"No, it can't be true." The suddenness of suicide, the fact that it so often takes the survivors by surprise, makes it difficult to accept the reality of the death, let alone the reality that it was an intentional death. The night her son killed himself with a shotgun in an upstairs bedroom, Joan remembers asking over and over, "Are you sure he's dead? Are you sure he's dead?" Although she knew her son was dead, she couldn't believe it; she kept clinging to the hope that he was still alive. Chris recalls hearing the news of her brother's suicide from her mother: "I said, 'He was in an accident.' I wouldn't even let her tell me. . . .And then I said, 'Well, how did it happen?' And she said, 'He was in his car. He started the engine—' And I said, 'It blew up.' I mean, the furthest thing from my mind— I couldn't believe it."

Even in cases where the suicide was preceded by a long period of self-destructive behavior or previous attempts at suicide, the survivor is left feeling that it can't be true. The reality is simply too horrible to take in at first. Survivors often search for another explanation—murder or an accident. As Natalie says of her mother's leap from an eighteen-story building, "[Suicide is] so unbelievable that a lot of unbelievable thoughts come into your mind. Suicide seemed as bizarre as the idea that she might have been having an affair with some person and he pushed her. They're all bizarre!" Other explanations may take on a reality of their own and be easier to imagine and accept. However violent and horrible, an accidental death or even murder does not carry the stigma and the sense of abandonment that suicide does. It is easier, after all, to accept that someone one loves was taken away than that he or she chose to leave.

By its very nature, suicide is an act of profound violence, yet some suicides are more violent than others. Combined with the suddenness of the loss, a particularly violent death can add to the unreality of the experience for the survivors. Natalie says, "The violent aspect of [my mother's] death is something I can barely keep in my consciousness for more than a second at a time." She tells about her fixation on the height of the building from which her mother jumped: "For the longest time, whenever I passed a tall building, I'd start counting—one, two, three— trying to figure out whether it was as tall as the building my mother had jumped from. Most of them were not eighteen sto- ries. I'd count the stories and it would be fourteen, and I'd think, 'Bigger than that?' "

Because of the extreme violence of her son's death—a shotgun blast to his head—Joan never saw his body. Moments after his death, she wanted to go into his room and see him, but she couldn't bring herself to do it. Later, when she decided she really did want to see him, the police, her children, and the undertaker all said, "No, you don't," and she never did. As she puts it, "I never got to say good-bye to him." Several months later, she still feels sometimes as though the death of her son is not real but a nightmare from which she will awaken to find him alive and safe. Seeing a car like his approaching the house, she slips for a moment into the expectation that he's returning home: "Every time a red car comes down the road, I think, 'Oh, it's not true.' But it is. The car goes by, and he's not coming home."

Catherine also did not see her lover's body, but she chose not to (as she explains in her continued story in chapter 3):

> I think the boys and I are more comfortable with the memory of her alive than with some image of her dead. I didn't need to see the body to know that she was gone. That doesn't mean that I don't think I see her on the street all the time. I think that's true for anyone who loses someone close. You think you see the image of that person in all kinds of different situations and places.

Yet she sometimes wonders whether seeing the body would have helped her begin to understand the reality of the death.

When Laura saw her husband's body in a funeral home in Wales, she found herself looking for a telltale wart on his hand: "His hands were folded, and I remember checking. The wart was there, and then I knew that it was Stuart, that he really was dead. If I hadn't seen him dead, I think I would have had active fantasies about him coming back. I *still* had fantasies. . . ." Seeing the body does not necessarily preclude those fantasies, nor does it erase the unreality and disbelief, but for many people, it is an important first step in being able simply to take in the fact of the death. In addition, it is an opportunity, however imperfect, to begin to say good-bye.

Words, Rites, and Secrets

Even though the stigma surrounding suicide in our society has diminished considerably over the past century and particularly in recent years, it may still influence the survivors' decisions about what to tell people. For some, the decision not to reveal the truth about the death is motivated by a need for protection, whether it is the desire to protect the memory of the person who has died or a need to protect the surviving family members. In either case, the survivor anticipates public and private judgments about the person who has died and about those whose lives are linked to that person.

The problem with not telling is that it forces the survivor to maintain the secrecy of the suicide, making it much more difficult to grieve openly and fully and to feel supported in doing so. For Catherine that problem was magnified twofold. Not only did most people not know that Marion had killed herself, but they were also unaware of the true nature of Catherine's relationship with her. Not knowing that the two women were lovers, they could not know the depth and extent of Catherine's grief after Marion's suicide. The effort to maintain the secrecy of a suicide can become an enormous burden for the survivors, keeping them isolated and magnifying the darker feelings that so many people experience in the wake of the death—shame, anger, and guilt. Moreover, secrets have a way of being sensed, if not guessed outright, and they often spawn speculation and rumor, so that, ironically, the kind of hushed murmuring that the secrecy is meant to avoid is actually encouraged.

Even if the cause of death is not covered up, suicide, like other taboos, is both fascinating and fearful to the onlookers, inviting speculation and even fabrication to explain the forbidden act. Laura recalls the rumors surrounding her husband's suicide: that he was a victim of incest and that she, since his death, was having an affair with her friend Judy. "People were really curious about my life and just how deviant it might be. I had a sense that I was like a freak show. . . . They wanted to know, but they didn't want to get *too* close." The rumors that are generated serve the dual purpose of explaining the suicide and keeping it at a safe distance: there is a simple reason why this suicide happened (and why it happened in that family), which has nothing to do with me (or with my family).

Many survivors feel a deep sense of shame, and even if the suicide is not kept a secret, there may be a tendency to retreat from public exposure. As Laura says, "Part of me wanted to open up to the world . . . because I felt I was containing so much. And then there was part of me that really desperately needed to hide because of the shame that I was carrying and the sense of failure." Any whisperings and rumors only add to these feelings.

Natalie found some relief from her sense of failure when she talked with her mother's former therapist: "[I felt as though] my mother had somehow said, 'You're not okay enough for me even to stay alive for.' When her therapist saw me afterward, she didn't say, 'You're the daughter? You're the cause of this. You were terrible!' She still treated me like an okay person."

The rites of death—funerals, wakes, sitting shiva—help guide the living through the initial shock of loss. They provide the survivors with a series of stepping-stones through the first hours and days after the death. In the face of a loss that cannot yet be fully taken in, let alone understood, the survivors must make a series of concrete decisions about how the death will be acknowledged, from choosing a casket to deciding who will lead the funeral service and what will be said. These decisions can help provide substance and structure during a period that may otherwise feel like a void. They also help the survivors begin to take in the sheer reality of the death. Most important, the rites of death provide a social channel for offering—and receiving—comfort. By attending the funeral service, visiting the survivors, bringing them food, sending cards expressing their sympathy, friends and acquaintances acknowledge the loss for and with the survivors, letting them know they are not alone.

But after a suicide, the sadness and regret for a life that has come to an end are colored by the feeling that the way in which it ended was all wrong. Moreover, if the survivors are carrying a burden of secrecy and shame, if they blame themselves or fear being blamed, the rites of death may be a source of further pain rather than comfort. Joan found no comfort in the rites surrounding her son's death: "I only had the wake one night, because I couldn't take any more of it. I wasn't going to have anything. I couldn't see any purpose to it. He was dead. Having a wake or a funeral could not change things; it only hurt more."

For Natalie, the most important part in planning her mother's funeral was that her suicide not be hidden: "The only thing I insisted on was that [my mother's] letter be read. Other than that, I said [to the rabbi], 'Do a funeral.' " Yet the rabbi chose not to read the last part of her mother's letter, in which she said simply, "I can't go on."

Catherine, Andrew, and Samuel chose not to acknowledge

Marion's death as a suicide at the memorial service. What was most important for them was that they plan every aspect of the service together. With Marion no longer there as the central link between Catherine and the boys, the three of them had to create their own sense of family together, and the way in which they planned and carried out the memorial service was a first step in that process. The service, which consisted of music and readings that they chose together, was deeply satisfying to Catherine: "We really made an effort to take all the fragments and make them whole again and share with people our view of who Marion was. And I know that we were successful in doing that."

For Laura, Stuart's funeral service was a mixture of pain, humor, and comfort. She felt that the religious rites observed at the service were a betrayal of her husband, who had been an atheist. The sight of the organist, with her blue hair, bird's-nest hat, and clip-on sunglasses, was similarly out of keeping for a service in memory of her husband, yet the humor of the scene somehow served as an antidote to the pain: "In the midst of all the pain, she was playing the organ. It was almost as if Stuart was [looking] over my shoulder. I could hear him making some funny, biting remark." And during the service, Laura was able to draw comfort from a memory of her husband that was emblematic of what she loved in him. She even found comfort in the sound of the machinery that moved the casket: "I remember thinking it was amazing the way life kept getting in the way of death. We just could not send him off as flawlessly as he had sent himself off. That was very reassuring to me." In a sense, it was not the ritualistic elements of the service that were comforting so much as the glitches in it and the opportunity to remember and cherish the humorous, light side of her husband.

Death makes the living hold on to one another for comfort and support. We need that contact to reassure ourselves that we are not alone in our loss and to reaffirm the connections that remain in our lives. After a suicide, the survivors may choose to close their doors, to protect themselves from public exposure, especially if they are harboring feelings of shame or guilt, or if they have decided not to reveal the true cause of the death.

But the survivors are not the only ones who may retreat; those from whom they would otherwise expect to receive comfort may do the same. Susan's boyfriend never called her while she was away planning and attending her father's funeral—a time when she was most in need of his support. Catherine had a similar experience: "Some friends made a real effort to continue to stay connected, and other people ran like hell. They just couldn't connect anymore, didn't know what to say and didn't know what to do." As Philip, commenting on his roommate's pointed absence, puts it, "People run from the very idea of suicide like they do from fire and high places."

Suicide brings all of us face to face with the possibility of despair and loss in our own lives. By acknowledging that suicide happens—in our midst, among people we know—we must confront our own vulnerability to self-destructive impulses, however close to or far from the act of suicide they may seem. Moreover, the pain of the survivors—of a mother whose son has shot and killed himself, of a wife whose husband has taken a fatal overdose of drugs, of a daughter whose mother has jumped to her death—is frightening to witness. Not only do we not want to be reminded that some people decide to end their lives, but we also do not want to imagine that any of us, not just the survivors, could suffer that kind of loss. Suicide is an inescapable reminder that we are all, in some measure, susceptible to the failure of hope in our own lives and vulnerable to the consequences of that failure in other lives.

If Only . . .

"But if I had not let the guns in the house, this never would have happened." ". . . if we hadn't seen that movie [that night], maybe she could have changed her mind at the last minute." Much of the wisdom that we gain in our lives comes after the fact, in hindsight. After a suicide, the voices of hindsight can haunt the survivor: if only I had done this, if only I hadn't done that, he (or she) might still be alive today. The if onlys whisper or shout in the survivor's mind, intensifying the pain of the loss as the survivor becomes convinced of his or her own culpability in the death. Hindsight imbues memory with the imminence of things to come, and as the survivor remembers all that preceded the suicide, the death itself—its inevitability—looms over every word, act, and circumstance. Knowing what I know now, how could I not have known then?

The if onlys that come from hindsight lead easily and quickly to blame, whether the target is oneself or someone else. Particularly after a suicide, which is a death that, perhaps more than any other, robs us of any comfort in understanding, blame is enticing, because it provides an explanation where we fear there is none. It gives us a way to frame the loss in reasons that we can point to, that have not been taken away from us: it was my (your) fault; I (you) should have known.

Why and Why and Why?

The act of suicide leaves trails of questions in its wake, questions blazed in the minds and hearts and guts of those left behind: "Was she cold?" "What was he thinking?" "Why that night?" Why? Even after years of pain, unhappiness, and perhaps other, unsuccessful attempts at suicide, the act itself is so inconceivable that it leaves the survivors speechless with questions. Why and why and why? None of the trails has an end. Each leads to others, which turn this way and that, leading to more questions and back to earlier ones. Natalie recalls going through her mother's trash looking at torn up pieces of paper: "I was desperate for answers, desperate to know, desperate to feel connected to [my mother]."

The smallest questions and the largest feel equally important after suicide. No ordinary scale applies. "Was she cold?" is just as important as "Why that night?" and "Why did he do it?" At their core, the questions are the same. They gnaw at the survivors, part of the struggle to bring the enormity of the act into some imaginable sphere of human thought, feeling, and action, because suicide—self-murder—is one of the most unimaginable acts that a human being can undertake.

When someone dies, the material signs of that person's life loom large for those left behind. How can these things still be here when the life that inhabited them is gone? They seem infused with the person, and at the same time emptied out of that life. After suicide, the survivors, in their search for answers, may fix on these things, as if by shaking them, by turning them upside down and inside out, they might shake out the answers they seek. The smallest thing—a coffee cup, a pair of boots— may hold a message. That thing is neither small nor insignificant if it is all that is left.

Voicing the Words

Suicide wipes out all the assumptions and explanations we normally rely on to give meaning to our lives, both hour to hour and over the years. It leaves in its wake a void that is frightening to the survivors. The litany of if onlys and the intense and prolonged questioning are responses to that void, an effort to make some sense of a loss that feels fundamentally senseless.

Giving voice to these responses helps make the loss real, bit by bit. At first, just the mechanical process of forming the words and speaking them—hearing oneself speak them—can help let in the reality of the suicide in a way that is tolerable at least in that moment of speaking and being heard. Gradually, the questioning becomes a way for the survivors to try to fathom the loss and its meaning in their lives. "Why did we see *that* movie *that* night?" "How long had he planned this?" "What did she mean when she said———?" "Why didn't I make him get help?" "If she really loved me, how could she hurt me like this?"

Survivors need to be able to voice these questions in the company of people they trust. But it can be difficult to find listeners, people who can bear to stay with the survivors as they give full voice to their grief. Family members may fill this role for one another, as Natalie and her sister did: "I don't think I could have made it without my sister. We had different ways of coping . . . but we had always been very tight, and through the initial period after my mother's death, we were incredibly close." But sometimes family members feel too vulnerable in their own grief to be able to listen fully to others. And in some families, the currents of guilt, blame, and shame leave the survivors feeling estranged from one another rather than drawn together. This was Joan's experience: "You'd think that something like this would have brought the kids closer together or tied the family tighter. I have a daughter who won't come down to the house unless I can guarantee that I'm not going to be depressed. I can't guarantee that." Suicide has a way of magnifying any pre-existing tensions or conflicts among family members. What might have been subterranean and avoidable before the death may now loom large for the survivors.

Laura drew on her close friends as "witnesses and anchors." They not only listened but accepted the chaos and confusion of her grief, reassuring her that what she was feeling was normal and okay. "I would say, 'I can't even grieve right.' And [my friend] would say, 'You're doing this just right.' "

Catherine and Joan found listeners by joining support groups for survivors of suicide. The experience has helped Joan feel less alone with her loss and less responsible for it: "I don't feel as though I've done something drastically wrong. I'm not alone, and I'm not the only one who's lost a child." In the group she joined, Catherine felt a special connection with a woman whose husband had killed himself several years earlier. The opportunity not only to tell their own stories of loss but also to listen to other stories can help survivors feel less alone and isolated in their grief, more connected with other people who are struggling with similar feelings in the wake of suicide.

Therapy is another source of "witnesses and anchors." Catherine was able to tell her therapist of her own suicidal feelings and her fear that she might end up making the same desperate choice that Marion had. She found the reassurance and support she needed to help cope with the frightening feelings she was experiencing after her lover's suicide: "I was completely blown away and didn't want to live anymore myself. . . . I kept struggling along and verbalizing my frustration with therapists and with the boys and trying to understand why I was left in this situation."

The questions that suicide leaves behind cannot be fully answered, yet the search for answers is not easy to give up. When so many vital questions about the life and death of someone whose loss has overwhelmed one's own life remain unanswered, how does one stop asking? Perhaps the most difficult part of grief after suicide is to be able to give full voice to all the questions and then put them aside, unanswered or not fully answered. It takes time, a long time, longer for some than for others. It also takes people who will listen to these questions.

They need to be spoken out loud to people one trusts, not simply held within. Silent questions reverberate much more loudly than those spoken aloud. Like so many other elements of the aftermath of suicide, questioning that is silent and solitary becomes harder to put aside with time. By giving voice to the questions, the if onlys, and all the confusing and frightening feelings that suicide leaves in its wake, the survivors start to find the words for their loss; they can speak that which feels unspeakable. They can begin to find a language for their grief.

3

In the Midland

The six stories in this chapter trace the midland of grief after suicide, as the survivors start to return to their own lives. Several of the stories are told in full here and contain within them accounts of the early aftermath of suicide, but from the vantage point of the midland. One story, told by Catherine, is continued from chapter 2, and another, told by Joy, is started here and continued in chapter 4.

Prologue

OCTOBER 27, 1981. I escaped the first anniversary of my mother's death, or so I thought. I had been dreading it ever since the heat of August had disappeared into September. On the day of her death, one year later, my father, my daughter, and I were in Bermuda, enjoying a pastel-colored, balmy world far removed from New England in the fall. But we returned to the news that my mother's close friend had died two days before, on October 27. The day after our return, my father and I sat side by side at another service. We seemed, for the first time, to be able to hold on to each other and cry together.

I ached at the difference between these two deaths. My mother's was a desperate out. She chose it, planned it secretly, and died alone. The good-byes were all on her side, and she said them silently to herself. Her friend's death came after a two-year struggle with cancer. She savored those last two years of her life and died at home with her family. The good-byes were said out loud, on all sides.

It took me a long time to allow myself to feel angry at my mother for leaving me in the way that she did. At first, I channeled the anger elsewhere: at the medical examiner, for taking so long to arrive and pronounce her dead; at my father, for climbing back into the car she had died in and wanting me to do the same; at my brother, for being so far away and so silent over the months and years that followed. But slowly I began to let myself rage at my mother: how dare she leave me like this, the very person who had given birth to me and launched my life? I might be an adult, but I was still her child. One day, I took out her note to me and reread it: "I know that someday there will be happiness for you." The irony of that statement was unbearable. How could she talk so assuredly of my happiness when she was just about to leave me with more pain than I had ever imagined having to bear?

I remember a nightmare: my daughter and I were in a house somewhere, and my mother, murderous, was coming after us. We were running from room to room, trying to escape her. As she got closer, I could see that one of her hands was missing, a saw blade in its place. I woke up at that point, terrified that my mother would overtake me. I think I was afraid not only of her anger but also of my own, afraid that I might someday slam shut the door to my life, just as she had done to hers—indeed, that I had already closed it partway and was simply going through the motions of living a full life.

I think I was also afraid that if I let myself feel how angry I was, that's all I would be left with—the dark weight within me. But I found that as I was able to air some of the anger, bit by bit and mostly in therapy, the weight lightened. Gradually, it became easier to live with all the paradoxical pieces of this loss: that my mother abandoned me, that she was in desperate pain, that she was both the murderer who had taken my mother away and the victim who had been taken away.

*

Catherine: A White-Knuckle Ride

[Continued from chapter 2, page 79]

It has been a year and a half since Marion's suicide. Catherine is now enrolled in a graduate program in children's literature.

We somehow got through the first year. It was a real shocker for me, because people kept saying, "If you make it through the first year, everything gets better after that." So I guess I thought I'd wake up the 18th of July a year later and I'd be all better. I was worse. Not only did I not feel better, I was totally frustrated and upset that the pain hadn't gone away.

Although my life-style isn't straight, I'm pretty straight in many ways. I don't drink, and I don't take drugs. They gave me Xanax [an antianxiety drug] when Marion died. I took it for two days, and then I took myself off it, because I just couldn't cope with the way it made my body feel. I have not found any way to anesthetize myself to what's happened in my life other than listening to music and watching Windham Hill videos. That's what I've used to go to some other place and find some relief from the pain. And I've gradually begun to be able to function a little more normally.

The boys and I waited a year before we had an interment. We went very quietly through the process of deciding where we were going to bury Marion and when and just didn't force ourselves to make those decisions until we were comfortable doing it. We had the interment on June 21, which was the first day of summer, because we wanted to go through all the seasons before we let her go.

When we were looking for a place to bury her, we put a lot of thought into it. Where had we been happiest? What was most important? We went to an old cemetery [where a plot] was available. It's in an area where we had summered for two years. We had had some wonderful times there, so it seemed like a perfect place. And, coincidentally, Marion had honeymooned in the same area. The cemetery is midway between the place where we would spend summers with the boys and the place where she spent her honeymoon. So there's some kind of joining of her life there.

We stood on the site [of the plot and looked around us]. The name on a [nearby] headstone was the same as Marion's maiden name. Another stone had a name that was the same as the name of the college where her son was going, and another one said "Boston," which is where we'd been all our lives. It's almost a mystical experience for us, that there were familiar things in an unfamiliar place that connected her to that place. And this is coming from people who are not terribly religious but open to the kinds of connections that one can make to ease the passage through the pain and have some feeling of letting go in a place where she would be happy, where she would be truly at rest.

I still don't know what to do with Marion's suicide note. I thought about burying it with her. Maybe at some point I will set it on fire somewhere near her grave. The message the note conveyed, that she was releasing us from the burden of having to care for her, was not terribly helpful for us. I think we all felt in some way responsible that she felt she had to do that. I know where the note is, and I just don't know what to do with it. It's a constant reminder of the reality of her pain. I think it's necessary to release the note in order to release her pain and release us from that bond of her pain. It certainly isn't something that I'm going to drag out in twenty years and show the grandchildren.

We have all her poetry and essays, and we have sketches that she's done. I would rather have those to hold on to than the note, which is almost a testament of her madness at that point. I don't want to have that memory of her being mad and being at the point of feeling as though suicide was her only alternative. I'd rather have the positive creations of her life to hold on to. The boys and I have talked at different times about what to do with the note, and just like with everything else, when we don't know what to do, we don't do anything. Somehow, during the past year and a half, we've found the answers. We've taken each piece as it's come up, and I'm sure the time for deciding about what to do with the note will arrive, and we'll deal with it at that time.

Last July, the first anniversary of her death, I took Andrew and Samuel to Europe, took them to all the places where their mother had lived and studied when she was in Europe. It was kind of a tribute and a way of letting go and trying to give the boys a feeling of something positive to replace the painful memory of the year before. It was a very difficult trip for me. They had one another, and they had other young people they met along the way. I was alone, feeling the loss in a very real way.

The boys and I have gone through a realignment since Marion's death. Andrew's primary emotional support was always his mother. She seemed to be more on Andrew's wavelength, and I seemed to be more on Samuel's wavelength. Andrew didn't need me particularly, because he had his mother. But now we've had to deal with his feeling resentful of Samuel's relationship with me, and Andrew and I have had to figure out what our relationship with one another is going to be. Driving him back to school after Marion died, I said to him, "We don't have any reason to have a relationship anymore. The last eight years you've been tolerating me because I was your mother's lover, and you felt the only way you would have access to your mother was to have tolerance for me. You don't have to play that game anymore. I will understand if this isn't what you want." He said, "I love you, and I want to work it out." We've struggled, fought, and cried through a lot of stuff in the past year and a half to be able to get to a point of mutual caring and respect. And the same, I think, is probably true for Samuel. Although he and I were the ones who were more closely aligned, his mother was always in the background, and I think he had the confidence and the knowledge that she would come to the fore when and if he needed her. After she died, he no longer had that kind of emotional safety net. So all of us have had to readjust to one another.

We were like a three-wheeled cart for a long time. I was the tire in the middle of the front, and the boys were the two tires in the back. I'm still trying very hard to be the caring adult in their lives and to let them know that I care about them unconditionally. They can be up and down and off the wall and crazy and irresponsible and emotional and all kinds of other things, and I'm still going to be there. Particularly because of the way their mother died, they've gone through some torment, asking themselves, "Is it me? Was it me?" I think we're all arriving at some kind of acceptance of the fact that it wasn't our fault, that we can take the blame for a lot of things, but we can't take the responsibility for someone else's life. And I think that's a really significant step in the right direction for us.

Until the very end, Marion and I were a very loving couple. I'm not idealizing—we had our ups and downs, but we learned to accommodate one another. I would have done anything—and thought I was doing everything I could think of—to make her want to keep going. I really felt that her sister's suicide would stop her from ever killing herself, because I knew she was tormented by that. The boys and I have gone over this a million times. I would say, "Well, if your mother wasn't happy with me, at least she had you." And the boys would say, "Well, if we were disappointing Mom, we know she was happy with you." We've gone back and forth. What else can you do? At least, at some level, there was a check and balance there, that if one of us felt like the negative part, we saw the other side as positive and motivation for going on.

It's a little scary when I think about not only what Marion was going through but also the impact that it had on me and the boys. I spent probably the first eight months after her death sleeping. I'd get up and go to work and do what I had to do and come home and pass out. I never really understood the drain of trying to sustain someone who didn't want to live any longer. I was, I guess, incredibly naive, thinking that I would give Marion something to live for, that I would love her enough and would make life interesting and exciting enough that she'd never want to give it up.

The house renovation was part of that—creating a space and doing designs that Marion had always wanted to do in a place. I went right along with it—whatever you want to do. And we made a great team, you know? We took this fairly unattractive house and turned it into a very attractive place and put a lot of energy and effort into it. When she died, it was about 70 percent complete, and it's taken me almost two years to finish it. After she died, I threw everyone out and said, "I don't want anyone in the house." They came back gradually, and I'm finally at the completion phase now. I had to plaster, I had to paint, I had to finish the roof, I had to put fixtures back in, I had to put the kitchen in and put up walls—just a tremendous amount of work that still had to be done on the house, and I didn't want to do it. It didn't make any sense. The whole purpose for doing it was gone.

It's still very difficult to be there. Every day I drive by the sign for the pond where they found her. But I feel that I have to make the house a friend before I can leave it. I have to come to peace with what's happened before I can go and be in another place peacefully. Although I wanted desperately just to say, "This is it. I'm going to sell the house and go to another place," I've hung in there and gone through the pain and the suffering and the inability to cope and to make decisions at times, because I know in my mind and I feel in my being that I can't successfully go on with my life until I go through all the stuff I have to go through to understand this and accept it.

Sometimes I think I should have seen Marion's body so that I can understand that her death is real, but as time has gone on and we've talked about it, it's not as much of an issue. I think the boys and I are more comfortable with the memory of her alive than with some image of her death. I didn't need to see the body to know she was gone. That doesn't mean that I don't think I see her on the street all the time. I think that's true for anyone who loses someone close. You think you see the image of that person in all kinds of different situations and places.

The past year and a half have been about accepting Marion's death and also accepting my limitations, trying very hard to understand that other people can take care of me sometimes. And people have had to take care of me since Marion's death. I would have to say that losing Marion was probably the first time in my life that I lost control. I was just an emotional basket case and made no secret about it. When you fall apart, the vast number of people seem to retreat into the bushes. And when you really fall apart, they're in the deep woods. You can't even see them anymore. There are very few people who stand out in the clearing with you. I've certainly found that to be true. There have been very few people who have made a sustained effort to hang in there with me, people who, when I call them and all I'm doing is crying on the phone, just listen. That's all you want them to do. You don't want them to say, "Stop crying, it's going to get better. You don't have to do this to yourself," or "I'm sick of listening to you." You just want to know there's another human being who's there for you.

My father couldn't do that. He was great at the time of the crisis, but on a long-term basis, he couldn't sustain the commitment. He really handled the police—he's a police officer himself—and the reports in the newpaper did not indicate that it was suicide. With something like this, the level of activity in looking for Marion could easily have made the news, but it didn't. And I'm very grateful to my father for that. It was a real protection that he provided for us in that situation. He drove us to the church the day of the service and was available that whole week. But when I'd call him later on and I'd be crying, I'd get this, "Life is for the living. You've got to pull yourself together. You can't be carrying on like this." He made me feel ashamed of my feelings, that something was wrong with me because I was emotional about what had just happened.

My sister is very good about calling me on a regular basis. My friend Barbara has been there for me, and a couple of other friends who have been there since I was a teenager. They pick up the phone, and even if I'm not there, they'll leave a message on the machine: "Hello. We're checking to see if you're okay. We love you. Give us a call." Even if only the machines connect, it's crucial to me to understand and appreciate that they're there. There are no judgment calls about how much is enough and how much is too much.

Having had to deal with coming out in my life, as far as my sexuality is concerned, I've had some experience with alienating information. I've had to live in a world where I can't be open with who I am or feel I can't be without compromising myself professionally or compromising the children. I certainly am not going to go howl from the rooftops about my sexuality any more than I'm going to go howl from the rooftops about the true circumstances of Marion's death. It's been a double constriction. In a situation where someone didn't understand my relationship with Marion, didn't understand the enormity of my loss, that person wouldn't understand the extent of my grief.

But there's also the more positive aspect that, having had to deal with coming out, I've had some experience with stigma. I've already been rejected by different people in my life because of my choices, so for the most part, the people who are in my life aren't going to reject me. People who care about me and don't necessarily know the full story have at least responded to the pain that they see I've been in, because one of the things that I have not been able to do is hide my pain. So my own life experience has maybe been a benefit in trying to deal with this. But that doesn't stop people's general discomfort around death, especially suicidal death, which just sends them off into the hinterlands.

I've made sure that the people who can give the comfort and the caring are part of my life and the people who can't are no longer. I think that's another painful stage you have to go through, the realization that people who could accept you before the tragedy somehow can't accept you after it. You're already feeling rejected when someone has killed herself, and to have to deal with the rejection that you feel from the people who are still here is pretty hard. And I do think that when you become a little bit more receptive to your own emotions, you tend to gravitate toward other people who are emotional. Maybe I have to assume some responsibility for having had relationships in my life before that just were not adequate. But my needs were different, and what worked then doesn't work now. You can't fault those people, because they haven't changed, but you have. And you have to go on. That's another subsidiary of the grief, I guess—the losses of other kinds of relationships and connections.

As I accept what happened more, I think I'm able to be more open with it. Probably losing Marion was the first time in my life that I actually experienced my feelings. I have usually been more of a reactive person. If something's broken, you fix it—always looking for a solution. And here's a situation in which there isn't a solution, so you have to let go and find a direction wherever it comes from. There's no logic; there's no reason.

After almost a year and a half of trying to understand and cope with this whole thing, I'm expecting that I'm not going to understand, that it's always going to be a very painful aspect of my being. I am not going to recover fully, but on a continuum my life will probably get better, and there has been some movement, some growth since Marion's death. I still feel, for whatever reason, that there had to be something that I could have done, a feeling that I think is absent when someone dies from chronic illness or accidental death. I've tried to accept the notion that for someone who's mentally ill, suicidal death is not really that different from the death of someone whose body is wracked with cancer.

I vascillate between feeling that Marion's suicide was a natural progression of her illness and feeling that I have to protect her and her integrity by not sharing the true nature of her death. And I think it's all tied up in society's lack of understanding of mental illness. I can't change the world, but I'm still living in it, and so are the boys, and we're very cautious about sharing what really happened. There are guys who Samuel has spent two years partying with at school who have no idea what's happened. That's a tremendous burden for him. I think the burden for me has come not only in wanting to protect Marion but also in not being able to be public about my grief, since not everyone knew the true nature of our relationship. I guess the people I felt comfortable sharing the truth with were people I thought would not be judgmental. In a couple of instances, I've told people six months or a year later, because I felt that during that time they were accepting and supporting me, so I thought it was okay to tell them the truth. There has to be a tremendous amount of trust before you can really tell someone the truth. I feel very vulnerable, and I want to protect Marion's memory.

There are still situations and circumstances that bring back the pain, and I can anticipate it. I went to see *Love Letters* [a play by A.R. Gurney] last weekend. The female lead in that play struggles with alcoholism and depression and loses custody of her children. It's implied that she kills herself. As soon as I connected with the desperation that this woman was beginning to feel in correspondence about her own life, the tears were rolling down my face. I had no control over it. It's almost as though I knew what was going to happen next. And it happened. It's weird how different situations will just bring it back to you.

The capacity for intimacy—I'm not sure how that's going to work out, how in the long term I'm going to fare in terms of being able to make a commitment to someone again without constantly feeling like she's going to leave me. I don't want to surrender and not have a life. I want to have a life beyond this experience. I certainly didn't spend eight years with someone because I didn't have the capacity to care and to make a commitment.

Nobody prepares you for death. Certainly no one ever warns you about the possibility of suicide. Literally overnight, your whole life changes. For someone like me, who has always felt that I had everything under control, Marion's death has taught me that there's really very little that I can control. And at some level, the more I've surrendered to the notion that I can't control very much about my life, the more freedom I have had to be open to the possibilities. Some days are better than others. Some days I feel I'm being consumed, and other days I feel I'm going to be okay. My hope is that you gradually get to a place where there's a balance.

But I think, in a very real way, every day of your life you have to make that choice again. It's saying, "I'm going to get up today and do it again." I don't think that any of us can take it for granted. I don't like it, but I keep doing it! I can hear my therapist saying to me, "Even if you don't really want to go out, just make the effort, just go. If you only stay in the room for five minutes, do it for five minutes." For the last year, I've done a lot of things I didn't want to do, and I recognize that a lot of the recovery is doing things that you have to do and not doing things that you want to do, because if you did what you wanted to do, you'd just sit down and die when it first happens. You have to go on living and somehow get to a place where it's less of a chore and it begins to feel natural to live again, because I did go through a period when I didn't feel like I should be alive. Nobody could feel that awful and still be alive.

One thing that has been really important to me in the process of recovery is acknowledging and developing some type of spirituality as part of my life. When Marion died and we were struggling through those first couple of weeks, that was probably the only time in my life that I can honestly say I was grateful for having been brought up a Catholic—not because the Catholic Church did anything for me, but because I was somehow open to the possibility of some kind of spiritual life. I found that very comforting. About six months later, I was talking to my friend Barbara about it, and she said, "There's a church that I think you would really like. It's a mixed group of people, a very creative community. I think we should go there sometime." We've been going to that church together ever since.

The ability to acknowledge some kind of spiritual life in me has been a very freeing experience. I think it's another level of acceptance, that there are powers that we have no control over. The same power that took Marion from me can, I feel, work in positive ways to bring me closer to acceptance, but it's a matter of finding that energy and making it real. It feels like a very natural thing. I'm not a Bible thumper, but it just seems like a place where I can be at peace and accepted for who I am.

One of the ministers from the church went to the funeral home with us when we picked up Marion's ashes, drove to Maine with us, and did the service for the interment. A year before that, I had no connection with any kind of religion or any kind of spirituality. It felt really comforting to let go of her in the presence of a minister, someone we felt could release her and release her spirit. It took me a year to get to that point. I had resisted it because it didn't feel, particularly in this society and to some extent in a lesbian life-style, like something I wanted. It's not politically correct! You know, there's all this bullshit about the patriarchy of Western churches. But it doesn't feel that way. I've found a place and a community of people I'm comfortable with.

Throughout this whole thing, I kept thinking about the notion of the equal and opposite reaction: there's so much pain that if you can ever get through it, maybe you'll be happier than you've ever been before. I haven't gotten there yet, but my sense is that it might be true, because I certainly experienced more emotion in this past year than I've ever experienced in my life. So I'm hoping there's a part of me that's been opened to more positive things as well. I think you only start to accept it when you begin to take whatever positive stuff you can from the experience and carry that forward, as opposed to the anger and resentment, which I think all of us feel. All of us have experienced the ultimate abandonment. It doesn't get any worse than this, I don't think. It's so far down, you have to look up.

Joy: Knowing Suicide from a Young Age

Joy was a nineteen-year-old student at a boarding school in northern New England when her mother, the poet Anne Sexton, died from carbon monoxide poisoning in 1974. The story that follows is the one Joy told me in 1983. Married and in her late twenties, she was a student in nursing school at the time. Her continued story, told five years later, is in chapter 4.

For Joy, the aftermath of suicide has in many ways been framed by her experience of growing up with a mother who was self-destructive and made numerous suicide attempts. Whereas many survivors feel the force of their abandonment only in the wake of suicide, Joy felt it throughout her childhood. Among the many other responses to her mother's suicide, Joy's sense of relief was strong.

When suicide marks the end of a long period of self-destructive behavior and severe depression, many people feel relieved. The years of living with someone who does not want to live can take their toll on other family members. Survivors may be ashamed at their relief, yet it is natural and quite common to feel it. Relief often goes hand in hand with anger, sadness, regret, and a host of other responses to suicide.

I thought I knew how I felt about suicide, but when I really began to think about talking directly to another person about it and I began to look at my feelings and my doubts about my mother's death and her illness, I came up with contradictions all over the place. I don't know whether that's normal or whether there is even a normal feeling to have about suicide. I kept trying to come up with some statement that would sum up all my feelings. There isn't one. It's not something, first of all, that people feel comfortable talking about. It's not a normal death that you can process with other people and get through the way most people can with the death of a parent. People just want to forget about it. It's too touchy. It's hard for people to talk about.

My sister and I talk about it a lot. We go through different periods and different stages when we feel relieved and sad and angry. I don't feel so much anger anymore. Well, I haven't felt that way in a long time—who knows what will happen in five days. I think it's something that never remains constant, that never gets completely resolved.

My mother's suicide was not a first attempt. There had been many others. They were always geared around a time when people would find her, or at the last moment she would say, "I don't want to do this. I'm not ready to die," and she was saved. The circumstances surrounding her suicide were different from any other attempt. She'd always tried to kill herself with pills before, pills and alcohol. And each attempt had been preceded by a serious depression. Her death was 180 degrees different, and for a long time I was convinced someone had murdered her.

It just made no sense to me. Things had begun to go well for her for the first time since she had divorced my dad. She had given her best reading about two weeks before her death. People said it was phenomenal. She'd gone to her psychiatrist the morning of her suicide and had had a good session. She had lunch with her best friend, Maxine Kumin, went home, got in the car and turned on the radio, got a drink, closed the garage doors, and died. She'd called her answering service for messages. I mean, there were things that made no sense about it whatsoever. So both my sister and I were convinced that she had been murdered. I'm sure it was purely our need to find a reason that didn't say "suicide."

It's awful to say, but in many ways I'm glad she did it. This is where the contradictions come in. My life has clearly improved since she's no longer alive. She was a very, very difficult person to live with. Her sickness made it a bitch for me to grow up. I was tired of her poisoning my life, and if she was going to do it, then get it done with and let me get on with my life. From the time I was very young, I understood what suicide was, and I lived in constant fear of it. I knew what it meant, and I knew what its implications were, the guilt that she used: "I'm depressed. Fine, go out." "Well, if I go out, are you going to try to kill yourself again?" It was impossible to say, "It's your bag of shit. You deal with it." Children don't have that ability to separate. I think for a long time I saw myself as the cause of her mental illness, which started just after I was born.

There had been so many attempts, it was almost as if she had been dying of cancer. If I were to say twice a year for fifteen or twenty years, I don't think that's an exaggeration. It was constant, it was relentless, it was exhausting. So when I say, "Enough already," that's really the way I felt. Too many scares, too many close calls, times that were kept from me, and other times when they tried to keep it from me but I knew. Afterward, she would apologize, and my answer was always, "Don't ever do it again." "I won't, I won't, I won't," she would say. "I promise, Joy, I promise." Too many broken promises.

I was nineteen when she died. I'd been away at school and had come home the summer before. My sister was away for the summer, and my parents were divorced. My mother was the craziest I'd ever seen her that summer. She was incapable of really taking care of herself. She wanted someone to sit with her while she took a nap in the afternoon. She wanted someone to cook for her and eat with her. She wanted someone to drive her to her psychiatrist. And I wouldn't get sucked in. Her demands drove me crazy. It was a horrendous summer for us, for our relationship.

That summer there was such anger, and when I remember that time, I feel the anger again. There was part of her mental illness that I just didn't buy. One side of me accepted the mental illness and the suicide and understood it, as far as saying, "If you're going to be miserable, then do it and get it over." But there was another side that said, "You have the power to change that. If you want to be crazy, you can be crazy. If you want to be sane, you have the power to be sane." I still struggle with that.

One night that summer, I went upstairs. She had taken a lot of sleeping pills and was talking with her psychiatrist on the phone. She was almost asleep. You could barely understand her, her words were so slurred. I picked up the phone and said, "Do you think she's taken an overdose?" The psychiatrist reassured me that she'd only taken a normal amount of pills. So I went downstairs and was going to go out, but I didn't feel comfortable about it. I was angry. I had a date that night, and I wanted to go out and have a good time. I went back upstairs and she was sleeping, but she looked like she was sleeping really deeply, and I was concerned. At that time, she had a nurse who would come and stay with her during the day, because I had basically laid it out that I could not do that. I called Joan, the nurse, and explained the circumstances. She said, "Go up and take your mother's pulse." So I went up and took her pulse and talked to Joan. She said, "Wait fifteen minutes and take her pulse again and call me back." I waited, did that, and it was considerably slower. Joan seemed to think there was reason for concern. She came over, and I called the police. The ambulance arrived. They were taking my mother out, and she was screaming, "I haven't taken too many pills. I just took my normal dose." I rode with her in the ambulance. It was a horrible experience. The doctor at the hospital said she'd taken the pills so long ago most of them were digested, and from pumping her stomach, he couldn't tell whether she'd taken an overdose. My mother took a lot of pills. She'd been taking them for years.

They were going to keep her overnight. The doctor asked me if I wanted to go in and say good-bye to her. They had put something in her mouth to keep her from swallowing her tongue. Her whole body was arched, and she was gagging and obviously not in any condition to say good-bye to her daughter. She was having some kind of seizure. I got halfway into the room, backed up, and collapsed.

The next day I visited her, and she was mad at me. She said, "I didn't try to kill myself." I said, "I didn't know. What was I supposed to do, go out and come in the next morning and find you dead in your bed? How do you think that would make me feel?" The next night Joan said, "I have some bad news. Your mother's escaped. She must have taken a cab home." I was furious. The next morning my mother said to me, "I can't drive to the psychiatrist today. Will you drive me?" I looked at her and said, "You walk. I've had it. I can't do it anymore." And she screamed and ranted and raved and told me to get out of the house. I left, and for the last four weeks of the summer, I stayed with some friends and with my dad. I went home just before going back to school and kind of made peace but not completely. I still felt that she had ruined that summer for me. The last time I saw her was the day before I went away to school.

She died on October 4. I remember we used to watch the eleven o'clock news at school, and they wouldn't let us watch it that night. They made everyone go up to bed, and I didn't understand why. Early the next morning, my adviser came into my room, woke me up, and said, "I have some very, very bad news for you." I said, "What's happened?" And he said, "There's been a death in the family." I said, "It was my mother, right?" And he said, "Yes." And I said, "It was suicide, right?" And he said, "Yes."

And I think, following that, there was the shock and the disbelief that everyone feels. I don't think the shock and the initial stages that you go through are any different for someone who's committed suicide or someone who's died in an auto accident. With a long, drawn-out death from cancer, it might be a different feeling, because you're more prepared for it. It's the lack of preparedness, the surprise and the shock. What's strange is that there have been so many deaths from automobile accidents in my family. My grandmother's first husband, my father's father, and my father's sister all died in car accidents. And my mother killed herself in the car.

The most joyous experience was emptying all the drawers and all the pocketbooks of sleeping pills. We ended up with a shopping bag half-filled with pills and flushed them down the toilet. Good-bye! I really despised the pills. I remember when I was a kid, they were all over the house. It's only been in the past three years that I've been able to look at the causes of her death and see alcoholism as one of the prime causes. I think if she had stopped drinking, she would have been able to get to some of the more intense problems that she had. The drinking helped her stay away from all that. She drank all the time, and toward the end, she was a full-fledged alcoholic.

She couldn't get close enough to the problems of her childhood—all those issues she never resolved. And they're tough issues—I'm not saying they're not—but there's a way to get through them and beyond them. There's a point where you accept it, and you move on. That's what frustrates me, that she could never move on. She stayed stuck. I don't know how anyone could stand staying stuck for that long. My feeling was that she always took the easy way out, that she was lazy about most things, except her writing. But I think, toward the end, her poetry got worse as she drew back more, as she took more pills, as she lost touch with reality. Her poetry reflects that. I think it was perhaps fear that really kept her from moving on, accepting and moving on.

One of her close friends told me, "I asked your mother once if she didn't think about her two daughters when she wanted to kill herself. And her answer was, 'I have to kill her.' Not 'I have to kill me,' but 'I have to kill her. I have to get rid of her.' "

My mother was terrified of being old, and I think she was absolutely terrified of dying. There was this fear of death that drove her, which said, "I can't stand to get old and die. I just need to do it." I guess that's how I see her— I was about to say "her final suicide," as if she'd really died a million times before. Finally, she said, "Enough. I'm going to do it, or I'm not going to do it. If I really don't want to live, then I'm not going to live." And in that I admire her. Of all the last things she did, that was her most courageous. She has a poem: "Live or die but don't poison everything." Do one or the other. Either decide to live and be happy about living or don't.

They asked us at the funeral home if we wanted to see her body, and I couldn't deal with it. Now, looking back on it, I wish that someone had made me. I remember that I was kind of manic, laughing and smiling a lot. I don't think I cried once during the visiting hours.

I did cry at the funeral. I don't really remember it very well. A number of people got up and read things. I've blocked a lot of this out. Part of my memory is that someone read some of her poetry, but I'm not sure. The funeral wasn't really satisfying. I was too tense, too freaked out, out of touch. I was also exhausted from not sleeping.

No one would sleep at the house, so I stayed there alone. I wanted to be there. I didn't want to be anywhere else. I wanted to be in my bed. The problem was that I couldn't sleep. Never in my life had I had insomnia. I think I was just so freaked out. I would go through phases of accepting and not accepting, believing and not believing. It came in waves. It can't be true, it can't be true. And you'd forget about it and feel as though everything was normal and whole and complete, and then it would hit you. And that's what would happen when I tried to go to sleep. I couldn't stop thinking. I cried a lot, too. I remember my eyes stinging and being swollen for days.

I still sometimes have those waves. They still creep up on me, waves of feeling sad, of disbelief. Maybe now it's more sadness that I've grown so much and come so far, and I wish she were here. Usually when I take a monumental step—when I went back to school, when I went back into therapy—when I know that she would have been proud of me, those are the times when you want your mother there.

I remember my sister and I had a fight shortly after my mother's death. She was trying to talk to me about why I was upset. I said, "You can't take my pain away. My pain is mine." I didn't understand that, but I remember distinctly saying it. I needed to harbor the pain for a while. I needed to feel sorry for myself. I needed to be angry, and I was afraid that if I let that anger out, I would lose something.

My relationship with my sister was very distant at first after the suicide. We were still kind of sparring and going through our teenage jealousies. Now she's my closest friend. We really worked through it. It was hard. There were times when she drove me nuts and I drove her nuts. But there's a sense, after you lose someone in a family, that life is tenuous, life is fragile, and that not to fully appreciate and love and give to each other while everyone's alive and healthy is only to feel awful afterward. She still drives me nuts in many ways, but we're so close. There were things that my sister and I did together as kids. We did puzzles a lot. We fought like cats and dogs a lot, too, but there were periods of time when we were very good playmates. We decided that we wanted to hold on to that. My sister and I basically said, "We are going to maintain the family. We're going to maintain a lot of the tradition and rituals that our family had."

I really believe that if my mother hadn't died, my sister and I wouldn't have become as close. It would have been easier to continue on our separate ways. I think maybe my mother was a real blocking point between us. I was jealous of my sister because she was closer to my mother, and my sister was jealous of me because I was closer to my father. When my mother died, my father had to move into a central position, the primary supporter. Instead of the four of us being separated into twos, the three of us formed a triangle and worked off each other. I don't think my father knew where he fit in. I think he was really at a loss. He saw himself as being a supporter for my sister and me, and the grieving that he did after my mother's death he did very, very privately.

Anniversaries of my mother's death used to be unbearable. She had wanted her ashes scattered on the ocean. We planned to do it, but it was painful, and we put it off and put it off. Her second request was that, if she couldn't have her ashes scattered on the ocean, she wanted to be buried in the family plot. That we decided to do. Another request was that we have the palindrome "Rats live on no evil star" engraved on the family headstone. We might do it someday, but my grandmother didn't want it on the headstone. Since it made my grandmother happier, we decided not to do it. Maybe after she dies and my father dies, we will. I don't have any great feelings that when people die, they're still around. In my head, when people die, they die. And Mother is not going to know whether "Rats live on no evil star" is on the headstone or not.

We waited a long time, two and a half years, to bury her ashes. The box of ashes had been kept in my father's closet. I felt horrible guilt over the fact that there were ashes—my mother's bones—in my father's closet. We put them in the ground and said our last words and cried. And then I went back to work. I can't believe I went back to work, but I did.

A few years ago, I realized I was in some trouble. I wasn't doing very good things for myself. I started seeing a therapist and just stopped three months ago. It feels good. I don't feel I'm finished for life. I think that at some point I'll come to a new stage when I'm ready to resolve things over again, but maybe I won't. It would be nice to think that I won't need to go back, but that's stretching it.

Therapy really helped. Who knows whether I would have gotten where I am had I not gone into therapy. I think that it sped the process. I learned to look at things in new ways. The new feelings that I was having didn't seem to have so much weight. They weren't so intense. They were manageable. In many ways, therapy gave me the mother I didn't have. It gave me someone to talk to, someone who could listen.

My mother didn't like being a mother. There was really never much question about that. She loved us when we were teenagers, but she didn't really like us as kids. She wanted to be a writer; she didn't want to be a mother. I suppose that's what I feel angry about. Hey, fine, but sorry, you're a mother now. Whatever way you can do both the best is fine, but when your children suffer because you're spending your time writing and not being a mother and doing things with your kids the way a mother should . . . I look at my friends now and see what they do with their kids. I would never have asked, because I know I wouldn't have gotten her to sit down and color or read a story. I was never read to as a kid.

I don't think that my mother could have written if she hadn't been selfish. I don't really think that she wrote for anyone other than herself. She wrote when she had inspiration, sometimes for four or five days straight, and then there'd be months when nothing would happen. To me, those were fine times. I was just as happy when she wasn't banging away at the typewriter. We couldn't walk into the room when she was writing, so I really resented her writing.

I was embarrassed about my mother for most of my life. No one had a crazy mother in the town where I grew up. Everything was nice, and no one talked about that stuff. And my mother wrote about it. I had friends who couldn't come to my house because of the poetry my mother wrote. Her death was the final embarrassment. She did it in a way that made it impossible to talk to anyone about it. When I went back to school after her suicide, I wanted to talk, but people tried to avoid the subject. No one could deal with it. These were sixteen- and seventeen-year-olds. They weren't in a place to deal with a kid talking about the fact that her mother had died and that she had killed herself.

I don't know whether I've ever felt suicidal in the way that my mother felt suicidal. I've been depressed and had fantasies of jumping from trains or in front of cars, never of taking sleeping pills and dying slowly. My fantasies have always been for shock value. They've usually happened when I've been hurt by someone or felt left or lonely. It was not really that I wanted to die but that I wanted to make someone else feel bad because I felt bad, and I didn't have any other way to say it.

I think every little girl grows up thinking that she's going to be like her mother. I think that's really normal. And when your mother kills herself, it's scary. Is this what I want to do? But my fear never was, "Am I going to kill myself?" It was, "Am I going to be crazy like her?" The whole time I was growing up, I was terrified of getting depressed. I couldn't let myself be sad, ever. If I was depressed, I never let it show. If I had, that would have meant that I was like my mother, that I was crazy. It still scares me sometimes, although I feel so much more in control of my life than I know she ever was. At least I'm in touch with reality and able to see things from the past clearly and separate myself from some of that stuff and say, "It wasn't my fault. It wasn't my birth that made my mother go crazy."

I'm planning to go into midwifery. I considered psychiatric nursing, and maybe someday I would be able to do it, but being with crazy people is still very hard for me. I would like to be able to do it ... I guess I really want to work more with healthy people. To give birth isn't a sickness. It's something to rejoice in; it's life. I've always been fascinated with pregnancy. When I was a little kid, wherever there was a cat having kittens, I was there with my nail clipper, clipping cords. Once I realized what a pregnant woman looked like, I was absolutely fascinated. I'll listen to the story of anyone's labor and delivery, no matter how awful or good. Tell me every detail!

[Joy's story is continued in chapter 4, page 205.]

Chris: Being the Only One

Chris's brother, Tom, was twenty-two when he killed himself on January 4, 1988. He was living at home with their parents at the time. Two and a half years older than her brother, Chris had recently completed a master of business administration (MBA) program and started a new job in another state. I interviewed Chris at her apartment in December 1988, almost a year after her brother's suicide.

Tom's death left Chris the only child in her family, and her story is about the "circle of emotions" that she feels about her brother—anger, guilt, sadness, fear that she will forget him—as well as a heavy weight of responsibility for her parents. Suicide often leaves siblings feeling doubly burdened. In addition to their struggle to accept their own loss, they may feel the need to protect their parents and somehow make up for the parents' loss as well.

Chris's story also tells how important pastoral support can be for some survivors, particularly when the priest, rabbi, or minister can help them acknowledge the fact of the suicide and is attuned to the survivors' needs in its wake.

Tom had been having a hard time for a number of years. We didn't realize the extent of it. He had been going to college and had pretty much flunked out. My dad said, "Look, take a year off, try to work, and then maybe you'll want to go back." So he took a year off, but he couldn't find a good job. He realized that he needed school, so he went back in September of 1987. It sounded like things were going well, but apparently he was flunking out again and didn't want to tell anyone.

I had been away a lot and had come home in May, after I had gotten my MBA. This was the first time Tom and I were getting to know each other as adults. He was very moody, very abrupt. If you looked at him, his face would get so full of anger, and he'd just storm off. You couldn't carry on a good conversation with him. I just thought, "Well, that's the way he is," not realizing, because I was getting to know him. My parents were a little concerned, but they talked to other parents who would say, "My son went through that and then came out of it."

Right before Christmas, he had a hernia operation, and I think maybe that affected him; he wasn't feeling well. And then a registered letter came from the university; [it was being held for him at the post office]. My dad kept saying, "Have you picked up the letter?" And Tom kept saying he hadn't picked it up yet, he had forgotten or whatever. Well, the letter said that he'd failed out of school and could not go back. Later, my dad found out that he'd picked it up on the 24th of December, which means he went through Christmas and New Year's knowing this. We had no idea. The 4th of January was a Monday, and he knew that he couldn't lie to my parents any longer about not getting the letter. There was no excuse for him not to go pick it up on that day, and he could not face my parents that night and tell them that he had failed.

He had washed his car that day. It was spotless inside and out. Now, do you think he wanted to leave a clean car? I don't think so. I think he was just doing something. My priest said that he was probably being so meticulous, thinking, "Well, as soon as this is over, I'm going to kill myself because there's nothing left," but he was taking his time because he really didn't want to do it. That's why everything was spotless.

We had this sweeper that you use with a hose to clean the inside of the car. And I guess he got the idea from using that to hook up the hose from the exhaust pipe into the window of his car. He had a candle sitting next to him, and there were several lit matches. We figure he was lighting that candle so that he'd know when the oxygen was gone, as a check that he could get out. Someone said that maybe he was having some kind of ceremony. No way. I think he said to himself, "I'm going to do this, but I can get out if I want to." And that's the only reason he got into that car, because he knew he could change his mind.

And he apparently did, because he had gotten out of the car, walked around to the back, thrown up, and moved on. The garage door opener was on the other end. He had to walk around the car and cross the garage to get to the wall. There was a kerosene heater there [which he probably had used while cleaning the car], and he must have tripped over that trying to get to the garage door opener and passed out. The coroner said, "You don't know how many people maybe change their minds in the car at the last minute, but they just can't move from the carbon monoxide." So that was a pretty incredible feat for him to have gotten out. And for us, we needed that sign that he wasn't so intent on killing himself, that it was kind of a mistake.

I had been in Boston over New Year's and had just gotten back to my apartment the night before this happened. It was seven o'clock and the phone rang. It was my priest from home. He said, "I'm at the hospital; something has happened. Here's your mom." It seemed like it took forever for her to come to the phone. All these thoughts were rushing through my head. I just knew it was something really serious and unexpected. And right away I said, "Mom, is it Dad?" I thought Dad had had a heart attack. She said, "No." I said, "Oh, not Tom." You know, right then I knew. He had so many problems. Right away I thought he'd had an automobile accident and was lying in the hospital, near death. And she said, "Yes." I said, "He was in an accident." I wouldn't even let her tell me. And she said, "He's not with us anymore." Right then my heart—it just— I fell to the floor. Your stomach just drops. You just know your life is never going to be the same. And then I said, "Well, how did it happen?" And she said, "He was in his car. He started the engine—" And I said, "It blew up." I mean, the furthest thing from my mind— I couldn't believe it. But then it made sense. All of a sudden, it made sense when I realized what he had been going through.

One of my biggest fears right away was that maybe he compared himself to me and thought that he had to do what I had done. I had gone through my four years of college pretty easily. I had gotten an MBA. I'd studied overseas. Those kinds of things were easy for me. I just thought, "Oh, God, I hope he didn't think that he had to do what I did, and because he couldn't, he thought he'd failed."

I had a really hard time getting home. It took forever. The flight was delayed. Somehow, I just felt that if I got there, it was going to be okay. I didn't get home until about 2 A.M. My neighbor picked me up at the airport. We got home, and what I really wanted was to see the body. I wanted to hug him. And I thought I could get home soon enough to get to the hospital, but it was too late. It makes me mad that I didn't get to see him in the hospital—in his leather jacket and his t-shirt—that I only saw him in the coffin.

My mom couldn't go near his room. She'd come up the steps and look at that end of the house, and she couldn't go near it. I don't know where I got the strength, but I just said, "Well, I'll do it." I opened up his room, and it was a mess. It was the most wonderful thing to see. I mean, it was him. Clothes were all over the place. It was so great that he left it that way. And I did things like go to his bed and try to smell him, anything that was there. I picked out his gray pants and a blue sweater that I had given him for Christmas, and my mom got two pairs of socks for him—she kept complaining that he hated the cold. That's what we laid him out in.

The next morning, we went to the funeral parlor and made all the arrangements. A lot of the siblings in the suicide support group I go to say that their parents did things without them. We made every decision together as a family, the three of us. But it was funny, because my parents weren't really making a lot of decisions and I was. It was weird. I picked the clothes. And when we went to pick out the coffin, we were walking around and I said, "I like that one." That's the one we got.

Seeing him in the casket was so hard. He was a little bit black—from the carbon monoxide, I guess. He had a big bruise on the side of the head. I think it must have been where he'd fallen. It didn't really look like him. It was hard, too, because I'd never been that close to a dead person. It was really hard to go up and touch him and kiss him.

We had the funeral in the morning. It was bitter cold. Was it in the morning? I can't remember. Isn't it funny how things become less clear? Maybe you just block some things out. I don't know. I thought I would never forget every little detail. I don't even remember what time the funeral was. I can't remember.

We had a little service at the funeral home. Our priest, Pierre, gave a talk, and it was so comforting. He started out saying, "The worst part, Chris told me the other night, is having to wait so long to see Tommy again. But the best part is that you will see him again," and he just went on and comforted us, telling us that he is in heaven and that there's no way God would deny him entering heaven, he was in so much pain. Then he said that we have to deal with the fact that it was a suicide. All Tom's friends were pallbearers. They were all on the left in the front pew. Pierre looked at them and said, "Just because Tom did this does not mean it's okay for you." I just think he covered everything. It was really great.

Tom had left a note in the car. It was scribbled on the bottom of the letter from the university. It said something like, "Life sucks. I'm a failure." I wanted to [know exactly] what it said, but my dad said, "I don't remember." How can you not remember? But the coroner took the note, and I never did see it. The second day of the wake, we were at home, making some sort of financial arrangements, maybe looking for his insurance papers. I was helping my dad in Tom's room, because no one wanted to walk into that room alone. For some reason, I pulled open the center drawer of his desk, and there was a note on a pad of paper. It said, "Mom, Dad, Chris, I'm sorry to do this to you on Christmas." Something about him being a failure and the grades proved it. And it said, "I know you love me, and I love you." That was the most incredible thing to read, just proving that he knew we loved him. That was so important. And the second paragraph said, "I never had anyone. I never knew what it felt like." And then he wrote, "I love you all. Bye. Tom." I had never realized that Tom was so lonely. I just didn't think it bothered him that he'd never had a girlfriend. I'd really like to see that note again, but I'm afraid to ask my parents, and I don't know where they put it. Maybe [when I go home to visit them] at Christmas, I'll ask to see it.

At the end of the week, I came back here. I had just started my job three weeks before, and I didn't want to ask for any more time. And besides, I was ready to go back. We couldn't sit around and do nothing any longer and just think about it. You have to go and do something. It wasn't too bad to be back here, because Tom had never been here, so there wasn't any memory of him here. I think I slept with the light on for a while.

I had all these books on grief. That's all I could concentrate on. And a lot of people called me. In fact, for a while there, I would come back to my apartment after work and be on the phone for five hours. I wasn't doing anything but talking with people. Then, after a couple of weeks, it starts breaking off. All of a sudden, you're not getting as many phone calls. I could tell people were getting tired of it.

I talked to my parents every day. This was long distance. You just can't do that. In the past couple of months, it's started really getting on my nerves. I don't want to talk to them every day. We weren't even talking about Tom, but it was like they had to talk to me. It hasn't been so bad lately. Now we talk every couple of days, which is better. A couple of times, my dad has called me at work and said, "Mom had a bad dream. She just wanted to make sure you're okay." What's hard is that I feel like I have an obligation to them. If anything happened, I'd be there for them. But now I'm the only one. Tom put this on my shoulders, and now I have to take care of them. And I don't like that. If I had always been the only one, it wouldn't have bothered me.

One night I was dreaming about Tom. I could see his face and the top part of his body, from the waist up. He had on that blue sweater that he had on in the casket. Well, he was yelling at me, and his face was angry. It was puffed and bright red. And then, all of a sudden, he changed and above him appeared the real Tom from heaven. I mean, I know that. Now there is no question. And I knew it then, in my dream. So here's Tom at one level, and above him appears the real Tom. He was in the same sweater, but there was a soft light all around his head, and it was white. His face was so peaceful; it was beautiful. I could see the contrast, and as soon as I saw him I said, "Tom!" And the first thing that came out of my mouth was, "Can you see God?" And he said, "He's holding out a limb for me. But I've told you too much." And I said, "Wait!" But he was gone. It wasn't a spooky thing; it was like it was meant to make me really believe and not to scare me. And the part about him saying "I've told you too much" just seemed typical of Tom. Everyone knew he could not keep a secret. I haven't had any more dreams about him, but that was really special to me.

I've gone to two different support groups: Compassionate Friends [a national network of bereavement groups for parents and siblings; see the list of resources for survivors, at the end of the book] and the suicide survivors group [a local group]. The suicide group I find very helpful, but it depends on my state of mind. You hear everybody else's story and the crazy things that happened, and that's really good. You see that there are other people in your situation, and they couldn't have done anything about it. That comforts me. So in that sense, the group is good. Compassionate Friends is okay. It's mostly parents, but that gives me a good perspective on how my parents feel.

At the last meeting of the suicide survivors group, someone asked me how I'm doing now that it's almost a year, and I said, "I'm to the point where I'm okay." People say, "How are you?" and I don't automatically think how am I because Tom died. How am I today? I'm okay. Once in a while I'll just have a really bad spell. But maybe I kind of push it away. I don't know. I noticed not too long ago that when I sit, I'm hunched. I was a dancer, so I always had good posture. I know I'm hunched, but it feels good, so I just do it. I don't think about it every day, and I go on with my everyday life, but when I sit, it's kind of like folding in, to feel safe.

One day I came back here, and all of a sudden I just started crying, and I had to find something that Tom had given me, like a new thing that I hadn't gotten to yet. I tore everything apart until I found two cards. And then it was okay. I don't look at them every day, but I had to do that. And it helped. It was October when this happened, and here, after nine months, was something new of him. When we were little, we used to tape our Christmases—you know, opening the presents and all. I'm saving those tapes, because eventually I'm going to want to listen to them. It's going to be something new of him that we haven't pulled out yet. That helps.

I like going into his room when I'm home for a visit. I just sit there and look at his things on the shelf. I open all his drawers, and I look through everything, and usually I take a couple more t-shirts. That makes me feel good. I like wearing his shirts. I don't know if he was even buried yet when I went into his closet and put on his sweatshirt. It's not that I always admired his clothes and wanted them. I never even thought of putting on one of his shirts before. But now I have to have everything.

I also like to drive his car when I'm home. My parents wanted to sell it, and I said, "No way." Now I've finally agreed to it, but they're having problems selling it, so it's still sitting there. The only place I drive it is to the cemetery. It's not that important for me to go there, but it bothers me if I want to and can't because I'm living here. My parents can go anytime they want. At first, my parents and I would always go to the cemetery together. But as time wore on, I got a bit tired of it. I don't like to cry in front of them, and that really bothered me. When I was home at Easter, I wanted to go by myself. I was trying to arrange it. I told them I was going to go shopping. My dad said, "I'll go with you." And I just burst out crying. I said, "Look, I'm going to go to the cemetery. You can go anytime you want. I never get to go by myself." I don't know if it hurt his feelings or not—he just looked surprised—but I went by myself. Now I always go by myself. I'll just say, "I'm going to the cemetery, okay?" And I leave. I would rather it be that way.

When I go home to visit, I usually get there in the evening. The next day, I have to go to the cemetery to say, "Hello, I'm here." And then the day I'm leaving, I have to go. The last time I was home, I was in a hurry and had to rush to the cemetery. It was not that I wanted to go so much as I felt I owed it to Tom. It's like a duty: I have to say good-bye to him. I don't know why I feel like that, because when I go, I just stand there thinking, "What am I doing here?" When I look at the stone, I get angry at him: "Look at what you are now; you're a stone on the ground." I still get so mad at him. And then other days I'll completely understand, because I know it was rough. That's what's hard—the circle of emotions.

I guess everyone finds that in hindsight there's just so much that seems to connect. Even when my mom first told me that he committed suicide, it kind of made sense. But at the time, you just don't see it coming. I noticed so many things. I don't know why I never did anything. There were so many signs, we should have known.

The guilt is horrible—thinking I should have been more deep with him instead of having him as a buddy, someone to joke with. We never had really deep conversations. I should have been there. I remember on Christmas Day, this was a week before he died, my great aunt was there and said, "Do you two miss each other when Chris is gone?" And I said, "No." I looked at him, and I could tell he was ready to say, "Yes." But because I took it lightly and joked, he didn't say anything. I really feel bad about that now. It would have been nice to say, "Yes, I miss you, Tom."

To me, it's really important to keep going over and over why and to try to understand. That's what's really good about the survivors' meeting. You dwell on that, and you talk a little bit about how to go on, and it always comes back to the events leading up, trying to understand. I think it's helpful. When I hear someone else say something that led up to that person's death, I think, "Oh, maybe that could have had something to do with Tom." You just think in ways that you may not have. We'll never know. That's what's really hard.

What's also hard is that he's different from us now. He has done something that no one here has done. And all of a sudden, he's distant because of that. Sometimes I think about ways that I could do it. I won't. But I could be standing in the shower and think, "Well, I could just drown in here." Or, "I could stick myself with a knife right now." I've had to put a knife down because I've been tempted. I don't know why that is.

Right after Tom died, there was the question about what to tell people. I guess it took at least a month before I could say the word *suicide*. I could say he killed himself, but to say suicide took a long time. When I called work to say that I was home, that my brother had died, the secretary didn't know what to say. She said, "Was it an accident?" And I paused and said, "Yes." This was the day after he died. You just can't deal with anything else. So I went back to work and no one asked me, but I didn't volunteer anything. I've since told a few people. I found out later that people just assumed that it must have been cancer. I told a couple of women I trusted. I said, "Please don't tell anyone."

But I've gotten to the point where I want everyone to know. I just want it to be out. But, you see, people don't want to carry your grief. I discussed this with a psychologist once, and he said people feel bad for you for a couple of days, but it's over with. They don't want to know any more about it.

One guy I work with didn't know for a long time. I eat lunch with him every day, and I was longing to tell him, but how do you just say, "Well, do you want to know how my brother died?" One day last September he said, "What are you going to do this weekend?" And I said, "Saturday, I'm going to a conference." "Conference?" he said. "On what?" I said, "On suicide. That's how my brother died." I wanted to shock him. I wanted him to know. And he never said another word about it. It felt good shocking him. I don't know why. It's like defending [Tom's death]: "Yes, that's how he died. What's wrong with it?"

I'll never forget the first time I was asked the question "Do you have any brothers and sisters?" It was about a month after Tom's death. I was so shocked, I just sat there, and then I said, "My brother just died." Now I've been asked that question a number of times, and I say, "Well, I had a brother, and he died. He committed suicide." I always tell people how, because I want them to know.

I think my parents are doing pretty well. They both work, so they're busy. They've started going out a lot, to the theater or whatever. And I've noticed that they've gotten very loving toward each other. It's funny—with Tom in the house, everyone was always kind of on edge. You never knew if you were going to say something wrong. We'd be eating dinner, and he'd jump up from his chair and storm out. And now, it's really terrible to say, but it's almost a relief. Everything is so calm, and the three of us get along really well.

My parents came out to see me in May [four months after Tom's death]. They had never been here or seen the apartment. They brought me all these presents. They bought me a microwave, they bought me bath towels, they bought me a sweeper. I was sitting here opening these things, and I didn't want them. I don't know if they would have brought me all those things anyway—maybe, probably—but I didn't want them. I didn't think I deserved them. I wanted Tom back, I didn't want these things. And I didn't want to feel that I was benefiting because Tom was dead, that maybe they felt since I'm the only one left, they can afford to give me more or give me more attention. I just felt horrible, and I didn't want them to think that I was ungrateful. I'm sitting there opening these things, and they're all excited seeing me open them, and I'm just thinking, "I don't want this," and I'm practically in tears. One of the things my mother gave me was a picture of Tom and me. She had taken it, and I had said I'd like it. And then I was able to cry, and they thought I was crying because I saw the picture.

A couple of days after Tom's death, I could smell him on the sheets, and everything he had said was so clear to me. And after a couple of months, I could remember little things that he had said. His face was clear. Now it's not so clear. But when I think of him, I think of him in my dream and how he appeared. To me, that's the last time I saw him. He's always going to be twenty-two. That will be really weird. And as I grow older and I look at myself as a very changed person, he's still going to be the same. I was afraid for a long time that I would forget him, which is ridiculous now, I realize. But I thought, "He's just going to disappear. I'm going to forget I had a brother." A friend of mine had a sister who died of an aneurism. It had been a couple of years for her, and I said, "Do you still think of Miriam?" She put her hand to her forehead and said, "She's right here; she's always right here—in my memory." It was a good thing for me to hear that she is close and that I won't forget Tom.

Marcia: Like a Shadow of Pain

Marcia's husband killed himself in October 1987, leaving her with their son, Jaron, who was just a few weeks old. I interviewed Marcia, a dancer in her early thirties, in June 1989.

For Marcia (pronounced Mar-see-ah), the pain of her husband's suicide was compounded by the realization that he had abandoned their son. Spouses who are left alone with children in the wake of suicide must not only shoulder the responsibilities of parenthood alone but also bear their children's loss, as well as their own.

Marcia's kinesthetic experience of her loss is reflected in the language of her story. Two other people whose stories appear in this book (Chris, in this chapter, and Laura, in the previous chapter) also mention the physical effects of their grief. One of the striking things about Marcia's story is the way in which her body has been the central reference point for her movement through grief in the year and a half since her husband's death.

Also like Laura (whose story is continued in chapter 4), Marcia finds herself falling in love with another man while she is still making her way through her grief in the wake of her husband's suicide. The accounts of both women suggest that loss, grief, and reconnection are not necessarily tidy, sequential experiences. Survivors may discover the beginnings of reconnection in the midland of grief, not just toward its end.

Tom had been suicidal before. I caught him once making the motions, I would say. I'm not sure how serious he was. In retrospect, I think he probably was much more serious than I thought at the time. He talked about having been suicidal and what that meant. He got very depressed. I guess I just never understood suicide. It was almost as if I didn't believe it existed, that maybe people thought about it, but nobody I knew would ever really do it.

I protected him a lot. I think that was a problem in our relationship, that he needed a lot of protection. The other side of him was that he was one of the most brilliant people I've ever met and very creative. He was an extraordinary person, on the creative level, and I think this is part of what made him crazy. I don't know if *crazy* is the right word. He was so delicate. When he was really being open and creative, it was as delicate as . . . It was there, but it could be broken. And when it was broken, he really went far. It was like falling off a cliff every time.

He ended up killing himself at home. I went into the basement and found him. I thought he was asleep. He was all curled up in a very dark corner in a fetal position. It was five o'clock in the afternoon in October, so it was really dark. I went and shook him and said, "Tom, wake up. You're okay. I'm right here." That's when I noticed. He'd suffocated himself with a plastic bag. I felt him, and he was completely cold. I touched his neck to get a pulse, and it was like touching a wall. I think that something happens to the psyche. I just backed away. I didn't think, "Oh, he's dead," and I don't remember thinking, "He's going to be all right." I erased myself. My first reaction, physically, was yelling. I was yelling, "No," and I was lying on the floor—this is my memory—just yelling, "No, no, no, no, no!"

Then there was the police interview—to make sure this wasn't a murder, I guess. I knew him well enough to know that he had killed himself. There wasn't a question in my mind that this is what happened. They asked me was he suicidal and where could he have gotten hold of the garbage bag and did I hear him and did he call me and when did I last see him and did he ever try to do this before. Those are the things that I remember. And they asked me what kind of a relationship I had with him and were we fighting. I remember answering without anger but trying to figure out what the answers really were. I didn't think he had been murdered, but they were asking questions that I needed to ask myself.

I wasn't really angry at them yet. I did get angry later. I said to the detective that I wanted to see my husband, and he said,

"You don't really." And I said, "You can't tell me what I need right now." It was the combination of being really sure I wanted to see him and say good-bye and the detective having no relationship to me at all. You know something that I need? Forget it. I had already seen him dead. This was not going to be the first time. This was not going to be the last time either. There were people hanging around the stretcher, and I said, "Go away." They said, "It is illegal for us to go away." It was as if they were saying, "This dead body is ours." I was furious. I just said, "You are going away. This is my husband. I have more of a right to be here right now than you do." So they just went a few feet away. I stroked Tom's hair and talked to him, said I was really sorry, and I just cried. As soon as I started crying, they pulled me away. Why is it so bad to cry at that point?

I saw Tom's body again in the funeral home. It didn't look like him. He was lying down in a way that he never would. I burst out crying. I think that the good thing about seeing the body is that it really is empty. There's no denying it.

I had a lot of people around me after Tom died. I couldn't sleep alone. I couldn't go into the bedroom. I didn't allow anyone else into that room. I couldn't stand that someone else was going to erase him. Lots of his friends came. I called everyone he was really close with, and I called all the people I was close with. Mostly I said, "I have really bad news about Tom. He killed himself." I don't think I ever just said that he was dead. I found out later that many people don't say that it was a suicide. It didn't occur to me at the time. But a lot of people reacted by saying, "Are you sure?" Even now, when I tell them, some people say, "Are you sure it was a suicide?" Why is that so hard for other people to take?

In the first few hours, I probably made twenty calls. I think partly I was telling myself over and over and over that this was true. And now, in talking about it, I still feel this. It's like a shadow of pain but not the pain itself to talk about it. And in remembering it, I remember the pain itself. I guess I remember it kinesthetically. I remember that my body felt frozen. I began to freeze up little by little as I admitted it more and more. I can feel that shadow in me, in my jaw.

Now, in talking about it, I don't have to recreate the feeling exactly. I can really talk about it without crying, without being completely confused—somewhere between admitting that this is true and not being able to deal with it all at once. Now it's a part of my life, and it will never not be a part of my life. It will change. My feeling will change. I can see it's changed a lot. But it's now a part of my life, and then it wasn't a part of my life yet. Tom killed himself, and my life stopped. For the whole first year, it was like my life had stopped, time had stopped. But I had a child who was growing up fast. There was this bubble of experience I was having with Jaron, which was an incredible joy and so lucky for me.

I have also been lucky because I have lots of friends, and my house was full constantly. People were feeding me and feeding each other, and there was always someone to hold the baby, who was happy as a clam. Had I been the kind of person who is socially separate, I don't know what would have happened. But I was very cushioned. There was a big couch in the living room, which is a metaphor for what it felt like. I just sat in the middle of the couch, and there was always somebody with me. I'm sure I was not a pleasant person to be around. I was exhausted, drained physically and emotionally. And I think I was really demanding—nothing was enough, I needed everything from everyone. I have this image of myself sitting on the couch and just going from one thing to the next and not seeing what was next to me or behind me or in front of me.

That whole period was healing for me. I didn't have to deal with other people's grief all the time, so I didn't have to put my own away, which I think I would have done, because it's my nature. I really got to indulge. I'm not sure whether I could have done anything else. I had a lot of support with the baby. My family stayed for a long time. And I have a community of friends who got together and made a list of people and their phone numbers and days they were available. So I was never alone, day or night, for two months.

After Tom died, one of the first things I said was, "What am I going to do now?" Part of that question was, "How can I be alive when this has happened?" The other part was, "What am I going to do financially?" This is, I assume, common for widows, but also I had an infant. I didn't have a cent, and I didn't have a job. They set up a memorial fund—actually, not a memorial fund but a fund in Jaron's name—and there was a benefit dance.

I received checks in the mail from people I'd never seen before. And that meant that I could just survive right then without thinking.

There was some shame that I had. I mean, suicide is this very terrible thing in our society. My whole neighborhood knew, and I couldn't leave the house. I felt so exposed. I felt people identifying with me, thinking, "What if this happened to me? What if I just had a baby and my husband killed himself?" And when I thought of it like that, I thought, *how* does one live through this? People would hold themselves apart, as if it were catching. I felt like the symbol for everybody's fear. If they understood too much, they would be afraid their husbands or their lovers or their parents would do the same thing.

I had different experiences with different friends. Some people couldn't tolerate being with me at all. People I'd been close to for many years just cut me off. And then other people I wasn't that close to were just so available. I have a good friend who had a miscarriage the day Tom died. I had a good talk with her, and then she didn't correspond with me for a year or more. She finally wrote and said, "I'm sorry I haven't been able to be in contact with you. I'm not really sure what it is, but it has been hard for me to be in contact with you, and I hope we'll be able to figure this out someday." That was all I needed: for this friend, whom I've known for fifteen years, to say, "I'm sorry, I just couldn't." That's really enough. I have another friend whom I've known for sixteen years. I've written to her twice telling her, "It doesn't matter how much time has gone by, if you feel like it's too late. It's never too late to communicate with me. This is a lifetime friendship; that's what I expect. It's okay." But she hasn't been able even to write and respond to that.

Maybe the raw emotion is too hard to face because it's a mirror. None of us has an emotion that another person can't recognize. I described my feeling at the time as having my face inside out—the masks are completely gone. You can't pretend to think or feel or do anything, and you don't even try.

I felt terribly guilty for a while. As I get stronger and feel more . . . acclimated, I guess I separate myself from the part of me that felt I should have been able to help or I shouldn't have had the child.

I went through constant questioning from October [when

Tom died] till June, going over and over and over the last conversation, and going over and over and over the last day. And then in June I spent some time working on a dance piece, a ten-minute solo called "For Tom," and that really helped my transition from all the questioning. My whole experience of his suicide was that he probably didn't really want to do it. He only wanted to kill that part of himself that was depressed, and he could have changed it. Didn't I make him happy? Couldn't he feel loved? Why didn't he love me enough? And at that point, in June, I felt that if I professed to accept him in life—which I really did—then I wanted to find a way to accept his choice to die. So I made a dance piece about accepting him. It was about pain and as much understanding as I could have, given that I can only understand suicide up to a point. And ever since then, I've released my guilt, I guess. I'm lucky to have had that avenue, being able to create something like that.

That changed my life, that whole process. I had a serious piece of depression later, around the anniversary of his death. And it continues to be painful in different surprising and not surprising ways. But that whole thing of accepting him also allowed me to separate and accept the range of feelings, that they weren't attached to whether or not I could figure out why he did it. I just can't figure it out, and I can't spend any more time doing it.

The first anniversary was horrible. It was a combination of Jaron's first birthday, which I could barely acknowledge, then Tom's birthday, which was three weeks later, and then the anniversary of Tom's death. And in between, Jaron had an asthma attack and was hospitalized. He has this condition, but I think it was exacerbated by my being a basket case. I just couldn't see the signs, and he felt the incredible pain and maybe had some of his own; he was sort of vulnerable and open. So I had this really big set of things. The first year was over, but it didn't feel like it was getting better—it was worse. I started getting depressed in August, when Jaron's birthday was coming around, and it didn't quite settle down until December.

I went to a support group for suicide survivors around that time. I felt that all my friends were burned out. I couldn't go back to them and say, "Can I be a mess for a while?" One friend was incredible. She wanted to give me a day—we called it a fall-apart day. She said I could do whatever I wanted and that it would just be her and me. Just knowing that I had that changed my whole feeling. It ended up happening in November. All we did was watch my wedding tape, and I also had a video-tape of Tom with Jaron when he was a few weeks old, which was just incredibly intense and very sweet and horrible to watch. And we talked. I don't know if that was all I needed, but that was the only piece of what I got that was really right at the time. I think the rest I just muddled through. And going to the support group was really useful.

I wanted to write about the first year. It was not just that I was trying to do something that could be useful and productive but that if I wrote it, I would be finished with it, that somehow I wouldn't be finished until I did this project. That's not the right motivation for writing, but if it keeps me writing, I suppose it's okay. Now I don't feel that way as much. I probably have to get rid of that feeling entirely before I can really do it, because there is no ending. I know there were times when I heard that and felt really depressed about it. I thought I was in this forever. I'm just beginning to understand that it's a part of me, a big part of me. It will change, but it's still pretty new. I can imagine in ten years still having it be a part of me, but it will be so different. I met a woman whose husband killed himself, and ten years later she has two kids and is married again. That was the best thing, to meet her.

I really wanted to dance through some of this. It's a good way for me to get clear and not hide things in my body. I think we all hide things in our bodies, and it's just that I happen to have a communication with my body or something. I went through the first few months being really frozen and then just coming out of it slowly. I had a big chunk taken out of the frozen part when I did that performance last summer. And then in the fall I went back to being really depressed and having no idea what I wanted to do. I didn't feel quite as frozen, because I guess I wasn't as well protected. And I felt even more emotional than I had at first. In some ways it was worse, because I couldn't turn to all those people anymore, there wasn't some-body sleeping with me every night. It was like reliving a different layer of it, and it was unexpected. I didn't know how to deal with it at all.

Now I'm starting to become alive again. And I'm frustrated because I'm not there yet. The one place that I have come through is that I feel I'm falling in love again, which is like a miracle. I can't believe it. And it's been so painful, because the deeper I love, the more I have to cry. Just a few nights ago, I cried for an hour about Tom. I just have to do that constantly. It's as though I have to make the transition.

The place where I haven't been able to come through—and I wonder if everybody has different places where they stay frozen for different periods—is work. I haven't been able to work. I haven't been able to perform again, except for that one performance, and I haven't been able to teach again. The only thing I can think about doing right now is writing. I'm just writing, writing, writing. Sometimes it's two words in three hours of sitting there, and sometimes it's ten pages in one hour of sitting there. I don't really feel that I need to start doing something. I live on Social Security, and I'm renting my house, so it pays for itself. I'm really kind of in limbo.

I don't know what Tom's legacy is. I've saved certain things of his—his wedding clothes and his bicycle helmet and his glasses, funny things—so that Jaron has something of his father's. When Jaron gets to know about his father, which he will periodically at different levels, he can go through the stuff, see pictures and clothing. I guess what I recognize, now that I'm talking, is that I still have some anger, quite a bit, every time Jaron— As he gets older, I think, "You weren't here for this. Jaron was sick in the hospital, and you didn't come!" All sorts of things around that. I think I accept Tom, but maybe I haven't yet forgiven him. I assume that that's another part of the process, when I really forgive him for doing this to his son, not to mention me, because his son is going to have to heal from this later. I'm healing now, and I'll heal more later, but Jaron hasn't even begun, and that makes me mad.

My son not only looks like Tom but has some of the same potentialities that Tom had. Jaron has Tom's last name, which is not my last name. Yet he has no relationship with Tom, and I don't know whether he will feel it's a stigma to have his father's name, a father he did not know and who killed himself when

Jaron was born. The farther away it gets from that time, the closer the birth and death seem.

I haven't yet gotten to the place where I can say, "I chose Tom as my husband—we chose each other—because of an extraordinary connection that we had and the depth that he was able to go and the person he was. He was a really valuable and much-missed person for a lot of people." Once I get to the point where this is what's left, then my ability to talk to Jaron about him will not be overshadowed by, "And he killed himself when you were a baby." I haven't gotten to that place, and when I do—it's a relief to think about it in this way, to assume that I will, because I think I will—then Jaron can make whatever choice he wants. Tom was his father, he is his father, and he will always be his biological father. He gave Jaron life, and other men in his life will be his father in a different way . . . a more important way, I think. But that doesn't change the fact that there's somebody I chose to be his father. So I'll come to that, I think, but I'm still mad. Fortunately, Jaron's not even two, so he's never asked.

To be present is really the only way to integrate this, and the lack of integration is what keeps people from finishing. Finishing doesn't mean that the person leaves your experience, but it means that you are no longer living inside it. The sadness no longer takes me away from my life the way it did. It makes me feel alive in some way, too; I'm alive and Tom isn't. But the sweetness of who he was and what was good, that I can still be sad about. I don't mean just now—because now I'm sad about it a fair amount—but later.

I think suicide in the family is different from suicide in the marital relationship. I can't replace Tom, the person or the relationship or the choice that we got married—any of that. But I can replace that part of my life. Tom's mother can't replace her son. It's not that anybody's grief is really worse or better, but there's something different about the experience that I have.

The thing that was most helpful to me in the beginning was to be told over and over again that whatever I feel is okay. The guilt and the anger, the millions of things that you go through, including relief and joy, being able to laugh in the midst of it— all of that is normal and okay. That's the biggest single thing that helped me. The other thing that helped, in the next stage, was to know that everything changes—not really that this too will pass, because it doesn't feel like it will pass, but that it will change. The thing that's helping me the most now is to know that it's okay for the sadness to come up over and over again unexpectedly and that I don't have to wait for it to be over, that it only changes.

I think forgiving is the next thing. I've begun to forgive people who haven't given me anything this past year and a half. I've been writing letters and saying, "For whatever reason, let's not be cut off, because I'm still alive." But I think the next step will be forgiving Tom. And then there's going to be a big step when I let Jaron have his own life, meaning, among other things, his own relationship with his father and his own understanding of the whole thing. He's going to have another dad, I suspect, because I'm serious about this particular person I'm seeing, and I understand that I'm not really meant to be alone. I was alone until I was about thirty-one, and I just don't think that that's where I am anymore. So Jaron will have to deal with that. I can't protect him. I can only forgive Tom so that I don't poison it.

I don't feel damaged; I feel altered. I feel changed for my whole life. I was a glass that was broken. I had this home and these expectations of life, and I was filling up this glass with food and life and experience. And then it was shattered. Everything that I believed in spilled out and went into the earth, and I lost it. I had nothing left. I was lying in this puddle of water that used to be something. Just broken, I guess that's how I felt, broken . . . and shattered. But I have glue. You can see the cracks, because I have changed, but I hold water just as well as I did before.

Ellen: Such an Interruption

Ellen, a woman in her thirties, was a social worker in training in November 1988 when Joe came to the clinic where she was working and began therapy with her. He made a serious suicide attempt the following February and killed himself in April. I interviewed her two months later, in June 1989. The names in her story have been changed.

Ellen's story tells of the dimensions of loss for a therapist whose patient commits suicide. Even though the relationship with a patient is part of a therapist's professional rather than personal life, the connection can nevertheless be strong. Therapists experience many of the same responses—the questioning, the anger, the guilt—that other survivors do. Moreover, a patient's suicide leaves the therapist with a host of questions about responsibility, competence, and even professional identity. Like Ellen, many therapists, in the wake of suicide, question their ability to be of help to their patients.

I did the intake evaluation on Joe when he first called to make an appointment at the mental health clinic where I've been working as a social work intern. He was twenty-four and had graduated from college the previous summer. At that point, he was speaking about suicide. I didn't ask all the right questions. It was probably the first intake that I had done in which somebody had expressed any thoughts about suicide. I got off the phone and thought, "I should have asked other questions," and I really wasn't clear what. And then somebody said, "Well, did you give him the hot line number to [the psychiatric hospital]?" And I said, "Oh, no!" It was scary for me. I found out all this information that I should tell him and maybe some more questions that I should ask. I called him back, but there was no answer. This was a Friday afternoon, so there was no way for me to get in contact with him until Monday. It was just scary for me to think that maybe I should have told him more. I looked through the obituary page on Saturday and Sunday, praying that this guy would know what to do if he felt that desperate.

I ended up having Joe assigned to me for therapy. He was a very intense, dependent person. He felt that he wanted to see me more than once a week. He said twice a week. And my inclination was to say okay. As a result, even though it was a short period of time that I met him, it was very intense.

Sometimes you meet people and there's just a connection of some sort. I really can't put it in words. There was just, on my part and it seemed on his part, some kind of nice connection that occurred between the two of us. There was something really likable about this guy. He was very engaging, very articulate. The way he would articulate his thoughts and his feelings had this poetic fashion to it. He had a sense of humor. He was very bright. There were certain issues that I could even identify with, not to the same degree perhaps that he was experiencing them, but some of his issues were issues and feelings that many people who are right out of college would experience.

He would talk a little about suicide, and we contracted, in the sense that he said he would be able to call me or the hospital if need be, if he felt that he would act on his impulses. When I asked him if he knew anybody who had ever attempted or committed suicide, he said no. And then I asked him if anyone in his family ever had, and he said, "Oh, yeah, my brother, ten years ago, attempted suicide." It's interesting how people sometimes make a division between everyone else and their family members.

I was planning to take a week off during Christmas, and Joe was going to visit his family out of state. Even when we were parting, I just never knew what he was going to do or if he would return. I thought he might leave and not come back. It's kind of an odd feeling to say good-bye to somebody and not know if you're ever going to see him again, even though you make an appointment and even though you feel that you're building some type of relationship. There are some people you know are not going to return. But Joe would not return only if he was not going to come back to this state. He was very unhappy living here, and he had a girlfriend out of state. There was no reason to stay. He wasn't here through choice. He was here almost through lack of choice, lack of any other place to be. It's hard to work with somebody when you don't know if he's going to split town the next day.

He called during his vacation. I wasn't there, and he talked to my supervisor. He talked about whether he should hospitalize himself. He was talking about feeling depressed. That was a major issue: feeling depressed, feeling loss. There were real identity issues, as far as "Who am I?" He had great difficulty making choices, taking responsibility. But he didn't hospitalize himself, and he did come back. I contracted with him again, but I was never sure. Of all my clients, he was one I just didn't know. It got to the point where I didn't know what he was going to do when he walked out of the office. It never felt clear. I never felt comfortable. He just wasn't always there. He would go on and on and on with thoughts, but I never felt secure that *he* was secure in what he could do and not do. I talked about him to a variety of people, really looking for somebody else to meet with him. I was an intern. I just wasn't sure, and I was grappling. I was constantly grappling with decisions. It was too big a responsibility. I shared it all with both my supervisors, but no clear decision was ever made. So I just kept moving along and seeing where it went.

[Then one day Joe attempted suicide but survived.] I had seen him earlier that day, and there was no hint. I [found out] about it the next morning. I was devastated. I went over my notes. I looked, looked. What did I miss? I know I had asked if he was okay. I don't really remember that much more of the conversation. I didn't want to go to work. I didn't want to see anybody. I remember speaking to one of my supervisors. What could he say? I was just so distraught. I felt a sense of responsibility. Intellectually, yes, I could say I couldn't have done anything and it wasn't my fault. But I had this pain in my stomach. I felt that I had missed something or I should have done something or I should have gone by my gut a couple of weeks earlier and made sure somebody else saw him. I don't know, I should have done *something*. I remember that day at work, because I had another client come in. All of a sudden, she started talking about feeling depressed and how she'd thought about suicide. I didn't show it to her, but my antennae went up, of course, and a part of me said, "I don't want to hear this. Don't tell me; tell somebody else. Maybe I don't belong in this field." It was so hard to sit with a client and be focused on her issues, because I was having trouble just keeping myself above water.

I talked to people all day. I called my other supervisor. And people said, "You can't do anything about it. You can't change it. It's not your fault. People make these decisions independently of you, and we can't always stop people." But it was really hard to integrate that into my pit, my stomach.

I remember the first phone conversation I had with Joe after his attempt. I told him that the most important thing was that he was alive. He sent out double messages, which included, "I hope you don't get in trouble for what I did." And I responded, "Well, that's nothing for you to worry about. The most important thing is that you're okay." And I used to think, "What the hell was he trying to say to me? What were these double messages? Was he really angry at me and felt I should have done something and wanted me to get into trouble?" I don't know.

He was seeing a psychiatrist [at the hospital] at that point. There was a decision that he was going to continue seeing the psychiatrist after he was discharged, so it seemed like a good idea that we terminate therapy. We probably met three more times. We talked about his suicide attempt. Part of the problem, he said, was that he could contract with people, but he didn't know at that moment that he would be planning on committing suicide or attempting it two hours later. So he could say something at that moment, but his feelings or thoughts could change drastically. I found out later, through his father, that he had bought the hose that he used to try to kill himself before he saw me, on the day he attempted suicide, so he wasn't sharing that piece with me.

He was having a hard time saying good-bye. He said that there were only a few people out there who really knew him and that I was one of them, so that losing me was really tough. He was crying. There was a lot of emotion in that room—ending, saying good-bye, and hoping that he would be able to follow through with the psychiatrist and stick with it and come to peace with some of the issues that were bothering him. Again, there was always this feeling that I didn't know how much truth he was sharing with me at the time. What was just the outer façade? What was he just saying for effect? What was he really feeling? I remember at the end of our last meeting, I asked how much of him he felt was really genuine that day. He said, "A little piece."

Sometime later, I called the social worker at the hospital about something totally irrelevant to Joe. She was sitting in the office with the psychiatrist, and they had just heard that he had committed suicide. I was silent on the phone. I didn't know what to say. The only words that came out of my mouth were, "He's such an asshole!" What a waste! Why did he do that? There was so much inside him.

He hung himself on the bathroom pipes. And he had seen the psychiatrist the same day or the day before. She also didn't know. Every time he left the office, she didn't know. Would he be okay? You just never knew with Joe.

I was a wreck. I couldn't believe it. I really didn't believe it in some ways. I didn't want to believe that he had done it. I used to fantasize that I'd see him on the street or he'd call up or come into the office. It just didn't seem possible that he could end his life at age twenty-four and that there was so much promise and so much creativity and so much talent. Through my eyes, he had so much to offer people, and he just couldn't see it. He couldn't see the light at the end of the tunnel. He couldn't see that maybe in two or three years he would feel better. My gut feeling was "Asshole," but I just felt so much sadness for him. And that pain in the gut returned. People used to ask me, "Aren't you angry?" and I'd say, "No." To me it was just such a waste. I felt so sorry for him, that he couldn't see what I saw and what other people saw in him, that he had so much to offer, that he was really special.

I learned that his father had found a suicide note addressed to me. I thought, "I don't really want this." Part of me was afraid that he was blaming me and that he was angry at me, and I just didn't want him to be angry at me. Although the note wasn't dated, they thought that it was probably from the first suicide attempt. He had never made any mention of it. Every day I'd look in my mailbox, waiting for this letter to be sent by Joe's father. That's all I would go to work for, to look in my mailbox and see if the note was there. Finally, it came. I dreaded opening it, but I opened it. It was addressed to me, and it just talked about how much despair he felt and that he was finally making a choice.

I've never been able to cry about it, which seems out of character for me, and I never understood why I wasn't able to express my sadness that way. I just had this pain in my stomach. And I'd get all shaky and upset when I would share it with other people and just be at a loss for words.

I remember after his first attempt I spent the whole next day making all these long-distance phone calls. It was my way of reaching out to people, to talk to people about it. I was just so upset. I talked to a woman who's a social worker and has been somewhat of a mentor. She's one of my mother's friends, and I'm really fond of her. She told me, "Nobody's omnipotent. You have these messianic ideals. We can help people, but sometimes we just can't stop people who really want to go through with it." That was helpful.

About a month after Joe's suicide, or over a month, I presented his case to a group of interns at the clinic. I thought I would be able to do it and that I would be okay about it. What a mistake. I was shaking. I was *so* overwhelmed—such intense sadness and pain. I was reliving it all over again.

I talked to the social worker at the hospital about Joe. We talked about what he was like, different aspects of his personality. She was one person I spoke to who knew him, maybe at a different level than I knew him, but knew what I was talking about and saw what I saw and liked him. That was helpful, to feel that there were other people out there who really could understand what I saw and knew of him. It's different from talking to somebody who doesn't know this person from a hole in the head and can empathize with you, *may* know what it feels like, but didn't know Joe.

I didn't make any overtures [to talk to Joe's psychiatrist at the hospital]. I think I said something once: "Oh, we should talk." And she said, "Yes." We both responded the same way. Neither one of us made any overtures to do anything about it. And I know I could have made the time. That wasn't the issue, that I was too busy. And I'm sure if she had called, I would have made the time. But she didn't call, and I didn't call. In a way, I was grieving, and I don't know what it would have been like to be with somebody who was grieving about the same thing. I didn't really have enough energy to give to that person. I had enough trouble keeping myself going, focusing my healthy energies on myself. To try to give that to somebody else—I don't know if I could have done that. There had even been talk about having some type of group, a few people who had known Joe, get together and do some sharing. But it's never happened, and I haven't started it. If I were invited, I would go.

I still have the suicide note. My friend says, "Give it back. Let it go, just let it go." I'm not really sure why I have it, except that it's addressed to me and that . . . I'm not ready to let it go. I could easily put it in his file, and I probably will when I'm ready.

Joe's father sent me a letter also. He had read all of Joe's journals and a lot of his writings. He saw a lot of despair. There were identity issues, sexuality issues, loneliness, real confusion. And his father had never really seen any of that from what Joe would articulate to his folks. His father never understood why Joe was so upset, because what he was presenting to his father didn't seem that important. It seemed like the kinds of issues we can all deal with and get by. He thought that he knew Joe the best, and he said he guessed he didn't. He thanked me and said I was one of many who tried to help Joe, and he wished people had been successful in their attempts. There was such pain in the letter. It must have been so hard to write. I didn't respond . . . What do you say? "Sorry" sounds so trite.

It's easier now to talk about it. I guess I came to grips—I hope I came to grips—[with the fact] that I couldn't change the outcome [but] that I do have something to offer to people, and with more experience, I can be good in my field. I want to be able to help people if I can and to make them feel, at least at the time that I'm with them, that they're important and that their feelings are important and that their pain is very real.

It took me many years to go back to school and decide to go for my master's in social work. I was a probation officer and a VISTA worker, I taught English in Israel, and I worked for the Department of Social Services. All my work was related to people in some fashion. It just seemed that I was always leaning toward becoming a social worker, and I felt I needed more education. I wanted to understand why I was doing what I was doing, not just do it in a haphazard way. I wanted there to be thought behind it, and I wanted to try to understand more of where people were coming from rather than be in the here and now all the time. But it's been a difficult two years. It's hard going back to school and having yourself evaluated all the time. I always used to get positive feedback about whatever I did. Now I was seen as a student. I knew everything I was doing wasn't perfect and needed work, and I was very raw. But it was hard revealing my weaknesses and insecurities and putting myself on the line for something that meant so much to me.

Social work is a field that involves so much exploration of yourself, and sometimes you don't want to look at yourself, because it's really painful. I knew that I would have to look at certain issues of my own before I could even begin to deal with other people's. I knew it was coming; I felt it. I couldn't run away. I didn't want to run away from it. What would be the point? But it takes a lot out of you.

Part of [my reaction to Joe's suicide] was just questioning my worth as this up-and-coming social worker. I always used to have the issue of separating the professional me from the personal me. How do I integrate the personal into the professional and know where to draw the lines? In the past, especially, there was more of a tendency for me to take people's problems home. I couldn't separate my work life from my personal and home life. That's one thing I did achieve over the past two years—I was able to separate them. But I couldn't just leave Joe's suicide at work. I used to ask people, "How do you deal with suicide? How do you work it through? How do I *process* this?"—a favorite word in social work classes—"I don't even know how to begin." So I just talked. Talk, talk, talk.

It's so hard for me to believe Joe is dead. As he said, he made a choice. I guess I just wish he had thought there were other options out there. It's so final. I can't turn it back and change his mind. I guess most of us think about suicide at some stage. But for most, that's where it stops—just thinking. Most people feel that maybe there is a light at the end of the tunnel and things will get better. As my father used to say, life is full of valleys and hills, and most of us are probably on plateaus. I don't know what it's like to be down continuously and not be able at least to get to the plateau.

My grandmother died when I was about twelve or thirteen, maybe a little younger. That was the first time I experienced someone dying. I remember I was a wreck. I sobbed. And it wasn't even that I was that close to this grandmother. It was just that somebody was dying. That was it—it was so final. That was really scary. And that you never came back. I remember I sometimes would ask my mother what I could think about at night to go to sleep, because I always used to think about lying in the ground, dead. That was terrible.

The last year of my internship was with the elderly. The major issue was death. It was hard hearing, even then, that some people wanted to die. I would sit there, and I didn't know what to say to people. I felt I should say something. Some of the people meant it, and some of them half meant it, but it seemed as though there was a time when some of them were ready to die and it was okay. They were at peace with that thought. Maybe I grew to accept it because of their age and because they seemed to have lived full lives. I guess it was hard to accept that people commit suicide at an older age. People stop eating, and people will themselves to die at times. My grandmother waited until my cousin got married. We all knew. You could just feel it. She was waiting for this grandchild to get married. And she was really fighting at the end. She couldn't even make it to the ceremony. But that was all she needed. So people have many ways of letting themselves die. I guess with Joe it seemed as though he didn't go his full course. It was such an interruption. He was at the beginning; he wasn't at the end. I wish sometimes that I believed in reincarnation.

I guess I'm not ready to think about death, at least my own end. Death is saying good-bye, and sometimes it's just hard for me to say good-bye. I mean, how do you say good-bye to people you love and know you'll never see again? I have my other grandmother, whom I'm really fond of. I wish she could live forever, and I know she won't. I'm really crazy about her, and I can't put a hold on her. I've been taking pictures of her. I like taking pictures. I came out with two that I thought were really good. My boyfriend liked them, and his father, who's a photographer, liked them. So I enlarged them, and I brought them home during the holidays and showed them to my family. My mother said, "This is not her." I said, "What do you mean it's not her?" "It's not her." My uncle: "Not her." My grandmother: "Not me." It was amazing. Everybody else said they liked them. It was her. Who else was it? It showed some of the puffiness around the eyes. Some of it's not so flattering, especially when you enlarge a picture. And I said to my grand-mother, "When you look at yourself in the mirror, you see a certain person. But you don't look at yourself in the mirror when you're laughing and smiling. You look at yourself in the mirror, and what are you doing? You're combing your hair, you're brushing your teeth, but you're sure not laughing. But when I think of you, I think of somebody who's laughing and smiling. So when I look at these pictures, that's you to me, somebody who's laughing, who's full of life. And that's what I see in these pictures."

How do people live on? If they've done anything or created anything with their hands, stories, sometimes memories—I guess a lot of ways. But for me, one of the ways is pictures. If you don't talk about that person a lot, he or she dies. So if you see something and it's outside of your mind, some type of creation, that's always alive.

I know I'll miss [my grandmother when she dies], but she'll definitely live on in me. I'm older. I mean, I've had more experiences. It's nice that I've been able to make a special connection with her. I guess what I've learned is that we make connections with people. Sometimes we don't even know it. I felt there was a nice connection with Joe. I was there to listen and try to help him. He wasn't able to use what I could offer. It takes hard work to establish a relationship with somebody—family, friends, therapists, clients. You work on establishing trust with people all the time . . . And then it's gone. It just ends.

Richard: Being There to See Him Off

Richard's lover, Mark, took a fatal overdose of medication in June 1988. Mark was thirty-five at the time; Richard was thirty-three. Mark had been diagnosed with AIDS several years before Richard met him. At the time of Mark's death, Richard was working as a therapist with patients who had AIDS. He has since moved to another part of the country and is enrolled in a graduate program in mental health. I interviewed Richard in November 1990, two and a half years after Mark's death. Richard's name and others in the story have been changed; Mark's name has not.

The story Richard tells is unlike the other stories in this book in several respects. Perhaps the most important difference is Richard's sense of completion. Mark's death was no surprise; Richard had prepared for it, with Mark, both in practical and emotional ways. Moreover, he was with Mark when he died. Mark's suicide—he called it "self-deliverance"—was carried out not alone or secretively but in the company of Richard and all the other people who were most important to him. Before Mark died, they all had an opportunity to say good-bye to him, and he to them.

The loss for Richard has nevertheless been enormous, and his story tells, among other things, of his struggle to let go of his life with Mark, little by little, and to go on with his own life. Yet Richard's loss has been simpler and clearer in many ways than the other losses described in this book.

It got to the point where Mark felt he was just waiting. He kept saying, "I've never been very good at waiting, and this seems to be taking too long." He had pneumocystis pneumonia [an infection that is common in patients with AIDS] two different times and both times was able to recover fully. One of the things that was his downfall was a diagnosis of tuberculosis, which was not only in his lungs but also in his joints, and he had funguses and skin lesions that wouldn't heal. It got to the point where it was really hard for him to focus, because he had headaches as well. He had pain all through his body. We had him on morphine and Valium for pain. The quality of his life had decreased a whole lot.

There was a lot of grieving and crying that we did together. At one point, we were driving back from Cape Cod after his thirty-fifth birthday party. This was five or six weeks before he died. He didn't feel well the entire time, barely got off the couch, and was a pain in the ass for me, because he was so angry and confrontational. Driving back, he said to me, "What do you see happening here?" I took a deep breath and said, "I don't see you gaining back the ground that you've lost." We drove for several miles not saying anything, both of us crying. And then he said, "Does it seem like we were the last to know?" And I said, "Yes, it does. But I guess now it's our turn to face this and accept it in the way that we've demanded of everybody else."

That was really the beginning of it. He needed me to know that he was afraid to be by himself from that point forth, and I needed to make plans to take a leave of absence from work. It was hard. I even put off my leave of absence an extra week, because it was the last little bit of denial I could possibly hold on to. Then it just seemed to start happening very rapidly.

He'd look at me some mornings, when I'd take him to the bathroom, and he'd just say, "Why can't I die?" Often tears would be streaming down his face. And the only thing I could say to that was "You will die." And he'd say, "Well, when? Why is it taking so long?" And I'd say, "Well, let's get you back into bed." Basically, that usually worked, to get him back into bed, get him cleaned up a little bit, and he'd go back to sleep.

This went on for several weeks. It didn't seem so bad, and he said that he could do it for a while, because he finally had company there all the time. His big fear was to be left alone. I didn't see tremendous change on a day-to-day basis, although a lot of people who came to visit, including his mother, were shocked by how emaciated he'd become. He lost probably forty pounds.

One morning he just woke up, looked out the window, and said, "This would be a good day to die." I'd heard that so many times, I didn't pay much attention to it. He was always testing me to find out whether I had budged on this topic. He knew, pretty much right along, that I was not in favor of his doing that. I thought we could keep him pain-free with the medications and the information we had. On a number of occasions, when the topic had come up, we would get into heated arguments about it. I said that I had to honor my inner voice, which said that it was not right for me to help him do this. However, he also knew that I wasn't going to stand in his way. He continued to confront me on it to see whether I would change my mind, but it never happened.

That morning, when he woke up and said it was a good day to die, I was thinking to myself, "Well, it's more of the same." I went down and was doing the laundry. I came back to the apartment just as I heard the telephone buzzing. We had a pager system in the phone, and he was buzzing me to come into the bedroom. I went running in there as quickly as I could, and he said, "Get the bedpan, quick." I quickly got the bedpan under him, and then he just started crying. He looked at me and said he had had enough, he couldn't do this anymore. He broke down and just sobbed. He cried in a different way than, looking back, I had ever heard him cry, almost a mournful kind of guttural wailing. At the time, I was thinking to myself, "Oh, you're really working it this time. It's not that bad." Little did I know that this was the last time he was going to cry. I think what was happening at that moment was that the fear and the humiliation of possibly soiling the bed were so intense for him, and he began to let go.

I gave him some morphine and some Valium, and he went back to sleep. When he woke up, he asked me if I thought he still wanted to die. I said, "Well, you've said it a lot." And he said, "This time I'm serious." He said, "I want you to call the inner circle," which is how we referred to the people he wanted there at the end. So I made all the calls and said that I really felt it was important that we surround Mark right now. He needed to see the faces of all these people, and he wanted to say good-bye. Because we had had so many conversations like this in the past with our friends, they knew to come. In some ways, we had rehearsed scenarios in our minds, what part we would all play in it.

A few hours later, people started to arrive. I went ahead and got the things—like champagne—we had always talked about having when we had talked, kind of in a joking way, about what we would do for his last party. I picked up flowers and did the whole thing. I was on automatic pilot, feeling numb and sort of in an altered state. People were taking shifts staying with him, and he slept most of the rest of the day. Then at one point, he woke up and said that he wanted to call his mother. I cleared everybody out of the bedroom, dialed the phone, and held it up to his ear. I only heard his part of it, which was essentially that he was getting close to the end and that he wanted to say good-bye.

Our friend Sue called to say that she had missed her flight and was going to take a later one. It would mean a two-hour delay. Mark snapped at her, "Well, I guess you weren't supposed to be here for this." That was really unfair, because of all the people in the circle, she was the one who had taken the greatest care of him, coming to visit and cooking meals and just pitching in whenever he was convalescing. I said, "You're not going to do this until she gets here. We're going to wait." He looked at me, and I looked at him. And at that point, I felt like I had some control, and he was willing to trust my judgment.

Then it just became a waiting game. He mostly slept. At one point, he did wake up, because we had his favorite brie heated with almonds on top, and we were feeding him that with bread. It was the most I had seen him eat in a long, long time. He was just like a baby bird, opening his mouth for more, and I kept feeding him more. I don't know what was different, but he consumed a lot of it and really relished it.

Sue finally arrived. She went right in and crouched down beside the bed. Everybody in the circle knew better than to touch Mark, because he was in such pain. She just sat with him and cried. Then he gave me the signal to have them start preparing the medication. This was something else that had been determined ahead of time, that it would be better to put it in applesauce. Finally, it was ready, and we had a toast with the champagne. There wasn't much said, except "I love you, and I'm going to miss you," "I love all of you, and thank you all for being here," and that sort of thing. We clinked our glasses together and took a sip, and then somebody handed Mark the bowl with the applesauce in it. He sat up on one elbow, and it seemed to me he had just enough energy to eat that applesauce. It looked like he was fading so quickly that I wondered if he was going to be able to take it himself. We were all convinced that it was important that he eat it himself, not have it fed to him. And so it was almost like he had paced himself to the point where he just had enough energy to eat it himself.

After he had swallowed the last bite, he put his head back down on the pillow and closed his eyes, and that was it. I think five minutes later, I asked everyone to leave us alone. One by one, people kissed him good-bye and left the bedroom. I stayed in there with him for the next hour, and I listened while his breathing changed. It became more labored and got slower and slower. And then finally he took what I thought was his last breath. It wasn't his last breath—there was another one after that. Then he took a final breath, and seconds after that there was a tap at the door. It was one of our friends, who asked if everything was okay, if I needed anything. I said, "I don't know. Could you come in?" I asked if she could get a heartbeat. She couldn't, and she said, "I think he just died." We sat there for a moment. I don't know what happened after that. I think she went back out to tell everybody that he had died, and people came in.

Sue and I prepared his body. We dressed him in the clothes that we had picked out earlier that day and that he wanted to be cremated in. He was always very particular about how his nails looked, so she filed his nails. And I combed his beard. She took a lot of pleasure in pulling the IV out of his arm and taking the oxygen off his nose. The beauty of it was that everybody got to come in and sit with him and touch him and kiss him on the forehead while he was still warm. It wasn't a cold, awful, sterile kind of experience. It was very intimate. People had been there all the way through his illness and were there to see him off as well.

About an hour later, the man came to take his body. Having set that up in advance really expedited the whole process. Three of us carried Mark out of the bedroom. We sort of stood around, and he said, "If you need more time . . ." I said, "No, I don't think we need more time." I kissed Mark on the forehead, and everybody in turn kissed him or touched him, and they took him out the door. It was at that point that I broke down, when the numbness and shock were wearing off and I realized that this was really over. I went into the bedroom and started crying. One of my friends came in and grabbed my hand and said, "Talk to him." And it just started pouring out of me. I was saying all these things to Mark, how I missed him already and was so sorry this had to happen and so sad. It felt completely natural, normal, even in the presence of another person. And I think, if nothing else, that single moment was crucial to my grief. I never, to this day, have stopped talking to him. I often find myself just talking directly to him, though it's changed a lot with the passing of time.

I'm really lucky that that group of people was there the whole time after he died, for the memorial service and for the months and now years since he died. It's a tight-knit group of people who are just survivors, who have kept, in some ways, taking care of each other.

I really lost a lot of innocence with Mark's passing, because up until then I had so much hope. Of all the people I knew, he had so much more piss and vinegar and fight. He was determined, and he was just angry enough that he propelled himself through all kinds of very difficult illnesses and infections. He kept outliving all these other people with AIDS. He had been diagnosed in 1981, and here it was 1988. He had been living with this for seven years. So when he actually was gone, I realized how much hope I had to let go of and what an active process it was for me to make myself recognize that he was gone, along with all that hope that he was going to beat this. At work it was particularly difficult. Working as a therapist with people who have this disease, it was really hard for me not to see all of them as people who were going to have debilitating conditions and die. I started to realize that I wasn't as optimistic as I might have been before, and I was imparting some of that to these people. I had to be honest with myself in terms of my burnout.

I did a lot of soul searching. I decided it was really time for me to make a change, that I needed to leave. But in some ways I felt I wasn't completely ready to let go all the way, although it had been over a year and I'd started another relationship with somebody else. It was still very difficult for me to think about not driving Mark's car, not having the memory of the apartment we lived in, and not running into people who knew my story and knew his story. There was a big part of me that was scared to make the move. I kept thinking, "Well, maybe it's premature. Maybe I'm really foolish, because I have such a loving community here and the support is so great." But what really convinced me, more than anything, was that I felt I had a chance to start all over again. My energy was returning, and I was feeling rejuvenated. It was time to take on something for me now, which was the graduate school program. And I needed to start trusting that that inner circle of people would always be friends, that we would always be connected in a deep way, but that it was going to have to be a two-way thing. I wasn't going to be able to control how many of these people would actually stay best friends with me.

It was a really big thing to sell Mark's car. He took such pride in that car, never let anybody else drive it, and here I was advertising it in the newspaper. I kept thinking, "If I don't sell it, maybe I'll just hang on to it." I finally did sell the car. And then another thing happened as I was packing up the U-Haul to leave. I had underestimated how much stuff I had. The U-Haul was too small, and suddenly there I was in the parking lot of my building on the last day I was living there. I had all this furniture, things that weren't going to fit in, and some of the things were Mark's. A friend said, "You'd better decide what you're going to leave behind." It was a really difficult moment. I just about had a temper tantrum in the parking lot, saying, "I let go of enough things. I want to take these things with me. Why do I have to let go of them?" I ended up having to leave a couple of things behind, including a dining room table, which was Mark's. Well, there's a happy ending. The woman I sold it to agreed to sell it back to me, and some friends just moved out here and brought it with them. So it's funny how these things work out. But the letting go is such an active process, and sometimes I resist it so much.

I think part of the letting go now is not comparing, not thinking, "Well, this is the way Mark was, and why can't Stephen [the man I'm seeing now] be more like that?" Or I've thought to myself, "This is the attitude Mark had toward this," and I've held the same attitude. Maybe part of it isn't healthy or appropriate for me, but I've held on to some things in that way. And I do catch myself at times, when things come out of my mouth, especially impatience with people who seem not to have what I would consider problems, who dwell and indulge themselves and complain. Oftentimes I just feel that sense of Mark's impatience. So I'm aware that there's a ways to go. But part of what I'm trying to do is even more fully integrate some of those things that I think were unique gifts that Mark had into my own self so that they fit better and are more me. I'm thinking especially of his compassion toward other people who had AIDS. He had tremendous concern and care for people who were suffering from this disease. I've taken a break from that in lots of ways by moving out here.

John, an old friend of mine [who lives out here], is HIV-positive and recently became ill with a throat infection. When he got sick, I realized that in some of my dreams, I was having flashbacks to Mark being sick in the next room. And then I started to think, "My God, I'm just making tea, and I'm just running out to the store to get aspirin, but this is how it starts. Right here. I'm watching my friend convert from being HIV-positive to having ARC [AIDS-related complex], and it's going to go from ARC to AIDS." And I had this really sad feeling that I didn't think, emotionally, I could go through this again with somebody. It was just too soon, and this person meant too much to me. In some ways, we have a primary relationship, even though it's a platonic relationship. And he was in a very deep form of denial about what was happening. So there I was, talking to his family and running interference, the whole time thinking, "How do I reassure these people that he is okay when I don't know if he's okay?"

John and I have now broached the subject more than we ever had before, and he's finally let me see him cry. In some ways, it's been really bonding. But even though there was a lot to gain from accompanying Mark through that rare and final part of his life—the wisdom one gains from that journey—I also realize that there's a lot of wisdom in deciding when to share that and with whom. This may not be the time and place to do that again. What I've done is given myself lots of breathing room in terms of dealing with this on a week-to-week basis. And John has a good, strong, supportive community here.

I find that there are not a lot of people who have experiences like mine, who are survivors and willing to talk about it. Little by little, in situations where it's appropriate, I share a little bit about what I've experienced. Now I share the story much more selectively. It's such an integrated part of me that when I talk about it now, it's not because I need to realize it again and share it to make it real, to let go of it. I'm sharing it because I meet somebody who I feel could benefit from something that Mark and I did or some strategy we adopted or just somebody who's having a difficult time struggling with the whole issue of self-deliverance. I've introduced that word to so many people who have never heard it before. In many ways, that's Mark's legacy, because he wouldn't let me call it suicide. He demanded that we call it self-deliverance. When I tell people now, it softens it somehow and makes it less stereotypical, less angry, depressed. For many years, the word *suicide* pushed so many buttons for me. But now I find that if I'm talking about it and I say "self-deliverance" and then explain it, people get it. It's one of those ahas: yes, there's another way to look at this besides suicide.

More than anything, the difference for me [between self-deliverance and suicide] is that Mark's death was not a surprise. We had talked about it so much. What I had to say about it and what I felt about it were included in his expanded vision of what this meant. That really made a difference. I mean, I didn't feel powerless, I didn't feel punished, I didn't feel like I was being totally cut out of this. I completely understood.

Another difference is that it wasn't a big secret. All those friends in the inner circle knew. They heard from Mark firsthand that this was something he was considering doing. So I felt there was no stigma. There was no lack of a support group to talk to about this. And I wasn't ashamed. I didn't feel responsible, and people didn't blame me. I know the tendency is to feel that you could have had a bigger effect. And I think that was difficult for me at first, because I really wanted to be the perfect caretaker. I said to myself that if I had only been there earlier that morning, it would have been different. I went through some of those feelings—I didn't do enough, I could have made a bigger difference, if only, if only, if only. I basically did a little healing ritual for myself, which was to forgive myself and ask him to forgive me, and I moved on.

We didn't leave anything unexpressed. We didn't leave anything dangling in terms of the business that needed to be finished. And I think that's a big difference, too. I had a chance to say "I love you" and "I'm sorry," and there was nothing left to say. It was a wonderful moment when Mark went to sleep. I thought, "There's nothing else to tell him. He knows exactly how I feel, and I know how he feels. This is so complete. If it had to happen, at least it's happening in this way."

I still sometimes commemorate Mark's passing. I have my own little rituals to do around the day he died. I generally speak with his mother. She and I have stayed in very close contact. And other friends who were there that night—we've all stayed in close contact. On the anniversary of his death, we talk. A lot of it at this point is unplanned, which I have a greater trust of. For the most part, I think the best rituals are the ones that write themselves rather than being premeditated.

Having the holidays without Mark is different now. Christmas trees and the ornaments are easier to look at. The first year was terrible. I forced myself to put up a tree. It took me hours to do it. The next year was a little easier. And this year will be different—being here, being involved with somebody again, and all the new things that are happening.

The biggest change I find in myself now is a willingness to look at my own mortality. I realize so much more now that I only have a finite amount of time and energy this time through. It's been a force that's propelled me to move through things quicker. I think I let go of especially petty things, like parking tickets, much faster. I don't give them any weight, and I would have before. Part of it also has to do with the fact that I'm a little older now and I'm seeing changes in my own body, just natural aging. It's great to be healthy, to feel well and celebrate this time when I don't have any major illnesses. It's really a wonderful time in my life, and I'm lucky. I know part of why I'm savoring it so much is that I'm not always going to have it. It's not a guarantee.

I think I've really been lucky to get to face what I faced with Mark, because in some ways it was a dress rehearsal. I have an idea of how I would like it to be for me when that time comes.

And it's not something that I need to be so afraid of. Some of the philosophers have said, "If you don't think about your death in the morning, then you've wasted the morning. And if you go to bed at night without thinking about death, then you've wasted the evening, too." It's what I've adopted, this animal way of keeping death to my side, to my left or to my right, knowing it's always there and thinking of it as a companion, not something at the end that's waiting to devour me and change everything and make it all fearful. That was a great thing Mark gave me: he made me face death with him, and that's continuing. It's just natural to continue to face it for myself.

I've found myself a few times anticipating my own death and grieving and at times being really moved. It's not sadness, but I'll see something and think, "This is so beautiful. I'm so happy to be seeing this right now. I'll miss the time that's coming when I won't get to see it." I think what I'm basically trying to do is extract more from each moment, just not knowing where they're going to lead and when they're going to end. Deciding to go to graduate school was really hard. It was taking on a commitment into the future, which I've resisted because it seems counter to the way I want to be in terms of making plans. But I decided to face the fact that I just turned thirty-five, and if I continue to take care of myself the way I have, there's no reason to think that in the second half of my life I won't be a licensed therapist. It will be so different, and the opportunities will be so much more plentiful for doing it.

I find that this is a time of great expansiveness—and great tragedy as well—but I really feel [the gay] community is coming of age in many ways and rewriting so much that was way overdue, especially in relation to the death and funeral industry. I mean, it was time for us to design our own services and really pitch in. It's a remarkable time; there are many good things that have come from this. But I also feel that the lessons have been learned. Enough is enough; let's get on with a cure. That's the first thing I wish when I see a star at night. But I feel prepared, at some level, to watch everybody I know who's infected die.

Once in a while, some anger will resurface, just in terms of the injustice. I've done some very experiential things. I went to an Elisabeth Kübler-Ross workshop and really let myself get mad. And I think it has made a difference in softening some of the anger. It still resurfaces, but I'm much more willing to accept that there is some unseen natural order to all this and that there's really little control that we have over what happens, but we can control our reactions to it.

I had a lot of fear that I could be HIV-positive. I went through the whole thing of getting tested and was negative. And I think that really helped me feel not only a sense of relief but trust in my intuition, which said that to be involved with Mark was a rare and wonderful opportunity for me and I would never regret it. To find out that I was negative reinforced that what I originally suspected—that we used "safe sex"—worked. There is some sense that I was brave enough to face something that a lot of people shied away from, and that gives me a charge, too, to think that I will continue to take risks like the risk I took in that relationship with Mark. Though they're calculated, they serve me well, and my life will continue to be one amazing event after another. I haven't lost that zeal. I said something earlier about the innocence being gone. In some ways, I still approach situations innocently, giving people the benefit of the doubt. But I feel a sense of self-assuredness, and I'm less affected by what people think.

Recently, I came out of a movie theater, and the constellation Orion had just come back into the sky. It had been gone for a couple of seasons. Whenever Mark and I were separated, when one or the other was traveling, we would use Orion to join us. The other night, when I came out of the theater, I was seeing it for the first time this season. I was so thrilled and thankful that we had thought to use a constellation to unite us, because that's timeless. There are parts of the year when I don't see it, but when I do, it feels so familiar. There's much more metaphysical exploration that I do, as each year passes now, about what it meant to have someone in my life like Mark, who imparted things to me that I will probably spend the rest of my life integrating. I'm lucky, too, to have a couple of friends to remind me that he was a real shit at times. There's no way they're going to sign a petition to get him canonized! So that's great, too, that we can talk about the times that he was really an asshole.

I still have a couple of Mark's shirts that I wear, but now when I put them on, I don't think about him as much. Certainly I don't smell him. For a while, I held on to one of the blankets that he'd use when he took a nap. I would go to the closet occasionally and smell it, and it would make me feel something—sometimes sad, sometimes happy, but really emotional. I let go of that—it became a cleaning rag. And I'm surprised, because I thought I would hang on much, much more, but little by little those things aren't as meaningful. I wear his ring. After he died, I took it off his finger and had it stretched to fit my finger. And that's really the only thing I have that I strongly associate with him. I'm just glad I took my own time with it and didn't listen to anybody else's advice on how to do it. My intuition said, "I'll let go of these things little by little as I need to, as I need more space, or as other things come in to replace them."

*

Epilogue: Living with the Words

Finding a path through the midland of grief after suicide is the longest and, in many ways, the most difficult part of the journey. One begins to realize that the end is not near—in fact, it may not be anywhere in sight. The reality of the loss is inescapable, and its repercussions go deeper and deeper.

In the beginning, the shock is so far-reaching that nothing feels the same as it did before the suicide. All one can do is try to get through each hour and day in this strange land. Enfolding the survivor and sweeping everything else away, the strangeness even offers a kind of protection against the harder, deeper experience of loss. But in the midland, the survivor has resumed the daily routines and habits of living, and the contours of a once-familiar life are again recognizable. Yet the life lived within, deep down, is anything but normal. The midland is a frightening place, because one enters it expecting to be able to put the pieces of one's life back together again, only to find that they no longer fit together as they once did.

Time for Grief

Our society has little tolerance for grief. We expect it to be discreet, tidy, and above all short-lived. Memorial services, burials, wakes, sitting shiva—these are the appointed occasions for expressing loss and grief. Once these rites have been completed, the survivors are supposed to grieve privately and be done with it as quickly as possible. Our social timetable for grief is surprisingly explicit. Depending on the survivor's relationship to the deceased, a period of mourning might be expected to last for a few weeks or even months, but certainly by the time the first anniversary of the death approaches, if not well before that time, the expectation is that bereavement should be completed, and the mourner back to "normal" once again. More often than not, this timetable does not coincide with the actual experience of bereavement. Assimilating the loss of someone close takes time, much more time than we might wish, and for the survivor trying to assimilate the loss after suicide, the journey may be long and grueling.

Struggling through the first months after the suicide, people often assume that if they can somehow survive this initial period, the second year will be easier, less painful, and they will feel less swamped by the loss. Yet the experience is often just the opposite: the second year, in many ways, is more difficult than the first. As Catherine puts it, "I guess I thought I'd wake up the 18th of July a year later, and I'd be all better. I was worse. Not only did I not feel better, I was totally frustrated and upset that the pain hadn't gone away."

There are several reasons for this. First, survivors often have the same unrealistic expectation that others do—that they should be done with their grief after a few months, or at least well enough down its road that the end is near. This reflects an even more fundamental assumption: that grief has a beginning and an end, that the work of bereavement is to go through it, come out the other end, and then be finished with it. But the reality is much more chaotic than that, the landmarks more obscure.

Second, by the end of the first year, many survivors find that various forms of support have dwindled and been replaced by an uneasy impatience. Friends, neighbors, colleagues, and relatives want the survivors to be done with their grief, urging them to "let go" of it, to "return to the land of the living." Some friends may simply disappear altogether; others may make a point of avoiding any mention of the person who has died, let alone the manner of the death. For the onlookers, the survivor's grief is too uncomfortable a reminder of how susceptible we all are to the pain of loss and—in the case of suicide—abandonment. As a result, the promise of relief in the second year is often dashed: not only has the pain not diminished, but the survivor feels even more alone with it. Even Marcia, who was surrounded and comforted by many friends in the first months after her husband's suicide, was afraid that these same people would be "burned out" a year later, when she again needed their support: "I couldn't go back to them and say, 'Can I be a mess for a while?'"

In addition, the first months after the suicide are often taken up with a host of decisions concerning funeral arrangements, financial matters, personal possessions, and property—all the tangible threads of a life that need to be tied off after that life has ended. These tasks can weigh heavily on the survivors, each decision seeming insurmountable, yet they also provide an external territory of loss in the face of overwhelming grief. By the second year, most of these matters are usually resolved or at least no longer pressing, leaving the survivors less distracted from their internal experience of loss. For Philip (see chapter 2), the enormous tasks of managing his father's business interests and taking care of his estate persisted well beyond the first year, demanding his full attention: "I didn't cry for a long time. I'm pretty emotional. The tears don't come hard for me, for a boy, at least, growing up in this country. . . . But it took two to three years. There was just so much of a mess to deal with, I probably couldn't afford to do it."

The First Anniversary

Survivors often anticipate the first anniversary of the suicide with dread, at the same time hoping or expecting that it will mark the end of the worst part of their grief, if not the end of it altogether. Catherine observed the first anniversary of Marion's suicide by taking Andrew and Samuel to Europe to visit the places where their mother had lived earlier in her life. Having managed to get through the holidays and each season of that first year, she planned the trip as "a kind of tribute and a way of letting go and trying to give the boys a feeling of something positive to replace the painful memory of the year before." Yet the traveling brought Catherine face to face with her aloneness: the two brothers had each other, but she no longer had her partner. Part of the painfulness of the trip was the realization that she was not nearing the end of her grief so much as starting a new leg of that journey.

The end of Marcia's first year of grief brought several anniversaries: her son's first birthday, her husband's birthday, and her husband's suicide. She says,

> The first year was over, but it didn't feel like it was getting better—it was getting worse. . . . I didn't feel quite as frozen, because I guess I wasn't as well protected. And I felt even more emotional than I had at first. It was like reliving a different layer

of it, and it was unexpected. I didn't know how to deal with it at all.

The feelings that are touched by all the significant anniversaries—anniversaries of the suicide, birthdays, wedding anniversaries, family holidays—change over time as the context of the loss changes. Some anniversaries may be more bitter, others more sweet. Many survivors dread the winter holidays, afraid that their grief will overtake any hope of celebration. Certain family rituals may need to be changed both to accommodate the feelings of loss and to find new ways of celebrating the occasions that are important focal points for the family.

Life Without

The midland of grief is the place where the survivors must come to terms with the deepest, hardest feelings of loss. Whatever else it might be, suicide is an abandonment—of one person's life and of all the people who have been a part of that life. The experience of being abandoned leaves many survivors feeling deeply angry. Not only must they live without the person who has died, but they must also live *with* all the painful, frightening feelings that suicide leaves in its wake. Catherine says, "All of us have experienced the ultimate abandonment. It doesn't get any worse than this, I don't think. It's so far down, you have to look up." In the midland, the survivors struggle to come back to themselves and their own lives, gradually finding ways to accommodate rather than be victim to their loss.

For Chris, life without her brother has come to mean, among other things, that she is now her parents' only child, a burden that her brother has left her with. "What's hard," she says, "is that I feel like I have an obligation to them. If anything happened, I'd be there for them. But now I'm the only one. Tom put this on my shoulders, and now I have to take care of them. And I don't like that."

Life without her husband means that Marcia must raise their child alone, shouldering all the responsibilities of parenthood— and experiencing its joys—by herself. That her husband has deprived Jaron of his presence as a father touches a deep channel of anger within her: "As [Jaron] gets older, I think, 'You weren't here for this.' . . . I'm healing now, and I'll heal more later, but Jaron hasn't even begun, and that makes me mad."

Yet life without can also bring relief from the burden of living with someone who has been struggling with depression and self-destructive urges for a long time. In looking back on her life with Marion, Catherine says, "I never really understood the drain of trying to sustain someone who didn't want to live any longer." Joy found relief in life without her mother, who had made numerous suicide attempts throughout Joy's childhood: "It's awful to say, but in many ways I'm glad she did it. . . . My life has clearly improved since she's no longer alive. . . . I was tired of her poisoning my life, and if she was going to do it, then get it done with and let me get on with my life."

The death of one member of a family forces the surviving members to find new ways of being a family. At first, the focus on the person who has died may be enough to hold them together. But eventually that will not suffice, and they must find a different basis for connection—a "realignment," as Catherine puts it—or risk estrangement. That process is often full of conflict. Describing the struggle to find a new way of being a family after Marion's suicide, Catherine says, "[Andrew, Samuel, and I] were like a three-wheeled cart for a long time. I was the tire in the middle of the front, and the boys were the two tires in the back."

For Catherine, life without Marion has also meant living alone in a house that was theirs and that they were in the midst of remodeling when the suicide occurred. Catherine would like to move, but her instincts tell her to stay there until it feels right to move on in her life. At first, she brought a halt to the construction activities, but she has gradually resumed them and is now almost finished with the remodeling. The house, in some ways, embodies her grief:

I have to come to peace with what's happened before I can go and be in another place peacefully. . . . I've hung in there and gone through the pain and the suffering and the inability to cope and to make decisions at times, because I know in my mind and I feel in my being that I can't successfully go on with my life until I go through all the stuff I have to go through to understand this and accept it.

One's sense of time changes in the midland. Earlier, time is measured in days and weeks since the suicide, which swamps any sense of life beyond it. Now that scale changes to months and years. Marcia felt as though time stopped when her husband died, and her life froze. But as she has become aware of changes—in herself and in her infant son, for whom time cannot stop—she again has a sense of time and movement in her life. What helped her the most at first, she says, was to be reassured that everything she was feeling—guilt, anger, even joy—was okay. What has helped her the most since then is "to know that everything changes—not really that this too will pass, because it doesn't feel like it will pass, but that it will change. . . . that it's okay for the sadness to come up over and over again unexpectedly and that I don't have to wait for it to be over, that it only changes."

Memories change as well. Chris recalls that days after her brother's suicide she could smell him in his room. She could remember his face and things that he had said. But gradually these memories grew less clear, which was frightening to her: "I was afraid for a long time that I would forget him, which is ridiculous now, I realize. But I thought, 'He's just going to disappear. I'm going to forget I had a brother.' " She also realizes that her memories of him are caught in time—he will always be twenty-two—but she will grow older and her life will continue to change.

The Search Continued

In the first few weeks and months after a suicide, the struggle for the survivors is to take in the sheer reality of the loss. Later on, the struggle is to find meaning in it, a context for assimilating it and reclaiming one's own life. For many survivors, the whys persist into the second year and well beyond. They may change from "Why didn't I see this coming?" or "Why didn't she tell me how much pain she was in?" to the more fundamental questions that suicide leaves in its wake: "Why did he choose to die?" and "How could she leave me like this?"

The frantic searching of the first months gives way to the deeper questions, those that touch on our most basic assumptions: that short of an accident or illness, the people we love and work with and live next to will still be alive in the morning, that they will choose life over death, just as we do. Suicide robs us of everything we take for granted about our lives and the people we love. The most painful lesson of suicide is that each of us has the choice to live or die every moment of our lives. It is a choice that most of us are never even really aware of unless we are somehow touched by suicide—whether our own thoughts of it or the suicide of someone we love.

The search for answers is driven by a compelling need to understand how someone could face that choice and choose death. A gulf exists between those of us who are still alive, who with each breath continue to choose life, and those who have chosen death. The gulf is as wide as the difference between life and death, and as narrow as the realization that each of us can choose to cross over to the other side at any time. Chris says,

> What's . . . hard is that [my brother is] different from us now. He has done something that no one here has done. And all of a sudden, he's distant because of that. Sometimes I think of ways that I could do it. I won't. But I could be standing in the shower and think, "Well, I could just drown in here." Or, "I could stick myself with a knife right now." I've had to put a knife down because I've been tempted. I don't know why that is.

For many survivors, suicidal thoughts are a way of trying to bridge the gulf, at least in one's imagination, in order to get closer to the person one has lost to suicide.

The search for answers is also propelled by the contradictions that suicide leaves in its wake. Regardless of how overtly violent the actual means of death, suicide is an act of profound violence to the self and to others. It is murder, but a form of murder in which the perpetrator and the victim are the same. The person who dies by suicide has been overtaken by a despair so complete that it obliterates any sense of choice. Yet suicide is, at some level, a choice, and the choice to end one's life is also a choice to leave those who are an important part of that life. The struggle for the survivors is to find a way to accept and live with that paradox.

The drive to understand, to find answers to all the questions, can be as intense and persistent as the conviction that, without those answers, the pain of the loss will always swamp life. But at some point, one must put aside the search, realizing that the answers are elusive and that, more important, one's own life does not have to hinge on finding the answers to someone else's death. Catherine has come to that point: "After almost a year and a half of trying to understand and cope with this whole thing, I'm expecting that I'm not going to understand, that it's always going to be a very painful aspect of my being." Yet in giving up the search and accepting that the loss will always be painful, the quality of that pain changes. Gradually, it takes up a smaller, quieter place in one's life rather than claiming all of it, as before.

The Limits of Connection
and the Possibilities of Reconnection

To put aside the search for answers, for a full understanding of such an incomprehensible loss, is to acknowledge the limits of one's control over another life, even the life of someone with whom one has been intimately connected—a child, parent, sibling, lover, or close friend. Catherine says, "I think Andrew, Samuel, and I are all arriving at some kind of acceptance of the fact that it wasn't our fault, that we can take the blame for a lot of things, but we can't take the responsibility for someone else's life." In the process of acknowledging the limits of her control over Marion's life and death, Catherine has discovered within herself a strong spirituality, and this in turn has helped her accept her loss.

For Ellen, the struggle has been to accept both the reach and the limits of her responsibility as a therapist and to retain her conviction that she has something to offer those who seek her help. Joe's suicide has also brought her up squarely against her own mortality and the realization that she will experience losses in her personal life as well: "I guess I'm not ready to think about death, at least my own end. Death is saying good-bye, and sometimes it's just hard for me to say good-bye. I mean, how do you say good-bye to people you love and know you'll never see again?" What has been particularly wrenching in her experience of Joe's death is that he was just starting his life, not nearing its end. His death was not a natural or inevitable finish to his life: ". . . it seemed as though he didn't go his full course. It was such an interruption."

It is this sense of suicide as an abrupt interruption—a cutting off of life and connections with other lives—that makes it so difficult for the survivors to find a way to say a full good-bye. If our connections with the people we love most in the world are not enough to keep them alive, if we lack that kind of power in the lives of those who are important to us, how can we be sure that others will not abandon us in the same way? At a deep level, many of us experience suicide as a betrayal of trust, and if we are to be able to reinvest ourselves fully in our own lives and in our relationships with others, we must find within ourselves a source of trust once again. It is a delicate and difficult balance, to be sure, because suicide teaches us that we cannot take anything for granted. Yet making a full commitment to an intimate relationship with another person is also an act of faith. For Catherine, the balancing point is between the risk and the reward of intimacy, both of which she came to know in her relationship with Marion: ". . . I'm not sure . . . how in the long term I'm going to fare in terms of being able to make a commitment to someone again without constantly feeling like she's going to leave me. I don't want to surrender and not have a life. I want to have a life beyond this experience." Marcia is falling in love again and at the same time finds herself crying about her husband: ". . . the deeper I love, the more I have to cry."

And so it comes to this: to live one's life fully once again, one must find a way to say good-bye after the door has been abruptly shut. Letting go is a large part of that good-bye, relinquishing the hold that the loss has on one's life, as well as the hold one has on the loss. Marcia speaks of it as forgiveness: "I think forgiving is the next thing. I've begun to forgive people who haven't given me anything this past year and a half. . . . But I think the next step will be forgiving Tom." To let go is to forgive oneself—for that which is beyond one's control—and to forgive the person who is gone—for having shut the door. The process of letting go brings with it a sense of hope. Catherine puts it this way: "Marion's death has taught me that there's really very little that I can control. And at some level, the more I've surrendered to the notion that I can't control very much about my life, the more freedom I have had to be open to the possibilities."

Richard's story, though told from the midland of grief, is quite different from the other stories in this chapter. Having had the opportunity to say good-bye to Mark before he died, Richard has not experienced his death as an abandonment or even an interruption. Instead, it has felt like a "completion." Yet for Richard, too, the challenge is to let go so that he can be free to live a life that is open to new directions. He says, ". . . the letting go is such an active process, and sometimes I resist it so much."

All the stories in this chapter are about letting go: finding a way to accept and live with the loss of someone close. In every case except Richard's, the difficulty of letting go is compounded by the paradoxical nature of a loss that is the result of suicide. As survivors gradually find themselves able to accept their loss, they begin to recommit themselves to their own lives, and the stories they tell become more fully their own.

Then and Now

All the stories in this chapter are shaped by the passage of time; in each case, many years have elapsed since the suicide. Five of the stories are continued from earlier chapters. Two are told in full here: Karen's, which appears at the beginning of the chapter, and Rachel's, at the end. Since these two stories have not been divided between chapters, as the others have, each contains within it smaller stories from the beginning and the midland of grief. To put it another way, the five continued stories tell of now, then having been recounted in earlier chapters. Karen and Rachel tell of then and now as intertwined parts of one story, which is how all these stories were told.

Prologue

OCTOBER 27, 1990. Today the new chill in the air and the late-afternoon darkness, though familiar, seem more remnants of a long-ago season than a hint of things to come. Fall used to be my favorite time of year. I always liked the way it cleared out my senses after the heat-muffled days of summer. I would savor the crisp smell of the air, the sharply angled sunlight, the intense colors of the sky and leaves, the rustle underfoot. For me, fall, more than spring, was the season of new possibilities, so closely was it linked in my mind to the fresh feel of things, even memories of new books with stiff spines and blank notebooks. But since my mother's suicide, ten years ago, this time of year has come to embody other memories as well, and on the first cold days, I miss the summer days that somehow slipped quietly away, along with a certain innocence that cannot survive the sharper air of the fall.

The seasons of my life have changed as much as the air and light from summer to fall. I was thirty-one when my mother died; I am forty-one now. My daughter, then a child of eight years, is now a young woman of eighteen. We have a special companionship that is familiar to me. It has something of the feel of my adult closeness with my mother. I savor it but still miss being on the other end.

I wanted my mother with me in June, when my daughter graduated from high school, and in September, when I drove her to college. Mostly, I felt a deep sadness at her absence, but intermingled with it was the twinge of a sharper feeling that has never quite disappeared: that she *should* have been there. These are the scars of her loss in my life. I feel their ridges—I always will—but the rawness is gone, and the edges have blended into the surrounding skin.

There have been many changes in my life since my mother's death. Her suicide once ripped such a large hole in my small family that it was hard to see what was left. But her absence no longer overwhelms our presence as a family. We have grown, and we have grown closer.

My mother's suicide occupies a smaller place within me now. I feel her loss more as an absence, less as an abandonment. Her opal ring, which I first wore around my neck and later on my finger, is now stored in a small wooden box on my bureau. Yet her suicide has remained a permanent, gut-level part of my being. As little as I can know of what propelled her to make such a desperate choice for herself, I know, inside out, what it is to be left in that way. And that knowledge has changed me. I pay greater attention now, but I no longer need to keep myself braced for the next loss. In struggling to find some meaning in the way my mother's life ended, I have come to know much more of my own life—the darker, the lighter, the deeper regions. I am toughened and softened, more attuned to the possibility of loss and more willing to risk it for the intimate connections with other lives that make mine feel rich and full.

Ten years later, the need to mark this October day, the day of my mother's death, has faded. In its place I find the wish to celebrate her life by marking her birthday, on the 14th of January.

*

Karen: Having Lost So Many Things at the Same Time

Karen (not her real name) is from Denmark but has lived in the United States since her father's suicide, when she was eleven years old. Now in her early thirties, she is a graphic designer and an art therapist. I interviewed her in January 1989.

Karen's story is one of childhood loss and its repercussions throughout adolescence and young adulthood. It is also a story of the multiple disruptions that suicide can cause in the life of a child. Shortly after her father's death, Karen moved to the United States with her mother and one of her two older sisters. Thus, she lost not only her father but also her other sister, her family home, her country, her culture, and her language.

Twenty years later, Karen is still trying to fill in pieces of her father's story that were withheld from her when he died—even exactly how he killed himself. For the child at the time of the loss and for the adult years later, it may be difficult both to ask questions about those missing pieces and to be given answers.

There's something about the whole aftermath of my father's suicide that was so isolating for me, the feeling that my family [my mother, my two older sisters, and I] just became these four people struggling to survive, each in her own way, almost in spite of each other. And that, I think, is the worst part of being a survivor.

My father was an electrical engineer. He worked all over the world. We lived in Denmark for a time, and then he went off and worked in England and the United States, Africa, and South America. He would come and go, come and go, come and go. It was a succession of jobs he would usually end up quitting for various reasons. As a result, my sisters and I went to all these different schools. Sometimes we were in boarding schools, and sometimes we were with our parents. We just moved around a lot, and it was pretty chaotic.

When I was maybe seven or eight, my father started getting physically ill. He had a bleeding ulcer and was hospitalized. He was in Liberia around the same time, and that was [where he made] his first suicide attempt that I know of. He tried to take an overdose of pills. They hospitalized him there and then sent him back to Denmark. I remember he was in our house, sick in bed, and looking terrible. He'd been gone for a while, so I was very happy to see him, because he was a very affectionate father. My mother's told me since that he had disappeared for a couple of days. She called up all the radio stations in Scandinavia and was going to get an APB [all points bulletin] out on him. About ten minutes before it was supposed to go on the air, he called saying where he was. She said what was so strange about it was that he just didn't seem connected. He didn't understand that people were upset. I think the story was that he'd been lying under some electrical power lines, just watching them and thinking about his life and driving around.

Then he got a job as the director of a hydroelectric power plant in Indonesia. I think he started becoming very discouraged, probably quite overwhelmed, by what he had to do. He had just turned fifty-one, and I think he knew it was his last chance to make it, and it was an incredible amount of money. There was a stopover in Thailand on his way to Indonesia. And at that point, he had what I gather to be an anxiety attack. He was afraid it was a heart attack. So he got off the plane and went to a hospital and then went back to Denmark. By that time, I think he'd started to calm down, but in his shame, he checked into a hotel in the town where we were living and didn't call my mother for a couple of days. He finally called her, and she would go over and spend the day with him and then come home and be with us and pretend that everything was fine. Finally, he contacted the company that had hired him and told them he wasn't able to go to Indonesia. This I just heard recently. There was some big meeting in Copenhagen where they yelled at him and told him he was fired. And then he came home.

The morning he killed himself must have been a Sunday,

because my [middle] sister, who is a year older, and I were ready to go out with him for hot chocolate, which we usually did on Sunday mornings. [My other sister was at boarding school.] My father always got up really early, and my mother was a late sleeper. But [that morning] my father never got up. It was late morning by the time my mother awoke, and we said, "Dad's not awake. Where is he?" All of a sudden, she had this look on her face like she'd been struck. She started to scream and tear around the house and knock on all the doors. We lived on the top floor of a very big, old apartment building. Our part was shaped like a big elbow, and way at the opposite end was my room, which was just becoming my room. It was being painted. My father and I had gone through this whole thing about what color to choose. Because it was being painted, I wasn't sleeping in it. I was sleeping in another bedroom.

My mother finally realized that was the door that was locked. She went downstairs and got this guy who worked for us and had him break down the door. I remember we were lined up in the hall: this young guy from downstairs, my mother, and then me and my sister. [When he got the door open] my mother just started screaming and rushed after him, but he held her back, and they had this struggle. My father had electrocuted himself. I'm not sure how he did it. It's still one of those big questions: how did he do it? But I guess he just took the socket off and hooked himself into the current. It's 220; it's enough to kill you. And the reason my mother knew, when she woke up, what had happened was that he had come in early in the morning and asked her for an extension cord. I imagine that one reason she was held back was that if she had touched him, she could have become part of the current and would also have been electrocuted. And even now— It was just so frightening, because I didn't know what was going on at all. She didn't say. I just knew that something terrible had happened. She was sobbing and carrying on.

I didn't see him. My sister rushed up and was pushed back, so I didn't even try. They closed the door. But I was about ten feet away, and it was in my room. After some time, they called an ambulance, and I saw his body with a white sheet being carried out the front door. I don't remember much after that. I must have just walked around somewhere.

I've never dared ask my mother exactly what she saw. What I imagine is probably worse than, or as bad as, what she saw, and it might be helpful for her to tell me. But most of the story that I've gotten has actually been when my mother has had a few drinks. I think she is very fragile in some ways, and I'm sure I've done a lot to protect her and to hold myself away from asking her a lot of things, to protect myself. A couple of years ago, I asked her for my father's suicide note, and she was unable to find it. She sent me instead a letter that he had written from Thailand. I really wanted the suicide note. She said that he'd written that he loved all of us and that he was sorry, something like that. That's all I know. Even now, there are still little pieces that I'm finding.

When the paint dried, I moved into that room. Not only was it the room that my father had killed himself in, but it was way down at the end of the hall, far from the other rooms. I slept out there by myself, hardly within shouting distance of the next room. I had a really hard time being there. I used to lie awake at night. I remember thinking, "I have to get used to this. I have to just be here and let it be." I'd try to numb myself out, but I was spooked to death there. I wonder what it is in me that made myself do that. I didn't say, "I can't sleep here." It was almost like this pretense that life went on as if the suicide hadn't happened.

Certain things became associated with my father's death. One was a dress, which had belonged to each of my sisters and which I wore to his funeral. It had these funny stripes on it, brown and red and black. I always liked it and was waiting until I could wear it. The first and only time I wore it was to the funeral. And I remember being worried because I thought it had too many bright colors in it, but then I thought, "No, it's okay, because red is his favorite color, so it's okay that it has red in it." I think I used to talk to that dress. Then we moved, and I outgrew the dress, and I forgot all about it. But it showed up many years later, when I was in college and went to my mom's house one time. She has a collection of handmade mahogany doll furniture that was ordered for her by my grandfather—a little piano, a grandfather clock, a table and little chairs, and a sofa. I always loved them. They were treasures, her little childhood treasures. But she had reupholstered all the furniture with this funeral dress material. It just freaked me out! I think she must have found it in a rag bag. It's funny—in this family where there's so much mystery, little things like that really shake me up.

My father's suicide was the beginning of what I see as the fragmentation of my family. It was the shock wave, and things fell out from there. My mother decided to move away. She had never really gotten along with my father's family, and [after he died] she stopped having contact with them pretty much. My father's brother started getting more and more depressed, ended up in a mental hospital several times, and is now divorced. My grandmother died three or four years after my father. Everybody says she was never really well after he died. He was the favorite son, and it broke her somehow emotionally. She lost interest in life. Now my two sisters live in Denmark, and my mother and I live in the United States. My sisters hardly ever see my cousins.

At the time of my father's death, we were living in a town of 40,000 [in Denmark], and people pretty much knew each other. My mother told me to tell people that my father had had a heart attack. So after a few days, I showed up at school again. People would say, "Oh, I heard your father died. How did he die?" And I'd say, "He had a heart attack." A friend of mine pulled me aside and said, "You know, you don't have to say that to me, because I know that your father killed himself." And I remember the sense of relief. I didn't even think to ask her how she knew, because this was all supposed to be secret. The ambulance people or somebody must have told her. It was such a small town that somebody just let it out. But it also created another lie. I couldn't go home and tell my mother, "Oh, forget this thing about the heart attack. It's just making it even harder." So I had to keep a secret from my mother, as well as supposedly keeping a secret from everybody else. It just made for another barrier. It started this thing where I don't feel that I tell my mother the whole truth. And ever since then, it's as though she doesn't hear.

[Not long after my father's suicide] my mother, my middle sister, and I moved to the United States, because my mother had the promise of a job there. My older sister stayed in Denmark, in boarding school. The move meant that I lost my language and my culture. It felt as though all the connections with my father that were part of my childhood were gone. My middle sister became very bitter. In some ways, when I look back on it, I think she had a healthier reaction [than I did]. She got really angry. She became rebellious and obstinate. She'd always been that way but grew even more so. She and my mother had fights—I mean physical fights. And then she stopped eating and ended up in the hospital. At that point, I started gaining a lot of weight. I was quite heavy during high school and just became a bookworm.

By the time I was eighteen, I was seriously depressed. I went to Denmark for three months, and I wanted to stay. Coming back was very hard. All the stuff with my father was starting to come up again in some way. I felt Denmark sort of became my father or became my childhood or became what I didn't get—I don't know what—but it just depressed me terribly to come back to the United States. My sisters, at that point, were both living in Denmark and had had fallings-out with my mother.

When I came back from Denmark, I was having trouble at school. I couldn't concentrate very well, I felt isolated, and I couldn't sleep. Eventually, I started to fall apart. It was the first time I let myself really fall apart. I spent a couple of days in the infirmary at college, and I was just scared, very scared. I wouldn't say that I became suicidal, but I definitely was in a place that was very, very fragile. I remember I went through a couple of days when I just didn't want to speak English to anybody. I didn't want to see anybody, so I would stay in my room in the daytime. I had these Danish tapes, and I would sing to them. Then I would sleep for a little while and go to the art studio. I would draw and paint pictures. I did a bunch of torso drawings of myself naked and then with different pieces of clothing on. I was just obsessed with that. [Gradually] I started going out more and talking English again. I also started doing a lot of artwork as part of it.

I ended up with a wonderful experience in therapy. The therapist I was seeing was an older woman. She had a wonderful face. I could just go there and love her face. I had had a good relationship with my grandmother, my father's mother, and my therapist had that same kind of gentleness about her. I love it when I find that, especially in older women. I remember one time I started to cry, and I saw tears come to her eyes, and it just did something to me. It hooked me in some way. I felt so touched by her response. I felt that she was crying with me, without pity. It just felt like this really clean thing, and it was great.

After I graduated from college, I moved to Vermont and lived for five years with a man I'd been having a relationship with. He became more and more of an active alcoholic. I think he was killing himself, and there was nothing I could do about it. When I started to realize I was again in a situation where I was watching somebody die, I got out, knowing that I couldn't help him. That was incredibly painful—all those issues about when do you help people, and when do you help yourself. I think leaving that relationship brought up all this other separation stuff.

Then I went to graduate school in Boston. I felt extremely lonely moving to a new town by myself. [Eventually] I hooked up with a therapist I'm still seeing. It's been very, very good. I still don't know what therapy is. I just know that it helps me. It's given me a lot of direction and support, and it's very challenging. The quality of my life is certainly a lot better.

Recently I've started feeling anger. It's very hard for me to get at anger, but a couple of times in therapy I've come pretty close. I think I'm incredibly angry at my father. I hope I'll be able to express that fully in therapy—to free myself from it, forgive the situation, and go on.

I sometimes have a feeling of being haunted by my father, almost as if there's a presence there, a ghostly presence. Sometimes it's really pleasant—it's companionship. Here's this person I went to for guidance when I was growing up, and in some ways, I still really want to do that, even though he is dead, so maybe I have this feeling he's with me.

My father used to say, "You have to be a brave soldier." In thinking about that now, I wonder if he [finally] paid a price for being a brave soldier. What's the message in saying, "I quit; I can't take it anymore"? Here is this man who abandoned his family because he couldn't take it. He couldn't take the heat; he couldn't take the shame. I can also say, "But no, he was crazy; he had lost all the things that he believed he could do. He felt there was nothing to live for. He was just depressed." All these things I forgive him for. But there's another part of it. I did some artwork once that really blew me away. It was full of these horrible images of spiders, Nazis, and all these things that I associate with the dark side of his death.

Sometimes when I get upset, I feel as though I have this mark on me. It's like the mark of Cain, being scarred by this thing for life—that I can never be married or have a child, or I'll pass on this curse. I call it the family curse. I also call it the black hole that he left—this little girl with a black hole in her who still hasn't really grown up. I think part of getting angry is being able to say, "Fuck off! This is my body. I am not a victim! I'm not going to be your black hole." And in saying that, it's almost like saying it directly to my father, as well as to myself. I'm not going to surrender to this. I'm going to live and be strong with it. That's the most painful thing.

Now there's a part of me that can soothe the hurt I feel and just say, "We'll get you through this. I'll take care of you." Before, I think it used to be, "Shut up. Stop whining. I can't stand it when you cry. Go away." I think that harshness has changed.

I believe that people have the freedom of choice, and I can really understand what would drive somebody to the point of feeling there are no alternatives. I mean, I can feel in my gut what that would be like. But I think that anybody who can get to that place hasn't had enough understanding that people can help, that there is hope. I'm not exactly an optimistic person, but I believe that there are always resources and there's always change. Maybe it's a spiritual belief, too, that we're here, that there's some purpose. Life is an incredible, mysterious process, and I don't feel it's within my right to take my own hand and kill myself, because then I'm wiping out every other possibility in my life and every person I may meet and experience I may have. On the other hand, philosophically, I feel people have a right to die and a right to choose their own death, especially people who are physically sick and who tell people and are able to face death and step into it. I really respect that. It's not an act of desperation. It's ethically very complicated, but I feel there are times when that seems like the healthier choice in a way.

But it just makes me think about my father. Maybe if he had felt or had some experience that the career problems or shame or whatever were passing things, maybe if he had felt there were other things to live for, his family . . . He needed to make some very, very difficult choices in his life at a time when he was confronting middle age, mortality. He had been sick. Those are all normal things, difficult, but I wish he could have just confronted them. I think that takes more courage, in a way, than saying, "I'm going to leave now." I guess it's given me a respect for people who go through really hard times.

From my experience with my father, I know how much pain suicide causes and that people never really lose that pain. In some odd moments, actually a lot, I see it as a peculiar gift that I've experienced that much pain. It certainly has brought me much closer to some things in life that I probably would not have been able to tolerate. It's triggered a lot of responses in me that have been very hard to deal with because they were so deep. I think it's also given me a capacity to empathize, because I'm not so scared of mortality. In some ways, I'm more scared, and in other ways, I'm not. In Western society, we're so afraid of death. I know people who are grown-ups who have never had anybody close to them die. I know I'm able to deal with that and that I have the strength to do it. When people tell me that somebody they know has died, I don't start feeling, "Oh, God, I have to stay away from you."

I've had my chart read, and I've had my palm read. People usually say, "Something traumatic happened to you involving your father. Did he abuse you?" One person said that there had been a "forced departure" of my father. Forced departure! It's odd, but I feel that there are certain themes in people's lives. We're colored by what we are genetically and by what we are exposed to, and then there are these events that happen to us that are these little red marks on the charts of our lives. My father's death is one of those red marks.

When I look at my sisters and myself, I realize we've all had problems with substance abuse, whether it's food, drugs, or alcohol. My older sister and I have spent several years, each of us, in intensive therapy. I feel that we are pretty honest with each other and talk about things. She's actually the best source of information. Last year, or maybe it was the year before, on my father's death day, she went up to the gravestone and had some pictures taken of it and of her with it. His death is an open subject with her, and she and I have had some good talks, whereas I still feel that my middle sister just can't hear about it or talk about it. She gets very angry.

It's funny being in Denmark now. I think I have an image of myself as another person over there; I have a Doppelgänger [a ghost of a living person, a double]. If my father hadn't killed himself, or if he had killed himself and we had stayed in Denmark and things had been processed differently, I wouldn't have lost as many connections. I think it was having lost so many things at the same time. I'm still not sure why I didn't decide to live in Denmark. I thought about it, but I felt I had already invested a lot of time [in the United States], and I just wanted to be in one place. Also, Denmark is a small place, and it's traditional. It's different now. It's been opened because there are so many foreigners living there. But ten or fifteen years ago, you had your place there, and if you were an outsider, you always stayed an outsider. Sometimes you're just not accepted back. My parents always felt like outsiders in Denmark. And I didn't know how to start over and make a place for myself, to settle down and start building friends and community connections all over again. You can be different in the States—everybody is different—whereas in Denmark there is more of a focus on conformity. Part of me feels comfortable being around other people who are also kind of oddballs—adrift or immigrants. I still miss Denmark, though, and I still really like it there. But I think it becomes almost unbearable to be in conflict all the time. You just have to choose one place.

[Karen wrote the following addendum to her story.]
My older sister and I had an intense visit about five years ago, when we discussed the pain of growing up with all this chaos and fragmentation. We acknowledged how much it had hurt us to be pulled apart from one another as sisters and how we had to bear secrets and pretense. At the end of the visit, we came to the point of making the semblance of an oath to one another: to be honest, to communicate, to respect each other, to build a relationship as adults. This has been very healing for me, to trust my sister and to know that we are both willing to speak truthfully through good and bad times. It changes my isolation and shame when I feel fully recognized and accepted. I can integrate

more acceptance as I speak more, and the shame is transformed somewhat to feeling that I am a member of the human race and that we share pain and loneliness as well as beauty.

Natalie: Dreams of Catching Her

[Continued from chapter 2, page 30]

It has been eight years since Natalie's mother killed herself. Shortly after her death, Natalie met the man she would later marry. She and her husband now have a young son.

It ends up being easier to talk about my mother and her history than about my experience of her suicide, because it is so painful to talk about how it actually felt to go through that experience. There are times when I feel it was like an out-of-body experience. I can hardly go back to it, because I think it's almost unbearable to touch. I'm sure there's a part of me that just doesn't want to. I put my whole life back together; I put myself back together. And as much as it's okay to feel the pain of it all or to think about it—and I do at times—you have to distance yourself in a certain way to be able to go on.

I felt incredibly angry at my mother immediately after she died. I thought, "How could she do this to me?" But then, at a certain point, I felt an even deeper anger that it really was cruel what she did to me. I don't think she did it to me purposely— "I'm going to make you suffer"—but her action had an irrevocable impact on my life that was cruel. For someone who supposedly loved me as she said she did, and I think she did in her way, she shouldn't have done it.

It feels better at this point not to be so angry. It feels better to know that after all that happened in my relationship with her, I loved her and I love her, and I would rather have had her here than not here. As much as I'd rather have her alive, it's also in part a relief not to have her alive. It's taken me a while to feel comfortable saying that.

It really upsets me now if there's something that isn't right between me and somebody else. I know that relationships can't always be problem-free, but I sometimes think, "If I never see this person again, is this the way I want it left?" It's taken a lot of willpower to allow myself to go through the downside in a relationship and not try to rush it, just stay with it rather than try to make it all better. It takes a lot on my part to realize that most people don't die the way my mother did. I don't have to worry every time I say good-bye to someone that I'll never see that person again.

My mother's suicide made me think about what it means to be a mother. I decided that if I chose to become a mother, I would be making a decision never to kill myself. It was very clear in my mind that I could not decide to be a parent if I could not make that commitment. However bad it might get for me, I could never do that to a child, even an adult child.

It's always felt very heavy for me to think about becoming a parent, and I'm sure that was partly because of my family life and having lost my father and then the experience with my mother. I think that's why I postponed having a child as long as I did. It's a huge commitment, a commitment to life. In the end, that's the commitment I wanted to make anyway, but I had to think it through.

After my son was born, I went back to the house I'd grown up in. I loved that house. It contained the memories of my whole life. We had moved there when I was a year old. It was the only home I had ever known. My father and my grandmother died there. It was my roots, everything. I wanted my son to know where I'd grown up.

Going back to that house was sad; it felt like a completion. We walked around the neighborhood and ran into some neighbors I'd known. I'd grown up with their kids, and they'd known my father. We had lemonade with them in their backyard. They were very sweet. There's a way in which I long for people who knew my life as it was when my family was intact. If there's anyone who knew me as a regular person, a regular kid, it says something—I mean, it makes me feel that something was normal. There's some documentation of things before they fell apart, which to me started when my father died.

Part of the experience after suicide is the loss of control. As much as you might have thought about empowering yourself and making your life work—all those terms from the '70s and '80s—you get to know how little control you have over certain things, and that's just the way it is. I feel jaded when I think of the innocence I've lost that I envy in other people. It's this hard-earned knowledge about life that I feel people get angry at me for sometimes. It's not that I think you have to crawl in a hole because life is awful. It's a comprehension of certain realities that you just don't comprehend until you really come up against it. Until you bump your nose right up against it, you just don't *know*! I guess it's hard to know and then be able to regain the positive and allow yourself to have your dreams.

It's another one of those balances. How do you acknowledge your powerlessness in the world and then feel powerful? Before my mother's suicide, I used to feel that I could do anything. I was young and energetic and into political movements, marching for this and marching for that—all things that I think were very important and that I still believe in. But I had a narrow vision of the world and myself in the world. My mother's suicide made my vision of the world open up. I got to see how big the world actually is and how much of it I don't understand. I used to feel that I understood a lot more than I do now. It's the old cliché that as you get older, you know less and less, but when you're young, you think you know everything. I had the whole world wrapped up at twenty-five; I had all the answers! You know—innocence is bliss. Yet when I think back on it, I don't know how blissful it really was. I have a certain contentment now that I never had back then. I see things more realistically. It's interesting to think of having less anguish now, after my mother's suicide, than before.

When people ask me about my parents, I say that they're both dead, and I don't have any trouble saying how my mother died. There might be circumstances in which I wouldn't tell, but if they're people I like and I'm getting to know, I want them to know who I am and what my life has been. There was a time when it felt pressing to tell people about my mother's suicide. I almost couldn't be with someone unless that person knew. Now it really surprises me to think that in the group of people I've met more recently, there are some who didn't know for a long time. I didn't have to tell them. I could be with these people and feel that they actually knew me without my having to say, "There is something terribly important that you should know about me."

Laura: Right at the Core of Life

[Continued from chapter 2, page 43]

Five years after her husband's suicide, Laura, now in her early thirties, works in a substance abuse treatment program and is preparing for her second marriage.

I was twenty-eight when Stuart died, and I felt like my life was over—*really* hopeless. I started to emerge from that when spring came. In the depths of winter, I was in the depths of despair. And then spring came, and I did a number of things. One of the things that helped me was career counseling. It got me reengaged in the process of thinking about my future and what I wanted for myself, and it culminated in my decision to go into mental health. I had read *Suicide in America,* by Herbert Hendin, and that book was what made me realize that I wanted to get into the field of mental health. It was more than just a reaction, trying to get some mastery over my experience with Stuart. It brought me back to an original passion that I had had.

Also, my in-laws and I had agreed the first time I visited them that I would come back in a year to see Britain, not through the fog of the funeral but in a better time. At the end of that first year, I was unemployed and had no income, but my parents said, "Do it." Stuart's mother and her husband had arranged to rent a cottage in West Wales. At first they couldn't get it, but at the last minute there was a cancellation. They called me and said, "We would love it if you could come." And I decided to do it. When I called to book a flight, the person on the phone said, "No, everything's booked. Sorry. Oh, wait a minute. A cancellation just came up on the screen." And I grabbed that flight. It was May 10, just before the one-year anniversary.

I was scared to death to go back there. I remember being afraid of flying, afraid of crashing, and not knowing what I was getting into. But as my sister-in-law put it, it was kind of a pilgrimage for me.

And it was very interesting, because I met my fiancé, Robert, on the way over. We sat next to each other. At the time, I had a passing fantasy that on the airplane maybe I would meet someone who was a little bit older than I and who was a therapist. I think I very much wanted to be taken care of. I wanted to meet somebody who was going to somehow rescue me from my sadness. Robert has not rescued me from my sadness, but he's given me a lot of opportunities to rescue myself. When we met, I was very attracted to him, and I thought, "I am not ready for a serious relationship." The juxtaposition of that meeting and the purpose of the trip was very strange for me.

In Britain, I was enlivened by the way in which my life was beginning to come up from the depths of despair, and at the same time, I was right back there confronting everything—confronting Stuart's home and spending time with his friends. I traveled, and I went to Bath and to the Y, where he died. It really was a kind of pilgrimage. It was a test, too, in a way. Can I survive this? Can I go and confront all this? It was also a dodge in some ways. I think I was desperate to be healed and to be able to face it and proclaim myself recovered and well. Robert's arrival on the scene gave me a way to do that, so that by the time the trip was over and I was back, it didn't take long for us to be in love.

It was interesting that my timetable never played itself out the way I expected. By the time the trip was over and the first-year anniversary rolled around, I was not in a place where I would be doing the anniversary reaction. I understood at the time that maybe that was going to come later. I was just in a space where I wasn't going to be connecting with those feelings, because I was falling in love. And it did come later. It's really come through the context of my relationship with Robert and through the first couple of years of being *terribly* frightened by intimacy. Robert really hung in there with me while I was quite ambivalent about giving myself over to a very risky way of being with another human being.

I gave myself more of an opportunity to connect with the feelings about Stuart at the second-year anniversary. Robert and I were in Maine on vacation, right at the anniversary of the death. I had brought Stuart's letter and some other stuff with me, because I knew I'd be thinking of it. I really needed to go through it. I went through this business again about the resentment [that Stuart expressed in the letter], and Robert put it to me in a way that I finally got it. Stuart felt that I had entrapped him into making promises he couldn't keep, that *he* would betray me, and that's what he was resentful about. Robert said, "You were a bystander." Here I was being so central in Stuart's life, blaming myself and feeling so guilty, staying connected to him through my guilt. That first year, I was so depressed and immobilized in my life, feeling that I hadn't done enough and I should have known. And what Robert said helped. It was a bitter pill, but it helped when he said, "You weren't so central to Stuart. You were a bystander in his life." So in that respect, what had been very painful in the letter eventually helped me to see what I hadn't been able to see so clearly [earlier]. I had seen it through *my* lens. It can be a real gift if you can let that in and make sense of it.

Last year, on the fourth anniversary, I did a kind of ritual. I took a couple of Stuart's things to Maine, and when we went out on our little boat, I cast them into the ocean. It will be the fifth anniversary this year, and I'll be getting ready for my wedding. What I've learned is that I need to carve out some time to have my feelings about Stuart, because I have a way of not letting myself do that and then paying the price later. It comes up at unexpected times. My experience has been that when I've tried to fend it off, keep it out, it just comes back in other ways.

I couldn't come close to getting angry at Stuart for so long. And when I did get a glimmer of it, even just a glimmer, it was so overpowering. How can you be mad at somebody who's dead? What are you going to do with that anger? If you really get as angry as you might get, you might sever whatever remaining tenuous connection you have. I sort of knew intellectually that I was mad at him about it all, and I wrote about that a little bit in my journal. But it was very threatening for me to access that rage. That's something that I think marks my life in general. I was trying so hard to understand Stuart, since he had clearly not been understood. I felt that was my job—not to abandon him and not to let him just fade into this horrible ignominious suicide.

I had a dream in which he was being really horrible to me and I was angry at him, and that helped. But it was in the first year of being with Robert that I really experienced the anger. I remember I was sitting on the bed, and something happened. It was something that Robert triggered. I felt a physical sensation of rushing backward and forward at the same time. I was just swept over by rage at Stuart for leaving me, for doing this to me. And then it was gone, and I was left with the echoes of it. What has permitted me to let that in has been working a lot over time in therapy.

I think pop culture is very useful, too, sometimes for these things. There's a singer named Jane Siberry from Canada. She sings a song called "You Don't Need." One of the first lines is about the slags of Merthyr Tydfil, which is a little town in Wales. And she makes literary allusions to Dylan Thomas and all kinds of Welsh stuff. But what the song is really about is how I don't need anybody, I don't want anybody to need me, I'm just moving through this tunnel. The tone of that song is Stuart's tone. It was as if this song had been written for me. Hearing it was like getting socked with the reality that here I was trying to make myself so central to Stuart's life and death, taking responsibility for it, and the fact of the matter was that I just wasn't that important. No wonder I felt blame and responsibility. I would rather feel guilty than unimportant. I loved him. I put up with so much and gave up so much of myself and my life for him. For him not to need me enough to stay alive was just intolerable. I kept trying to make him need me after his death, and he didn't even need me when he was alive. That is very grim, but it's also really freeing.

It's also only part of the story. There are whole pieces of the puzzle that will never be filled in, and that's really hard to live with. I think I've spent a lot of time making sense of it and explaining it and understanding it and understanding him, because it's very hard for me to tolerate the fact that I'm never going to know. I've talked to people. He left all these tapes, which I've played, thinking maybe he left me a message on one of them. I combed through his books. I read things greedily. I just tried to take it in. Maybe there'd be a clue somewhere.

I went to a support group for survivors last year. I haven't been back, and I'm not sure why. I went because I was writing a paper. I did it for the paper. I sat there and didn't speak the whole time. I spoke at the very end, but throughout the meeting,

I just sat there and cried. Everybody said why they were there, who it was they had lost, and it was like, boom, boom, boom! It felt big to me, and what also felt big was the fortitude, the survivorship! These were extraordinary people who had faced this extraordinary event in their lives, some of them more than once, and had survived. There was a part of me that still did the number that I do, thinking that what these people had been through was more horrific than what I had been through. But more than that, I felt I belonged. I *belonged*. These people understood. I felt I needed to go back to that group, but I haven't been back. I want to do that, but it's almost too powerful. There's a way in which I shy away from experiencing that too much.

I think I let the pain in more than sometimes feels safe for me. I used to become overwhelmed. I just couldn't protect myself from it. Even now, it comes upon me suddenly sometimes, and I don't expect it. Sometimes I choose it, but I choose it less now. There was a time when it was almost like having a sore place in your mouth, and you've just got to keep running your tongue over it, over and over and over. I don't do that anymore. And in some ways, I actively avoid it—not in a bad way, more like a self-care avoidance. I need to get through what I'm doing now. I don't need to stop and be flooded with pain. But I still have little secret ways of doing that.

I really believe that the unconscious doesn't lie. Just before you came, I got back here and I hadn't eaten. I wanted to have something to eat, and there really wasn't anything. I thought maybe I'd have some cereal. But I opened the refrigerator, and there was Branston pickle, which is British. That was Stuart— cheese and pickle sandwiches: cheddar cheese, Branston pickle, and bread. I don't eat that very often. I don't always like it. But all of a sudden, I found myself making this sandwich. I could have had cereal. But I keep Branston pickle in my refrigerator. So there are ways that I sometimes choose to let the pain in. And I think that's one of the ways of keeping Stuart alive.

My job has been very important to me. I work with people who look, on the outside, like they're trying to kill themselves. I don't think that's what they're trying to do. I think they're trying to survive. And that's helped me have a real understanding even of suicide as a way of having control over one's life.

The job has been very important to me in terms of not taking responsibility for other people's lives and letting people make their own decisions. Twenty-four hours a day, I've got my job, I've got my man, and I've got my therapist, so I'm always confronting this stuff. I've worked hard. And part of the work has been trying to get in touch with the anger, trying to feel it, trying to let it be, and trying to understand what I do not to have it.

It took what happened to Stuart to get me where I am now. I count myself so lucky. I mean, of all the pain I've been through and the horror, when the pieces finally came down and were reassembled . . . I haven't just healed from Stuart's suicide. I've healed from a lot of other wounds in my life as well.

Susan and Philip

[Continued from chapter 2]

Susan is now married and has just given birth to a son. She is a practicing psychotherapist. Philip, no longer so encumbered by his father's business interests, has recently completed his first novel. It has been almost eight years since their father's suicide.

Susan: Grieving Long Before He Died

[Continued from page 51]

I really do think that my father's decision was a rational decision. It was not at all impulsive. And in a lot of ways, I'm sure that made it, and makes it, easier to deal with. He wasn't going to get any better. It was very clear he wasn't.

I look back and say, "Well, if I had known what my brother knew at the end—" Maybe I could have. Maybe I didn't want to know, because I probably would have intervened. And I'm not sure that would have been for the better at all. From hindsight, who knows? I'm really glad I wasn't in my brother's shoes, but I don't think my dad would have chosen me to be, and I don't know whether I would have let myself be. It's a really awful position to be in, and I feel bad that my brother was put in that position. And yet he was much closer to my dad than I was.

My father had had a lot of losses, and he was really, I think, emotionally unable to cope with those losses. But the MS on top of it just really catapulted it into another sphere. Some days he was fine. He would be okay and could walk around, sometimes with a cane. Sometimes he'd need help, and sometimes people thought he was drunk on the street. Other times he couldn't get out of bed at all and needed to be in bed for weeks. It was totally unpredictable. I think that's one thing that's so psychologically debilitating about the disease: you just don't know. Now, with the baby, I realize how much I've enjoyed predictability and control in my life. My schedule has to fit him. Sleeping? Who's heard of sleeping at night? And how hard that is with something so wonderful. So with something that's terrible—that affects your self, your body, and your whole life—it's really hard. That kind of helpless feeling is behind a lot of depressions, and my father really felt helpless. He would always say, "I want to fight it" or "I can't fight it." He tended to set up these black-and-white dichotomies about everything.

For a long time after the suicide, I felt a compelling need to talk about it with people I already knew and even with people I was meeting and anticipated I might get to know. It was so much a part of where I was at that point that I felt I needed to tell them what had happened. I was embarrassed and ashamed that I felt that need so strongly. That's really changed. Now, with people I anticipate being close to, at some point I will tell them, but it's nowhere as close to the surface as it was. Even two years [after the suicide, when I first talked with you] it was close to the surface. That's changed.

I also watch people's reactions to that story. My in-laws, for instance, have never really asked anything about it. They're very kind to me, but they don't know who I am, and they don't really care to know who I am. They can't deal with anything emotionally troubling. I think they might know about my father's suicide, but they never really wanted to know. At one point, when my husband and I had been engaged for a while, we were visiting them. We were sitting in the kitchen [with my mother-in-law], talking about family members who had died. I started to talk about my father, and then my father-in-law walked in and [changed the subject]. That was that. He walked away, and then my mother-in-law started talking about the dances that they have in their groups. The clear message was "I don't want to hear about this."

I finally got rid of the stuffed animal my father had sent me just before he died. It was ugly. It was a cat in pajamas. In many ways, it was very endearing and sweet—his attempt to be close—and I recognize that. I can't remember when I decided that I didn't need to keep it or I didn't want to keep it. Maybe when I moved. I decided I could let it go.

There are other things that I have of his. I kept the note that came with the stuffed animal, because it was the sentiment [that was important to me] more than the animal itself. I kept some letters he had written me, pictures, and letters I'd written him that I found when we packed up his house. I also kept the note that his friend had written for him to say good-bye. There was no tone of hostility at all in that letter. It was very loving, which was not usual for his behavior. Most of my life, he wasn't able to express himself very freely in that regard, or it was always the kind of loving message mixed with all these directives and all this hostility and rejection. It took a lot of sorting out for me to realize that he did as much as he could in terms of trying to show his love for us. It's too bad that he couldn't do that in person most of the time.

My father left a sizable inheritance, which is the reason my husband and I can afford this house. For a while, I couldn't bring myself to use my father's money. I really couldn't bear to touch any of it. I didn't like my father's relationship with money. It was his way of manipulating people. He was so incredibly tight, he'd never spend money. I finally allowed myself to use it in a different way than he had allowed himself. He never traveled. And I decided, hey, why wait until I'm old and not healthy and can't walk? You never know what's around the corner, and we might as well do it while we can. So my husband and I took a trip around the world, and I'm really glad we did. It was wonderful.

My brother has been much more active in the business than I, much more interested. My father introduced it to him more than to me. And I've been very grateful to my brother for taking care of that. He's more comfortable with it. I've never been that interested, although I've had to learn some things about financial management and deciding what to do. But especially in terms of the real estate, I've not wanted to be particularly involved, and I'm very glad that Philip has, because someone needed to. We finally sold the property that had been my grandfather's. We exchanged it for some other property, so that tie to those particular buildings is now gone, which is fine with me.

When I got married, I wanted my father's name mentioned in the ceremony. That was important to me. I regretted that he couldn't be there and knew that he would have been happy for me. We asked the rabbi to talk about how we were grateful that everybody who was there could share our happiness and to mention both my stepgrandmother, who couldn't be there because of illness, and my father, who had passed away, and that we were sorry that they weren't there to be able to share that.

I went through a variety of thoughts about keeping my last name. When I was very young, I thought, "How could I ever possibly want to keep my last name? It's not my mom's last name, and I don't really like my father's side of the family at all, so I'd be glad to get rid of it." Then I went through a second stage, maybe in high school or college or even later, when politically it was important to keep my name. You know, the feminist thing of why would I take somebody else's name? This is *my* name. And then later on, I think I felt it was important to keep my name not only because of my career and the fact that I earned my degree under my name but also because it's a link to my past. It's a link to my father and my father's side of the family, and as much as I didn't always get along with them, that part is still there. I could throw out the stuffed animal, but I didn't want to throw out the name. It's a little odd having a different last name from my son. I have ambivalent feelings about that. But I don't think I need to distance myself from my father's side of the family in the way that I once thought I would want to. I kept my maiden name, and I'm sure there's a link to my father there that was important to me.

When I was pregnant, it occurred to me that a grandchild would have made my dad really happy. He would have been thrilled and might have had a less conflicted relationship with my son than he had with me. It was July when I thought of that, the month that he killed himself, and I thought, "No surprise here!"

In the Jewish religion, you name a child after someone you care about who is dead. We knew we were having a boy, and I did not want him to be named after my father. I kept my maiden name, and that link to my father was important to me, but my ambivalence was such that I wouldn't have wanted my father's first name to be that prominent [a part of my life].

I've been writing things down in a little baby book, and there's a family tree in it. I realized that my son's going to have a grandfather—my stepfather, who's been very much a father to me in my life. But his blood grandfather is my father, so in the family tree I put two different sides and wrote about both of them. There's a part of me that misses my dad, and I feel bad that he didn't have the opportunity to experience this. It would have made him happy. There really wasn't a lot that did make him happy at the end.

I will tell my son about his grandfather at a point when I think he's ready to hear it. I don't want to lie about anything. A lot of people hear distorted stories growing up, and I don't think that's healthy. I don't think he needs to know all sorts of gory details when he's really young, because that's a little scary and overwhelming to a kid. I'll have to figure out the timing, what he's ready to hear and when he wants to hear it. Kids are usually pretty good at asking at a level that they can hear. So I'm not going to hide it, and I'm certainly going to tell him. It will be a while. I have a lot of time to think about that.

I haven't visited my father's grave very much—maybe three times. It's not a lot. The first time I went alone. My mom wanted to go with me, but I wanted to go alone. I think she wanted to be supportive of me, but I felt that, considering her relationship with my father, I'd rather do that piece of mourning by myself. It felt more appropriate. I could *not* find the marker. I was wandering through this whole section of gravestones, and I saw the grandparents of people I'd known, because he's buried in a section where all the people belonged to one particular congregation. But I couldn't find my father's grave! And I had been there before, because it's right next to my grandmother and grandfather's plot. I'd been there twice before, when my grandparents had died. I laughed at myself, because I knew exactly what was going on as I was looking for the gravestone. I said to myself, "I couldn't really connect with my father in life, and here he's dead and I still can't do it!" And I haven't had an easy time finding it each time I've gone there. The layout of the cemetery is a little confusing, and it's huge. But still, I find it amazing that I always have a hard time finding my father's grave.

One time I went with my husband. I wanted him to go with me. And it's been important for me to tell him the stories about my dad and our relationship. Usually I feel sad visiting the grave. I haven't felt particularly angry. A lot of the sadness that I sometimes feel when thinking about my dad is sadness not for his death or how he died but for our troubled relationship, his life and my life.

I have a pretty solid relationship with my mom. I never went through a lot of the adolescent separation stuff that people go through with their mothers—I think because I needed her so much. My relationship with my father was so difficult that she was the person who was most there for me, and I was scared to test that in any way. So I've probably been unusually close to her for a long time. The most trauma, I think, that I ever went through with her was around my marriage. It was a very hard thing for her to deal with. I was furious. I don't think I've ever been as mad at her in my life, but we survived that. The anger that I went through with my father was more around the way we related, the way he related long term, and my feeling that he just missed the boat emotionally so many times. During the upset with my mom, I could understand where she was coming from. I certainly was much more direct about my anger with her than I had been with my father. I think growing up and living through my father's suicide helped make me realize that if you need to say something, better to get it off your chest, say it directly. I don't know if it was his death per se, but issues in my relationship with him and realizing where it had gone astray certainly led me to try to handle things differently in subsequent relationships. There are so many strands, and it's hard to say x is the cause of y. They're kind of interlocking strands, so it's impossible to sort out the fiber from the total weave.

In looking back, I realize what a different place I'm in now, how good my life is, how grateful I am that that torment has passed. I also feel that, as hard as it was, it enabled me to deal with other traumas and also issues around death in a different way.

I've had to work with a number of suicidal people in my

clinical work. Usually the circumstances have been different, but I always have to be aware of the part of me that wishes I could have saved my father and try not to let it interfere with what's actually going on. I also have to be cognizant of the other part of me that says, "All right, already, it's enough! He's better off and maybe this person would be better off." So going through some of those feelings that I had with my dad—the anger, the rage, and the hostility—sometimes has the potential of interfering with my clinical work. But I also think that having felt some of those feelings, having been in touch with both the sadness and the rage, as hard as that was, made me more open to the intensity of those feelings in others.

Philip: A Loss of Innocence

[Continued from page 59]

I've been to visit my father's grave twice in seven years. That's not a lot. It's funny, because it says on his stone, "He loved his children." I wanted to add, "Me thinks thou doest protest too much." He was always telling us how much he loved us. And what that does is it makes whatever you do back insufficient. It was always, you know, why didn't I come to live in St. Louis? Well, I couldn't have my career there. Or, "I've been keeping track, and the last two months I've called you twenty-seven times, and you've called me three times." I mean, it's ridiculous and crazy and wrong.

I don't know whether that's why I haven't been back more. I just don't have anything to say to the tombstone. The last time I was in St. Louis, which was just a couple of weeks ago, I thought maybe I'd go visit, but I didn't. I think that when you die, you're dead. I don't need to have the grave to conjure him up. My grandfather and grandmother are buried there, too. It's a spooky spot. It's a good spot, but it's . . . I don't know, I just don't make time to go out there and do it. I don't need to go out there and feel bad. I can do that all by myself wherever I am. And it wouldn't make me feel good, I don't think, in any way.

I'm a different person from my father, emotionally and psychologically—at least I hope I am. My father was not a generous man. He was not generous with others, and he was not generous with himself. And he didn't have the ability, the emotional flexibility and psychological ability, to weather what he had to deal with. I think there were probably some very early wounds that contributed, with the fact that MS is just a— It won't kill you, but it will make your life almost not worth living if you have a bad enough case of it. I'm going out with someone now whose mom has MS. As I was getting to know her [and I told her about my father], she said, "Well, why didn't you call the police and get them over there to the house?" Because I didn't want to do it. It wasn't respectful of what he wanted.

I never consciously, at the time, felt it was a burden [knowing that my father intended to kill himself]. I wanted to know. Now, looking back, I think it was an enormous burden, an extraordinary burden, and probably affected me in some fairly pernicious or subtle ways that I'm dealing with now. I mean, he was so incredibly needy. He turned me into the parent. When I was sixteen, sitting on this couch, and he said, "I've thought of the various ways to kill myself," probably at *that* moment, at that exact moment, I became his parent. I mean, there I was, eighteen or nineteen or twenty years old, trying to find ways that I could make my father's life worth living: "Well, maybe if you move into the city . . ." Or, "Why don't you change your job?" Or, "You can work less or work with people less fortunate than you." It's a real burden always to be the one *responsible* for someone else's success or failure or, in some ways, that person's life. Those things get integrated, I think, in a really powerful way.

But I don't know that it would have been any better had I not known anything about [his plan to kill himself], and one day he just did it. See, that's what you lose sight of if you just look at the fact that it was a burden to know. I think in some ways, it's more of a burden after death not to have known anything. I mean, I understood, I accepted it before it happened, and I tell you without guilt, I felt a lot of relief. I don't think that the level of my awareness of what was going on was bad. In some ways, it taught me some good things, too, about being honest and open and seeing your parents as people. My problem was that I saw my parents as people when I was five years old, when they got divorced. I never had a chance to have the illusion that they were anything but fallible human beings. I loved my father, but he was a bad guy in a lot of ways. And that makes it more understandable that he'd kill himself, because he probably didn't like those things in himself any more than anyone else did. It also makes remembering him much more of a mixed bag.

I can't imagine many worse feelings for a kid than to have a parent kill himself, because the very person who has given you life has renounced it. I think I was protected from the severity of that contradiction by the fact that it was so rational-seeming. I was old enough to understand, and it made sense and all that. But even for a young adult, the giver of life— There was no wife.

He didn't have parents who were around. There was no one. I mean, I sold the house, I sold the car, I cleaned out the closets. It would have helped if he had had a wife. It would have helped if there had been anybody else. Because the only relationship that was significant that was going on at that moment was kids and him.

It wasn't like I just lost my father. It was like I lost my kid, too, in the responsibility sense. And I think it probably stays with me in all kinds of ways. I'm very sensitive when people think I haven't done enough or criticize me for a lack of something that I've tried to provide. I'm very sensitive about that, probably oversensitive, in part because I never could do enough, could I? And he still died. What I'm saying is, 1 percent of that reaction—or 5 percent, 10 percent, who knows—I think is stimulated by the suicide. It's sort of like the bank of credit that we want to be able to draw on, especially if we've done all we could to try to keep our parents alive and they kill themselves anyway. And I felt I did all I could without completely ruining my life. I didn't move back to St. Louis. His life wouldn't have been any better, and he would have made mine worse.

When I was a young adolescent, I was fairly depressed, although I was the typical overachieving kid, getting straight A's and doing all this other stuff, but very sad inside. I thought about suicide. I don't know if I thought about it more or less than most young teenagers, but I did think about it—probably more. And somehow I had to stop thinking about it, because my father had started to think about it, to the point where, when I was sixteen, it seemed like he even took away the idea of thinking about killing myself. So I think that got transferred into the feeling that I wasn't going to live a long time. I thought I was going to die by the time I was twenty or twenty-five, which is also a defense against failure, because if you die, then no one can hold the verdict out on you. But that may have been the way I dealt with that same sort of feeling.

I've never engaged much in self-destructive behavior. I don't smoke. I've never taken drugs in a regular way at all. I don't drink that much. I don't drive cars fast. I don't drive drunk. I may go white-water rafting—that's about as close as I'll get. I'm very affirmative. In fact, I make people wear their seat belts. I can't even take it when other people do things that are self-destructive in my presence.

But we all have dark moments of the soul. I think the closest I got to feeling really that bad—not absolutely suicidal, but "I'm not so sure this is worth living"—was when my girlfriend split for good a year and a half ago, just a couple of days before Thanksgiving. From there, through those holidays, into the spring, I would say that I had thoughts the logical extension of which would be the consideration of suicide. By Christmas, I had gotten myself into psychotherapy, and I still felt very bad, because I was stuck on my book, halfway through it, and couldn't finish it. If you assume that you need to work and you need to love in your life, I didn't have either at the time, and I was living alone. Living alone and being alone conjure up for me all my father's living alone and being alone. It was really bad. I even took some antidepressant-type medication. I remember going to the pharmacy and coming back, the first time, with this medication. I started crying, just because of the idea that my father had taken all this shit. He was a walk-in advertisement for pharmaceuticals. And I used to go fill his prescriptions and bring them to his house. He was overmedicated. Susan talked once or twice to the doctors. She had more awareness of the different kinds of medications because of her psychology background. That was one area where she was probably more active than I was.

It was painful for me to think that I was following a pattern just by virtue— I wanted not to have to take anything. And I quit, in fact, the first medication I was taking and found something else. I don't know whether it helped or didn't help, but I found I was able to write, so I wasn't going to change anything until I finished my book, and then the day I finished my book, I stopped taking the medication. And, you know, it passed.

Suicide is your ultimate choice. I mean, I think it's a choice that I'm glad man has. A lot of people commit suicide, and it's not called suicide. They drink or take drugs—it's really what the crack addicts are trying to do. In my case, my father's suicide might dissuade me from suicide more than encourage me, because I wouldn't want to identify myself with my father. I've lived a lot of my life attempting to distinguish myself from him. If I killed myself, I'd really be my father's son, wouldn't I? I'd like to choose life, and I would like not to be defeated by the things that defeated him, although I don't know what I would do if I had a terminal illness. That's a heavy one.

Pain builds character, but at a certain point, pain doesn't build character anymore; it just destroys what character is there. Suicide arrested the pain my father was feeling. It allowed my sister and me to go on with our own lives. He had to stop needing things when he was no longer here, so in that sense, it was positive. I think that's the major way it was positive. I don't think life is inherently good or inherently bad. I think life is inherently biology and Darwin and struggling to create more life. My father's life was, by his own measure and by most people's measure, quite bad. Zero is more than a negative number, and in that sense [his death] was a real blessing. Everyone who knew him well said the same thing to me at the funeral: "It's for the best." I thought it was for the best.

This thing about suicide being a permanent solution to a temporary problem— The problem was as temporary as my father's whole life. It wasn't going to go away. So I think it was a permanent solution to a permanent problem—not the best solution but *a* solution, which is on a higher order than no solution, and that's what he had been wrestling with for years. Is a solution better than no solution, if no solution just means more and more pain and suffering and anguish, misery, loathing, self-loathing? Yes. *He* felt it was the only solution. I think there were others, but it was the only solution he was capable of. I think for all those people who choose suicide, suicide is inevitable. That's not to say I feel suicide is inevitable. But I think for the person who is choosing it, it is, and *that's* why the choice is made. So in that element, it's not a mystery. It's just so damned obvious to the person who's doing it.

[VA: The mystery is left for the people who still choose to live.]

Right. And, you know, I went through a lot of that, and I guess I still go through it sometimes. I went through it more immediately after his death: "How can I be alive if my father's dead? I'm just so young." Or, "How can I choose to be?" You get pretty existential. The questions are pretty big. I've always had a serious side, despite my deathmobile-type humor. I mean, it didn't serve to make me less serious. It probably served to make me more serious.

I had very little in me that took anything for granted before, and I think I probably have nothing in me that takes anything for granted now. The line of death is very close, and it can happen anytime, so you have to make life count. I've always been very life affirming. The things that I love are joyous things: art; architecture, which is probably the most optimistic of all art forms because it assumes a tomorrow; jazz, which is very self-affirming, the whole idea of the self involved in the group and what the spirit of jazz is about. And I think my father's suicide served to make me even more life affirming. But I'm trying to be careful about just the fact that he died and the fact that it was a suicide, because I'm not clear as to whether or not I would have had the same feelings had he just died.

I've tried to learn from my father's experience, too. I mean, the things that he wanted to do but didn't get to do? I've decided I'm going to do those things. I'm not going to wait. Like travel. Spend some money if you have it. I'm not in a profession where I'm going to make tons of money unless I get lucky on some book, so that's okay. And it's okay for me to use some of the money that he had, which is not an attitude he would have had.

After his death, I found it very difficult to focus on my own life. It was too painful at the time. And I think the form of death had a lot to do with it. I felt this was a terrible thing that had happened, and I wanted to take what I could out of it. At that point, the only benefit to anyone out of it was money. [So I became] very committed to helping other people. Because this was so bad, I had to make other things so good. There's a Buddhist phrase, "Take the poison and make it medicine," sort of like the Western idea that if God gives you lemons, make lemonade. So let me take his money and give it to artists who need it. And there were some real benefits for other people. He also had a foundation that gave to run-of-the-mill charities. I wanted to change that and make it a much more active thing, giving to individuals as well as organizations that reflected Susan's and my politics, which we've done. So I became very committed to trying to make something good come out of this bad, because I saw it as a bad thing, as a really painful thing. If it had been a natural death, I don't know that I would have had quite that same reaction somehow.

Sometimes I feel tainted by it, like it's something that doesn't quite wash off. I think I felt it more early on, when I was younger. People would look at me: "Twenty-three, twenty-four, and his father . . ." or something like that. Not so much now, as my father recedes into the distance and more people's parents meet bad ends. It's almost as though if you get angry about something, people may not give you the benefit of the doubt, because what you're really angry about is that your father— Almost like you're tainted in some way. It occurred to me that when my girlfriend split, maybe one of the reasons it was so painful was that it triggered something about my dad and everything else that I hadn't really worked all the way through. So in that way, there was a taint.

You're never completely innocent. I don't think the person who's had a suicide in the family is ever completely innocent about anything, in some way, because it is the ultimate question, to be or not to be. That's it. And when someone says, "Not to be," it's a refutation and a rebuke and a denial, and all those things that we know it is. But what it really does is undermine innocence, even in the way adults like to make believe they're innocent about certain things at certain times. It's not to say I have it on my mind all the time and not to say that, staring at Mount Everest in the moonlight, which I did a couple of years ago, I couldn't feel incredibly exhilarated. It was no less of an experience because my father killed himself. It's just that it creates a baseline that the rest of your life takes off from, and the baseline might be a bit lower than it would ordinarily be or more difficult, or you might be a bit more sticky with the past as you go about leaping away from it.

It lives with you. This sofa, this was his sofa, and I spent a lot of Sundays, growing up, sitting on it. He sat in a chair about where I'm sitting now, although not in this chair, and bitched about how horrible life was, which is one of the reasons I finally decided to get rid of the sofa. After seven years, I'm going to get a different sofa! This was his chair, that was his sculpture, and that was his table. It's more than material. So that's what I'm saying about a certain taint. There's a certain kind of continuation in terms of your whole emotional chemistry, and how it comes out is pretty subtle. I think I'm still learning about it. Maybe it makes everything more pointed, good and bad, in your life. And then there's just the simple fact of the death, you know? I mean, there have been times I've wished that he was around to see things that were happening, not so much because *I* want to impress him with what *I'm* doing or the good things that have happened, but because I know how much of a kick *he'd* get out of it for *him*. Not because it's necessary to make my parents proud of me anymore, but just because he lived for our accomplishments.

I think all strong life experiences are good if you can survive them. I guess it's my view as a writer. I'm thinking about this a lot now, because I want to write a novel that's much more autobiographical, more like a typical first novel, and the suicide would be the very center of the book. I don't know if it would be on the first page. It might be. Maybe the whole book takes place the night of the suicide. I don't know. I haven't figured out how to structure it. I haven't figured out how to *judge* it, because I've never written anything, other than poetry, that's so closely tied to myself. I'm not sure I could judge whether it's good or bad. But I want to deal with it. [I wrote an] article on teen suicide, [and doing that] was good, but it wasn't cathartic. It was significant, and I learned a lot and was really energized by it. I did a lot of reading. It was painful. I wrote 11,000 words, and they cut it down to 7000 or something. And my reaction was "You can't cut these words." Of all the stories I've written, it was the hardest. I did get involved in a way that was pretty good, but [doing that story] didn't exhaust it.

It's inexhaustible. You could say we'll talk about it for a half hour or we'll talk about it for thirty hours. I think there's the feeling that your parent's death becomes part of your own identity, or the suicide becomes part of your own identity in a way that another death does not. And the taint, just that question that people may have in their own minds about you, if you get sad or depressed. And the way you might worry about yourself. Last year, when I was going through the blackest, bleakest time of my life, maybe I put more pressure on myself to get well faster. I said to a couple of people, "You know, the lesson for someone whose father's committed suicide is 'Take it seriously when you start feeling so bad.' " So it becomes part of your identity. In some ways, it's almost like it's contagious. You've got to be careful. It's a really intimate thing.

And knowing [that my father intended to kill himself], which is really pretty unusual, I always know that I probably could have stopped it. I probably could have stopped it that particular time. If I had said, "I'm moving to St. Louis," I think I could have kept him alive. My life would have been horrible, but I could have kept him alive. By virtue of the fact that I chose not to, I was responsible for his death. And you always live with that. Do I think it was wrong? No. But still. Would I do it differently? No, because I'm not sick and I'm not a masochist, and why ruin two people's lives? But you can't deny that what you're involved in under the circumstances becomes part of your psychological frame of reference. And there are many, many, many, many days, most days, when I don't give it a thought. But I don't have to, because it's there anyway.

Joy: Knowing Suicide from a Young Age

[Continued from chapter 3, page 112]

Joy is now in her early thirties. It has been fourteen years since her mother's suicide. Five years have elapsed since she first told me her story in 1983. Joy works as a nursing administrator.

I think if there's anything different now, it's that my mother's death feels more like a death to me and less like a suicide. Going through the tenth anniversary of her death was tough, but it was good. I was nineteen when she killed herself, and I was thinking the other day that when I hit the twenty-year anniversary, six years from now, that's going to be longer that I've lived without her than I lived with her. That was a really strange thought, and I felt sad. I don't really feel sad about it anymore. I don't know, maybe time changes things, softens things.

My mother has a biographer, and I feel incredibly lucky to have her as a resource. The biography will be coming out in about two years. I've read a lot of the transcripts from it, and I guess that's contributed more to my understanding of my mother's illness than I had before. It's an amazing story, not just about a poet but about a woman who really had severe mental illness in a way that I didn't believe before. So maybe that's why the suicide now seems more acceptable to me or more realistic— not that it's a hundred percent that, but just the realization that her life was so filled with pain. She was incredibly ill, and yet she was able to do what she did. Reading those transcripts didn't completely take away my anger that she decided to remove her life from mine, but I guess I came to a different understanding of it.

The tenth anniversary was a time of looking back to see where I had been ten years before. Did it feel like ten years? No, it felt shorter—but no, it seemed longer. I'd made progress in that time, but it felt like yesterday, maybe because the feelings got kicked up, and that made it feel like it hadn't been ten years.

I've done so much personal growing and professional growing—and my relationship with my husband and what we've done together—that I wish she could have been around for. I guess in that way, it feels more just like a death than like a suicide. I think you'd feel that way about anybody who dies—missing her and saying, "Look at the parts of my life that she's missed." The other side of it for suicide is, "But in some way, shape, or fashion, she chose not to be here for that growth, for those changes."

Ten years of her being dead—I mean, in my mind, she's still forty-five years old. I have friends now who are in their early and mid-forties. When I was nineteen, that didn't seem so young to die. When you're nineteen, forty-five is old, but when you're thirty-three and you have friends who are forty-four and forty-five, that seems really young. That's been a more recent perspective. When my mother was my age, she had been in mental hospitals and in serious therapy. She was trying to manage life with children and with continued mental problems. But she was writing, and she was becoming famous. There was this whole side of her life that, being so young, I didn't see. As a child, you have a little ego that just surrounds you like a bubble. You don't see the other person's reality. That's what the biography has given me.

My sister gave birth to her second child on the tenth anniversary of my mother's suicide. She was two and a half weeks overdue. I remember talking to her the day before and saying, "You're holding on to that baby until October 4, 1984." For me that day now is always a mixture of feeling sad about my mother but also being able to wish someone congratulations for another year of life accomplished. In that way, it doesn't feel so heavy as it used to, because I call my nephew and wish him a happy birthday.

My sister and I are close on many levels, but we're different people. I don't understand quite how it's happened, but I think we have very, very different value systems. Maybe as we've grown older, our values have become more firmly entrenched. And the difference in value systems creates problems sometimes. It's not always easy for me to be with her, and I'm sure it isn't easy for her to be with me. We're still close, but maybe it's that my marriage is stronger now and I don't need that intensely close sister relationship to sustain me in the way that I used to. We're still close, and we talk on the phone and maintain contact. We reach out to each other when we're in trouble, and when we're really upset, we're there for each other.

I think both my sister and I are of the generation that says the buck stops here—the craziness and the alcoholism, not dealing with things, the lack of openness and lack of honesty. That's hard, because the tendency to repeat those patterns is always there. I think even in my marriage I feel them. But we're both working really hard to make that different. Not that we're going to be 100 percent successful but more successful than my parents were.

My grandmother died—of relatively natural causes—two years ago. I was incredibly close to her. For a large part of my life, she was essentially my mom. It was like losing another mother when she died. That was hard, but I guess I learned a lesson from my mother's suicide, and I applied it. The worst thing about the suicide was not being able to say good-bye and not being able to say thank you. I had some mixed baggage with my mother; I'm not sure how many thank yous there were. But with my grandmother, there were a lot of thank yous due. She was someone who had basically put her life on hold when she was in her fifties to take on a little baby—me at nine months— and to keep me for three years, and then she had to give me up. Only now can I contemplate the depth of what that must have done to her. There was clearly a struggle between my mother and her. She did not feel ready to give me up when my mother felt ready to take me back.

When I was in nursing school, my grandmother had a couple of heart attacks. After the second one, she was in the hospital and I spoke with her husband, my stepgrandfather. He said to me, "The prospect of her living is not good." I suddenly panicked. Oh, my God, what would happen if she died that night and I didn't get to talk to her? So I went to the hospital and got in through the emergency room [because it was late and visiting hours were over] and snuck up to her room. I sat on her bed and thanked her and said, "I just want you to know that without you I wouldn't be here. And a lot of what I've become is due to the unconditional love that you gave me." Not having been able to say good-bye to my mother, I realized how important it was to do that. So as a result, as much as my grandmother's death was incredibly sad and painful, it felt clean in a way that my mother's death did not.

Christmas is different now. I don't grieve so much for the loss of my family, because my husband, Stephen, and I are a new family. I wish Stephen had had a chance to meet my mother. There are still regrets, and that's one of them. I still have a couple of good friends who were friends then and knew her. My friend Susan felt very close to her, was a big supporter of hers, and there's another friend, Tim, whom my mother really developed her own relationship with. I'm still very good friends with him, and I still have kind of a connection through my mother. But I wish that Stephen, who's the person I'm closest to in the whole world, could have had a chance to be close to her, too.

I still feel sad when I visit my mother's grave. I think I feel more sad because my grandmother's there—they're buried in the same family plot. My grandmother's death is a lot fresher, and it's sadder in some way, because there really was no ambivalence for me with her. There was nothing I could do that was wrong in her eyes. No matter how crazy I got or what stupid things I did, she still loved me unconditionally. So when I go to the gravesite, there's more of an association to my grandmother than there is to my mom.

When we buried my mother, it had been so long since her death. We had the ashes, and we were going to scatter them on the ocean, but they stayed in my father's closet for two years. God, that seems terrible! They were in a little box at the top of the closet, next to old hangers and stuff. I think the whole family—my sister, my father, and I—felt a real need to bring that to closure, but it took a long time. So I don't really associate burying my mother's ashes that much with her suicide or her death. It was just somehow finally closing that chapter. But my grandmother did not want to be cremated, and we buried her body there. So that has a different association for me.

We didn't put the palindrome on the family headstone [as my mother had requested]. I could hear my grandmother roll over right now if we put "Rats live on no evil star" on the old English headstone! Not everybody's requests get met. You don't get everything you want. That was the other thing that came through to me in reading the transcripts for the biography: my mother was incredibly selfish. She just didn't have an ability to see things beyond herself. I always thought that her selfishness was just translated into our family life, but through the biography, I saw that it was translated in all sorts of other ways. I picked up this need for things to be balanced, always fair and equal, maybe because it felt so unbalanced, so unequal at home that I'll be damned if I'm not going to get my fair share now. And maybe it was that way for my mother as a child and that's how she overcompensated for it as an adult.

Sleep is still an issue for me. I had such terrible trouble sleeping after my mother died, and that was the beginning of insomnia for me. I don't have it that often, but I go through cycles of it. It's not a huge problem, but I hate it when I can't sleep.

I didn't dream about my mother for a long time, and I didn't dream about my grandmother for a long time. I think it takes a while for that reality to get into the back consciousness, that that person isn't there anymore. Now I still occasionally have dreams in which my mother comes back and says, "I never really died." It was all set up to look like she had died, but she hadn't. She'd been hiding out, and she'd come back. And then there was the waking up, the way it always is at first, waking up after someone's died and having to go through that again. Of all the things that I came to dread the most when my grandmother died, the worst was knowing that when I woke up, the reality of the death would come back—it would just be that sinking feeling early in the morning.

It's much harder for me now to conjure up an image of my mother that's not based on a photograph, a picture that I've seen. Images of her doing things—walking, eating, just doing everyday things—those images are harder to conjure up. It's very hard for me in my mind's eye to picture my mother being my mother when I was seven years old, eight years old. I can see a little bit more from when I was seventeen, eighteen, the last couple of years that she was alive, because I was alone with her so much when I was older. My memories of my husband when I first met him, when I was twenty-two, ten years ago, are sharp and clear, memories of conversations. That's what I don't really remember with my mother, which is kind of sad, because to say that her death feels clean to me or is done with—no, it's still painful. I guess I'm not so sad to see some of those memories go. Maybe someday I'll wish I had them back, but I'm not fighting to keep them.

I feel settled about my mother's suicide now. I don't feel that she was murdered. I know she killed herself. I guess I don't quite understand what made this attempt so definitive, so absolute, when her life really seemed to be in an upsurge. It still doesn't make a whole lot of sense, but I don't need to rationalize its not making a lot of sense by saying maybe she was murdered. I don't feel that way anymore. I think that she fully intended to kill herself, and this time she was just more sure of herself and sure that that's what she wanted to do. And she did it.

I still feel angry about that summer before she died, that I was her caretaker. I guess what I feel more angry about now is that somehow my last summer with her couldn't have been different. It was so unfair for her to have done to me what she did, at that age, considering all the past history. And I think what happened was that I was finally coming into my own enough to realize that that was totally unfair and unrealistic. For the first time, I was saying no to her. I had never done that before.

I guess my feeling is that life goes on. I would really like to have a family, my own family. It might be interesting to talk with me three years after I've had a child. I know my sister had a lot of issues come up right after she had her first child—mothering issues, the way that she had been mothered and trying not to repeat habits that she didn't realize were habits of hers but that had been habits of my mother's. I don't know how I'll adapt to that process. I really want to be a mother, but I'm realizing now that when you want it so badly, what you lose is the ability to have the ambivalence that's normal for anyone who's trying to have a child. When it does happen for me, I hope I'll allow myself that ambivalence—I really do—because I think that's part of giving up your singlehood.

Rachel: Needing My Best Friend
to Comfort Me

Rachel was twenty-six when she met Eva, also in her twenties. The two women (whose names have been changed) developed a close friendship that would last for five years, until brought to an abrupt end by Eva's suicide. Rachel, now thirty-eight, has since married, and she and her husband have a young child. I interviewed her in May 1989.

When Eva died, Rachel lost her best friend. Her story is about the aftermath of suicide in the context of the special connection that develops between very close friends. Rachel also tells of the different responses she had to her father's death from cancer and her friend's death from suicide. Years later, these two losses have in a sense merged; they occupy the same place in her life now.

Eva and I met in Toronto. We really liked each other, and we became friends. She rapidly displaced all my other friends, and I think I displaced hers, in terms of becoming best friends. It wasn't a lifelong friendship—only five or six years—but it was the most intense friendship I've ever had. I don't really know what made it work so well. I think we had the same disposition in some way. She was very lively, very smart, energetic, and looking for adventure. We frolicked, and we talked endlessly on the phone.

All the years that I knew Eva, she was, at least on the surface, a happy person, certainly ebullient and vividly living life. But there was always a piece of her that couldn't find something to commit herself to. She didn't have a man she felt attached to, and she didn't have a career that she felt was definitely the right one for her. She had been valedictorian of her class and had won awards, but nothing was right. So it wasn't that she didn't succeed; it was that she didn't feel as if she had a niche.

We made the decision to come to Boston together. She was in graduate school, and I was teaching. We were both in psychology, but she was in "shrinky" psychology, and I'm in experimental psychology, so we didn't overlap at all. I was deeply entrenched in my work, and she was always doubtful that she believed anything she was learning or cared about it at all. That seemed to trouble her deeply. So that was the first wrinkle. And it was a wrinkle—I mean, it was hardly an enormous problem.

In Boston, she dated wildly. Men lined up at her door—tons of them, always. And finally she met a man, and she said, "For the first time in my life, I'm going to be monogamous," which was an enormous decision for her. She made that commitment, and the beginning of the end was when she discovered that he had been having an affair with another woman. That seemed to be the crisis that triggered a profound depression. It is likely that there was a depression before that, but it certainly wasn't obvious. She was totally crushed, above and beyond anything that can be imagined—not necessarily because this was going to be the man of her life, but because she had made the commitment and had trusted him. She had never trusted anybody in that sense, and now she'd been deceived.

At first she just seemed like a kid who had been ditched by a guy—she was kind of upset, except that she was a bit more than kind of upset. But nobody took it seriously. She was seeing a psychiatrist at the time. I began to take it seriously, but it was only when she started showing true signs of depression, like not eating, that I knew things were pretty serious. Then she began to use morose language, saying things like she wondered if she wished she were dead but not actually saying, "I'm going to kill myself."

One night while her parents were in town—she had a very bad relationship with them—she called me and sounded distraught. We always had a telepathic kind of relationship, and [when she called] I had an *overwhelming* feeling—there was nothing that led to it logically, even in retrospect—that she was suicidal and had the means to kill herself that night. It was her voice. There was something disembodied about her voice. A friend of mine had just come in from California. I said, "Look, I can't just walk out of the house right now, but I want you to come over." So she left her parents and took a taxi to my place.

She walked in the door, and I got a *horrible* feeling again. I grabbed her pocketbook and turned it upside down, and it was filled with pills. She was not a pill taker, and I hadn't thought that I was going to find pills. I just felt that there was something in her pocketbook. I said, "We're going to a hospital." I didn't know anything about what you are supposed to do with someone who is suicidal except that you take her to a psychiatrist. I figured I should take her to the hospital she lived near. I guess we got there at midnight or eleven o'clock.

She had been all dressed up to go out to dinner with her parents—beautiful white dress, high-heeled shoes. She looked like a real debutante. She was a very beautiful girl. And I was dressed like I wasn't expecting to do anything. I was very upset. She was cool as a cucumber, and I was crying. When the psychiatrist came, he didn't want to see her, he wanted to see me, because I was obviously the one who was crazy. I was upset and disheveled, and she was so calm. He simply wouldn't believe me. It was impossible for anyone, even her psychiatrist, to look at her and take [her depression] seriously. She had a persona that was very put together. And she was always lively, even in her depressed state. One of the ways I knew how depressed she was was that she used to scratch her head, and there were rivulets of scars on her head from the scratches, but they were under her hair, which was shiny and clean and wavy.

I finally convinced them that she was seriously suicidal, but at that point, they had no place to put her. The choice was a locked ward or letting her go. She had no intention of going into a locked ward, so the choice was to take her home. Now, she had walked out on her parents several hours earlier, and they knew it was likely that she would come to me. I said, "Look, I can't hide you in the closet. We're going to have to come to terms with this situation. I work full-time. I can't sit next to you twenty-four hours a day to make sure you don't do this. You need help, and you don't need your parents." So I took her home and just sat there and watched her until daylight. I didn't blink. I didn't know what to do, but I knew that this was not a good idea, that I couldn't do this. In the morning, her parents came to get her.

I spoke to her psychiatrist, I spoke to the hospital, I spoke to her parents. Time passed. I guess her parents stayed with her for a while in her apartment. She didn't pull anything else, but she still wasn't eating. I spoke to her all the time and visited her.

The big event in her life at the time was going to be graduation. She hadn't really completed her [course] requirements, but somehow they were going to graduate her anyway. What was critical about that was that the guy who had abandoned her was going to be at graduation. He was a classmate. This was a bigger-than-life event for her. She didn't want to be there, because he would be there and because she was so ashamed of not having finished her courses. She was extremely achievement-oriented and was very down on herself for not having done things perfectly. She was a star and had always been a star, and even though she was having these problems, she was still doing beautifully. Nothing was really falling apart—that's what made it very hard for people to believe.

I remember we went to see a film, *Picnic at Hanging Rock*. It was a good film, but it was really somewhat ambiguous. Some kids disappear, and my interpretation was that they had gotten lost. Her interpretation was that they had died or killed themselves. I have an image—and I rarely have images in my head like that—of walking out of the theater ahead of her slightly in the crowd and turning around and seeing a blank look, a totally empty look, and being frightened by it. It was about eleven at night, and we talked until seven in the morning. I tried very hard to figure it out, talk about it. And we talked a lot about suicide, why and what. . . I never felt that the why and what were adequate. Her why was just that she had no place in the world, that she wasn't really committed to anything. It was always around this issue of commitment, that nothing, no one, mattered much to her, and that she didn't matter much to anyone either. The hub of it was that she hadn't found her commitment. I mean, that's what she said.

I don't think Eva ever really felt love. That was the difference that she and I always had. I had a difficult relationship with my mother to some extent, but my father and I were very, very close. Eva envied my unequivocal feeling that I loved him and he loved me, that surety. She thought that was such a gift. I knew lots of people who were insecure about such things, but they didn't kill themselves. I think there was a very large organic component [of her depression]. In retrospect, Eva was frenetic in many ways. I tend to be very disorganized, so when I'm distressed, it really shows, and that probably limits it, because there is only so far you can fall apart before it just hangs out too far. Since Eva could cover it so well, nothing ever limited her disintegrating. No one really knew. I knew, but I suppose it was really just incomprehensible. That's the other piece of it—that I don't think I really knew all along.

Eva's mother was manic depressive, on lithium, and her sister was manic depressive, on lithium. Although no one would have looked at Eva and said that she was truly manic, she sure was lively, and she did swing [in her moods]. But she swung the way I swing, and I'm still here. I think that she was organically a depressive person and that something happened that really did it to her. If she'd been properly medicated, it probably would have been okay.

It seemed like this period [after the episode with the pills] took forever, but I suppose it happened over a couple of weeks. Graduation came, and I'm pretty sure she went to it. As a matter of fact, her parents took her out to dinner afterward, and she passed a plant shop and very abruptly left her parents, walked in, bought a little plant, and brought it over to my house, which I later interpreted as "Here's something to remember me by." I still have the plant.

So she graduated, and the question was where she would spend the summer and whether she would go to school in the fall. Her parents made the decision that she should go back with them to Montreal, where she came from. I talked to them at length. I said, "Look, your home is not a happy home, and it's been a long-term source of difficulty for her. All her support systems are here; her friends are here. There is nothing for her in Montreal, and you're not good medicine for her. You should really leave her in a setting where she has as much support as possible." But they said—and I guess it's understandable— "Who's going to take care of her?" Eva was not wanting to go home—I mean, feverishly not wanting to go with them. She was an adult, but she was also impotent.

She arrived at my department one day, I guess to escape her parents. They drove up at the door and said, "We're taking her." I stood in front of their car and said, "If you take her, you will be murderers." They pushed me away from the car and drove away with her. I hated these people. There was a kind of iron will that they had. I'm pretty strong-willed, but I knew that I wasn't going to win this one. I put everything into it, but I felt I couldn't win it. The other thing was that if I won it, how would I protect her?

She was in Montreal for two weeks, three weeks maybe, and then she died. This is very hard for me, because I lost control of the situation totally. She was under psychiatric care there, too. I talked to her a lot, and as they often say about these things, she sounded fine. She sounded very balanced. She had gotten a job. She'd done this, she'd done that, she'd been shopping.

The weekend that she died, I was supposed to visit her. I wanted to see it—seeing is believing. She called me on Thursday night and said something about an opportunity to have a special interview on that Saturday, so she simply couldn't keep the weekend free, but could we do it the next weekend? Apparently, that same night she called numbers of people—everyone who might possibly show up in her life—to make sure that they wouldn't be there.

Eva killed herself on Saturday morning in her parents' home. She used pills—and I feel guilty about this part especially. When I had seen all the pills from her pocketbook, I had said to her, "You're an ass. You know pills don't kill, they mutilate. Do you want to be a moron all your life? Do you want to be paralyzed? You can't take pills and kill yourself." So when she killed herself, she used an enormous number of pills and alcohol, which she never drank.

I didn't find out until Sunday night, because I was away for the weekend. I had gone to visit some friends in western Massachusetts. In retrospect, I have figured out that within five or ten minutes of the time when Eva killed herself, I was telling this friend of mine that she was getting better. I was sitting in her kitchen. I remember exactly where I was sitting. I told many people after that last phone call that she was better.

Her parents wanted me to go to the funeral, but I refused. I did not want to console them. I was furious and felt that they had contributed to it. I can be softer about it years later. I realize it was complicated—what were they supposed to do? But at the time it was black and white: they were wrong; they had gone totally against her will. I didn't want her family in my life.

[For me, Eva's] funeral was my public declaration to many, many people. I bled publicly. I just wore it. I guess I felt that made it real. At that time, the most profound feeling that I had was that my daddy wasn't there, and he was the only one who would have understood.

I did have a friend I had met at a party, and she came and slept over that first night. It was a remarkable thing for somebody I hardly knew, and I needed that. She was very good to me, and I've remained friends with her over the years. But the poor girl could never be the friend I'd lost. I think she battled under that pressure. She knew she could be a kindly, stalwart friend, but she couldn't be *the* friend. She was one of the people who helped me the most. She was a caretaker. She really wasn't intellectually or psychologically very helpful, but she held the fort, which was necessary. I was just terribly depressed. I tend to reach out, so I made a lot of phone calls and got people to take care of me. I was lucky that there were people. Although, you see, that's the irony—I really didn't have another best friend, and I still don't. So there were people but not people of the same closeness. What I felt was that the person I needed the most to comfort me was my best friend.

When Eva died, I don't remember ever really feeling what they tell you you're supposed to feel—that you've been abandoned and you're angry you've been abandoned. I did have anger toward her parents, which I've stubbornly held on to, although now I think I can see more of another side. Anger also came in response to situations. I think that I overreacted in other domains, wildly sometimes. I got angry at one person at work. It was trivial, but there was so much anger, it had to go somewhere, and she was a good repository for it.

I think the predominant feeling I've had is a tremendous feeling of missing Eva. I haven't felt guilt as much as overwhelming helplessness. I just couldn't help her, and I didn't have any control over the situation. I tried to have control in as many ways as I knew. Even in retrospect, I don't know that there were that many more things that I could have come up with. *That* was enraging, not her. I didn't have rage toward her. I had rage toward my ineptness, some of that, but mostly that things can happen that you can't control.

I had many of the same feelings when my father was dying

of cancer—overwhelming loss and hopelessness. I was tremendously angry when I found out that he was going to die. Why me? Why him? I held on to that anger for a long time. He was supposed to die in six months, but he lived for five years, most of which were good. I started mourning when I was eighteen and had it constantly in my consciousness until I was twenty-two. The problem was that he had a brother who had died from cancer, and my father had said that if he knew he had cancer, he would rather kill himself than put his family through what his brother had been through. So we lied to him for five years. And that was impossible for me. I've always been a really open person, and I was very, very, very close to my father. I look back at it and think, "You should never lie." But the fact is when my mother finally told him, because things were starting to change, he became so depressed that it was downhill fast. He may have known all along, but he sure didn't act like he did. But my father and I had six months, at the end, of open discussion, so that got resolved.

There was one feeling I had about Eva's suicide that was different from my feelings about my father's death. I felt that her suicide revealed that our friendship hadn't been adequate for her. Had it been adequate, it might have provided that niche that she needed. Now I know that she might not have been able to have an adequate relationship. With my father, I always felt that he died satisfied with us. Very different.

The day my father died, I took all his clothing, ran laundries through the night, packed it all up, and put it out on the street. My mother was all upset, because [in the Jewish religion] you're supposed to sit shiva; you're not supposed to do anything. I wanted everything out. I didn't want to see a sock of his. I didn't want to be reminded that my father had died.

When Eva died, I surrounded myself with her stuff. I don't know why I wanted her around so much. Her parents asked me to dispose of the contents of her apartment. Most of the time, I went there alone, sometimes with a friend. When I took over her apartment—"took over" is probably a funny way to phrase it—I really looked around. I wanted clues as much as anything else. And one of the things I found, which I've held on to, is a diary, although it wasn't very helpful. [The entries stopped] well before the suicide, months before, so in the throes of the deepest depression, she didn't bother with the thing. But it did show the initial part, and much of what I know comes from there, even though she'd expressed it to me as well.

Most of her things we gave to Goodwill. Some of her clothing I took and wore. I never had any funny feelings wearing her clothes. I just felt like that's what we would have done—I always got her hand-me-downs. I still wear some of her clothing. I don't know what that is. Maybe it's attachment in some form. I don't know.

Eva and I really admired each other a lot, although we didn't necessarily admire ourselves. So we each wanted to be very much like the other one. She once said to me, "I can't live with your superego." She thought I was judgmental, that I had this very strict line of right and wrong, that I was too severe. But the flip side was that she felt I had a very clear set of values and knew what I thought was right and wrong, and she didn't feel like she knew that. She was this enormously in-control individual, and I very much wanted that. So I'm sure there was some identification going on, wearing her clothes. Some people said, "That's weird," but no one told me outright I shouldn't do it. If they had, I would have said, "But look at the good fabric."

I often thought there was just the slightest element of flirtation in our relationship. There was nothing overt at all, but just a shimmer or a glimmer of sexuality. Eva was such an extraordinarily sexual person, and at that time so was I, and it was in the air. But it was totally subliminal. So in a sense, there was a piece of it that was almost like a love relationship—not a major piece, but something like that. I never really thought of her as a sister. She wasn't a sister.

The irony is that she wasn't a good friend. She was fairly inconsiderate. She was so dramatic and interesting and exciting and everything else that I forgave it—very easily, fifteen times more easily than for anybody else—but she was very disappointing. She would make appointments and not show up. She did funny things, like throw a party and decide the ambience didn't quite fit for me to be there. Peculiar. It wasn't only with me. She would tell me all these things that she was cavalierly doing to other people. I would say, "Bad, bad girl, not good girl, bad girl," and she didn't want to hear it. That was a piece I never integrated into my feelings about her. I always said, "Oh, she's rebellious, that's her way." There are people who are that way, and there's nothing else. But she was definitely there for people when they needed her.

I have several images of Eva in my mind. Some of them aren't great, because I don't have a good memory for faces, so I have mostly images of the end rather than earlier, which is too bad. What I basically remember, when I think of her, is three images. I have an image of a disembodied face, which haunts me. It doesn't haunt me on a regular basis, but it used to. And then I have an image of a packaged, attractive, quasi-debutante, someone I would never have known if there hadn't been the third image, basically a very down-to-earth, ebullient, warm lady. I have all those images, all those sides, when I think of her.

You know, if you had asked me all this five years ago, it would have been so different from now. The first difference is me and my husband. He's just 100 percent best friend, and he's the only person who came close to replacing Eva, so that helped. And the baby makes a big difference also. So I feel like only for the last little while have I really begun to heal from Eva's suicide.

I still wish I had a woman friend, but I don't feel friendless, whereas prior to meeting my husband, I really felt friendless. I had friends from before and people I was meeting, but I felt friendless. Now I still feel that loneliness for a woman, but I don't feel the vulnerability anymore. I'm sure it has something to do with the baby. The commitment I have to work is strong, but it wouldn't carry me through a lifetime, and the commitment I have to my husband is powerful, but it's . . . effortful. I mean, I think any marriage takes some effort. But there's simply no question that I have this utter commitment to the baby, and I guess I feel protected from ever falling to Eva's fate. Not that I've thought of doing what she did, but I suppose to the extent that I identified with her . . . It was never really explicit. But I feel that now I'm really immune. It's peculiar. My reaction to complexity and frustration is to say, "Let's run, run, run," but actually, I never run. Maybe it's a feeling that in some convoluted sense I'm normal after all, so I don't have to worry about suicidal feelings sneaking up on me. I feel they snuck up on her.

I still burst into tears sometimes, talking about my father, whereas with Eva, I stopped crying probably about five years ago. I put them both in a bag now, and I cry for them both. I don't think she gets her own time anymore. He always hops in. It's for both of them.

*

Epilogue: Finding a Place for the Words

What is life like five, ten, fifteen years later? Is the grief finished, the pain left behind? What place does the suicide come to occupy in the survivor's life? The stories that survivors tell about then and now speak to these questions. The answers are as singular and, at the same time, as concordant as individual experiences of loss and life in its wake.

One of the differences between then and now is acceptance. Having struggled to understand the dimensions of loss in their lives, the survivors who tell their stories in this section have moved beyond that struggle. They are no longer driven to know why or how or why not—all the invading questions that are the language of grief earlier on. The healing has come in being able, gradually, to let go of those questions and the search for their answers. In relinquishing that search, people find that they can— more important, that they want to—go on with their own lives. And for this reason, the stories here are largely about moving on and following new paths.

Moving On

These stories tell of life and change much more than of loss, yet the experience of loss then has everything to do with life now. Adulthood, marriage, and parenthood have marked the transition between then and now in several of the stories. Karen was a child when her father died; she is a woman now. Joy was on the verge of adulthood and is now in her thirties. Laura is preparing for her second marriage. Several other people have married and had children. The transition has also been marked by changes in work. Philip's first novel is about to be published. Joy, in school when she told the first part of her story (in chapter 3), is now a nurse administrator. Laura has changed careers and is working in a substance abuse program. Susan has finished her graduate studies and is a clinical psychologist.

Such changes in themselves are certainly not unusual; they reflect the movement of lives as people pursue new directions in relationships, families, and work. Yet the stories in this chapter suggest that the experience of loss gives an extra dimension to the meaning of life transitions for the survivors. As Susan planned her wedding and later prepared for the birth of her child, decisions about names—choosing them, speaking them—tapped a mixture of feelings about her father. It was important to her that his name be spoken at her wedding and his absence noted as a way of honoring him and his memory. The choice of changing or keeping her own last name—her father's name—took on special significance because of her past struggles with her father. Earlier, she would have wanted to change her name, but now the sense of connection that it embodies has become more important to her: "I don't think I need to distance myself from my father's side of the family in the way that I once thought I would want to." Yet she did not want her child, a boy, to be named after her father: "I kept my maiden name, and that link to my father was important to me, but my ambivalence was such that I wouldn't have wanted [my father's first name] to be that prominent [a part of my life]." Susan's ambivalence is shared by many survivors; it reflects a need to embrace and at the same time contain the experience of their loss. Suicide becomes an important part of one's own life story, but having embraced it, one can decide how and in what measure it will be passed along to one's children. It is important to Susan that her son know about his grandfather, including his suicide, but it is equally important to her that the burden of pain she has felt not be passed along to her son.

For Natalie, the decision to become a mother hinged on a depth of commitment that she might not even have contemplated had her own mother not killed herself: "I decided that if I chose to become a mother, I would be making a decision never to kill myself. . . . However bad it might get for me, I could never do that to a child, even an adult child. . . . It's a huge commitment, a commitment to life. In the end, that's the commitment I wanted to make anyway, but I had to think it through."

When she was in nursing school, Joy talked of becoming a midwife. Now she hopes to have a child of her own. Married for several years and closer to her mother's age when she died, Joy now sees her mother's conflicts about being a parent and a writer in a larger context: "She was trying to manage life with children and with continued mental problems. But she was writing, and she was becoming famous. There was this whole side of her life that, being so young, I didn't see." Joy and Natalie, both the daughters of mothers who succumbed to suicide, approach motherhood with a profound sense of their own commitment to life.

Another important change in Joy's life has been the loss of her grandmother, who in many ways gave her the mothering that her own mother could not. As hard as it was to lose her grandmother, the loss gave Joy an opportunity she had never had with her mother:

> The worst thing about [my mother's] suicide was not being able to say good-bye and not being able to say thank you. I had some mixed baggage with my mother; I'm not sure how many thank yous there were. But with my grandmother, there were a lot of thank yous due. . . . I sat on her bed and thanked her and said, "I just want you to know that without you I wouldn't be here. And a lot of what I've become is due to the unconditional love that you gave me." Not having been able to say good-bye to my mother, I realized how important it was to do that. So as a result, as much as my grandmother's death was incredibly sad and painful, it felt clean in a way that my mother's death did not.

Two changes in Rachel's life have made all the difference between then and now: her marriage and her child. Her husband has become her best friend (". . .he's the only person who came close to replacing Eva"), and her experience of motherhood has sharpened the outlines of her commitment to life, both her child's and her own:

> . . . there's simply no question that I have this utter commitment to the baby, and I guess I feel protected from ever falling to [Eva's] fate. Not that I've ever thought of doing what she did, but I suppose to the extent that I identified with her. . . . It's peculiar. My reaction to complexity and frustration is to say, "Let's run, run, run," but actually, I never run. Maybe it's a feeling that in some convoluted sense I'm normal after all, so I don't have to worry about suicidal feelings sneaking up on me. I feel as if they snuck up on her.

Other transitions in these stories that have been important revolve around work. Making a change in her career was a watershed for Laura: "[Career counseling] got me reengaged in the process of thinking about my future and what I wanted for myself. . . . It brought me back to an original passion that I had had." Her work in a substance abuse treatment program reflects the healing that she has experienced since her husband's suicide: "I work with people who look, on the outside, like they're trying to kill themselves. I don't think that's what they're trying to do. I think they're trying to survive. . . . The job has been very important to me in terms of not taking responsibility for other people's lives and letting people make their own decisions."

The death of his father meant an abrupt change in Philip's work, as he suddenly found himself taking over his father's business interests. It was work that he neither chose for himself nor particularly liked, but he felt he had to do it. Eventually he was able to return more fully to his own work as a writer. He has since completed his first novel and is now thinking about writing the next one: "I want to write a novel that's much more autobiographical [than my first one], more like a typical first novel, and the suicide would be the very center of the book. I don't know if it would be on the first page. It might be. Maybe the whole book takes place the night of the suicide. I don't know." His passage through the aftermath of his father's suicide has brought him to a point where he can now contemplate writing his own story.

Underlying the transitions in work and family that are related in many of these stories is a clarity about choices in life that comes from a sharpened awareness that life itself is a choice. As Philip points out, that awareness can make one more rather than less life affirming, and many people feel a sense of renewal as they make decisions about what they want to do and how they want to live.

The changes described in these stories both reflect and contribute to the healing that survivors have experienced. As their lives have evolved over the years, their experience of loss has taken on different hues. Susan, for example, began to feel her father's absence in a new way when she married and became a mother, and Joy sees her mother's conflicts from the broader perspective that her own adulthood has given her. Yet the pain of the loss does not disappear. It is more intense for some than for others, but it remains, to some degree, in all these stories, however transformed by time and change.

For both Natalie and Laura, an important difference between then and now is the sense that now they have a measure of control over the intensity of the pain and they can permit themselves *not* to feel it much of the time. Then, there was no choice; the pain of the loss flooded life. Now, there is more of a choice, a greater sense of control in their lives. As Natalie puts it, ". . .as much as it's okay to feel the pain of it all or to think about it—and I do at times—you have to distance yourself in a certain way to be able to go on." Laura describes her need for distance as "self-care": "There was a time when it was almost like having a sore place in your mouth, and you've just got to keep running your tongue over it, over and over and over. I don't do that anymore. . . . I need to get through what I'm doing now. I don't need to stop and be flooded with pain." As much as survivors need to be open to their grief and to give it full voice if they are to heal from their loss, eventually they must move on from their grief so that they can continue to grow in their lives. Paradoxically, the very freedom to distance oneself from the pain now comes from having given it full voice earlier.

Looking Back

Years later, what is it like to visit the grave? How do anniversaries of the suicide change with the years? What happens to memories and perspectives over time?

Remembering his father now is a "mixed bag" for Philip. He has visited his father's grave twice in seven years, and each time the experience has evoked more negative than positive feelings. Even the inscription on the headstone ("He loved his children") strikes a painfully ironic note for the son who felt he had to be his father's parent when he himself was not yet an adult: "When I was sixteen, sitting on this couch, and he said, 'I've thought of the various ways to kill myself,' probably at *that* moment, at that exact moment, I became his parent." Only now, looking back over time, does Philip appreciate the magnitude of the burden he shouldered, knowing that his father intended to kill himself: "I think it was an enormous burden, an extraordinary burden, and probably affected me in some fairly pernicious or subtle ways that I'm dealing with now."

Susan is glad that she didn't know what her brother knew:

Maybe I could have [known]. Maybe I didn't want to know, because I probably would have intervened. And I'm not sure that would have been for the better at all. From hindsight, who knows? I'm really glad I wasn't in my brother's shoes, but I don't think my dad would have chosen me to be, and I don't know if I would have let myself be. It's a really awful position to be in, and I feel bad that my brother was put in that position. And yet he was much closer to my dad than I was.

Like her brother, Susan has visited the cemetery infrequently over the years. She is rueful as she tells of her difficulty finding the grave on her first visit: "I laughed at myself, because I knew exactly what was going on as I was looking for the gravesite. I said to myself, 'I couldn't really connect with my father in life, and here he's dead and I still can't do it!' " During these visits Susan has felt more sadness than anger, ". . . sadness not for his death or how he died but for our troubled relationship, his life and my life." Both Susan and Philip feel that their father's decision to kill himself was a rational one in the context of his severe, long-standing struggle with MS. And for both of them, this perspective has made it easier to accept his suicide.

Anniversaries also change with the years. They come to mean different things to different people, according to where they are in their lives and how the loss has changed for them. The first anniversary of her husband's suicide was not at all what Laura had anticipated, as she found herself falling in love with the man whom she will soon marry. It was at the time of the second anniversary that she made an important first step in the process of letting go of her sense of responsibility for Stuart's suicide. She began to realize how small her role in her husband's death had been:

Here I was being so central in Stuart's life and blaming myself and feeling guilty, staying connected to him through my guilt. That first year I was so depressed and immobilized in my life, feeling that I hadn't done enough and I should have known. And what Robert said helped. It was a bitter pill, but it helped when he said, "You weren't so central to Stuart. You were a bystander in his life." I had seen it through *my* lens. It can be a real gift if you can let that in and make sense of it.

On the fourth anniversary of her husband's suicide, Laura enacted a small ritual of observance that was another step in letting go, as she cast some of Stuart's belongings into the ocean. When the fifth anniversary arrives, she will be preparing for her wedding. Although the successive anniversaries of her husband's suicide have not been sequential markers of her grief and healing, Laura has learned that she needs to make room for her experience of loss as it evolves and is transformed by her changing life: ". . . I need to carve out some time to have my feelings about Stuart, because I have a way of not letting myself do that and then paying the price later—it comes up at unexpected times."

For Joy, the tenth and subsequent anniversaries of her mother's suicide have been times for taking stock of her own life, where it was when her mother died and where it has gone since then:

> I've done so much personal growing and professional growing . . . that I wish she could have been around for. I guess in that way, it feels more just like a death than like a suicide. I think you'd feel that way about anybody who dies—missing her and saying, "Look at the parts of my life that she's missed." The other side of it for suicide is, "But in some way, shape, or fashion, she chose not to be here for that growth, for those changes."

Joy's nephew was born on the tenth anniversary of her mother's death, which has altered the meaning of that date for her. Now it is not only a time to remember a lost life but also a time to celebrate another year of a new life.

Many survivors, like Joy, find that the anniversary of the suicide becomes less charged and potent with time, but it may still be a painful reminder of loss. The anniversary of her father's death each April is a difficult time for Karen, marking a series of losses in her childhood: "If my father hadn't killed himself, or if he had killed himself and we had stayed in Denmark and things had been processed differently, I wouldn't have lost so many connections." In more recent years, she has thought about making Denmark her home once again, but she is ambivalent about going back, giving up the connections and the place she has found for herself in the United States: "I still miss Denmark, and I still really like it there. But I think it becomes almost unbearable to be in conflict all the time. You just have to choose one place."

Natalie tells of revisiting her childhood home several years after her mother's death, and bringing her husband and son with her: "Going back to that house was sad; it felt like a completion. . . . There's a way in which I long for people who knew my life as it was when my family was intact. . . . some documentation of things before they fell apart. . . ." Like Susan, who brought her husband to her father's grave, and Joy, who wishes that her husband could have known her mother, Natalie was seeking a sense of continuity between her old family connections and her new ones. As different as life now is from life then, now has its roots in then, and many survivors, as they move on, feel the need to show those roots to the people who have become an important part of their more recent lives. It is a way of saying to those people and reminding themselves, "This is where I came from; this is the road I traveled to arrive where I am now, with you."

The Imprints of Suicide

What does suicide mean for the survivors years later? How have they changed in its wake? The experience leaves many people with a sharper sense of their own vulnerability to loss, as well as the knowledge that they have the strength to endure it. Philip feels that his father's suicide has made him "even more life affirming," although he's not sure whether this change is linked to the death of his father or to the manner of that death. But he also recognizes subtle interior changes that are directly linked to his experience of the suicide. He gives an example:

I'm very sensitive when people think I haven't done enough. . . . probably oversensitive, in part because I never could do enough [for my father], could I? And he still died. What I'm saying is, 1 percent of that reaction—or 5 percent, 10 percent, who knows—I think is stimulated by the suicide.

Her mother's abrupt departure has made Natalie acutely sensitive to the unfinished business that is a part, however large or small, of most intimate connections:

> It's taken a lot of willpower to allow myself to go through the downside in a relationship and not try to rush it, just stay with it rather than try to make it all better. It takes a lot on my part to realize that most people don't die the way my mother did. I don't have to worry every time I say good-bye to someone that I'll never see that person again.

Natalie, Philip, and Karen all talk about feeling marked in some way by suicide. Both Natalie and Philip experience it as a "loss of innocence." For Natalie, that means the realization of how powerless one is to keep someone else alive or to protect oneself from loss: "Until you bump your nose right up against it, you just don't *know*! . . . My mother's suicide made my vision of the world open up. I got to see how big the world actually is and how much of it I don't understand." Yet the loss of innocence can bring gains as well: "I have a certain contentment now that I never had back then. I see things more realistically. It's interesting to think of having less anguish now, after my mother's suicide, than before."

Philip feels that his father's suicide has left a kind of "taint":

> It's not to say that I have it on my mind all the time and not to say that, staring at Mount Everest in the moonlight, which I did a couple of years ago, I couldn't feel incredibly exhilarated. It was no less of an experience because my father killed himself. It's just that it creates a certain baseline that the rest of your life takes off from, and the baseline might be a bit lower than it would ordinarily be or more difficult, or you might be a bit more sticky with the past as you go about leaping away from it.

Describing a difficult period in his life when he became very depressed, Philip points out both the vulnerability and the opportunity for someone who has survived the suicide of a family member: "I said to a couple of people, 'You know, the lesson for someone whose father's committed suicide is take it seriously when you start feeling so bad.'"

Karen struggles against her feeling of being marked by her father's suicide: "I . . . call it the black hole that he left, this little girl with a black hole in her. . . . I think part of getting angry is being able to say, 'Fuck off! This is my body. I am not a victim! I'm not going to be your black hole.' " Yet Karen feels that her pain has given her a "peculiar gift" in teaching her that she has the interior strength to bear enormous loss. She has also learned to be more gentle with herself: "Now there's a part of me that can soothe the hurt I feel and just say, 'We'll get you through this. I'll take care of you.' Before, I think it used to be, 'Shut up. Stop whining. I can't stand it when you cry. Go away.' I think that harshness has changed."

Underlying Karen's story, like Philip's, is an awareness that her father's suicide has somehow become a part of her identity, making it all the more important for her to claim her own separate, different life, which she does not intend to fall prey to the "black hole" that brought an end to her father's life.

To Survive and Prosper

In the early aftermath of suicide, the stories survivors tell are of lost lives and lost connections. Many people feel compelled to tell and retell their stories—to put words to their loss and to speak those words out loud, over and over. With time, as people find their way through their grief, the need to tell subsides, and the stories of lost lives find their place within larger stories of lives that have survived loss. Reflecting this transition, the stories in chapter 2 are primarily biographical, telling of lives that ended in suicide, and those in chapter 3 are about the struggle to find a bridge between loss and life. Here, finally, all the stories are fully autobiographical. They tell of lives that have grown larger and stronger for having survived a loss that throws into question the very underpinnings of one's own life and links with others.

At the beginning of this book, I quoted *Webster's* definition of *survive*, which is to "continue to function" and also, perhaps, to "prosper." The stories in this final chapter hold out the promise that life in the wake of suicide can be much more than simply a matter of functioning. As people find words and listeners for their grief, they move through it and gradually come to lead whole lives again. The "peculiar gift" of the journey is the knowledge that in one's very vulnerability to loss lies the strength to survive it and prosper.

Is it ever finished? Probably not. We cannot leave our losses behind; they stay within us, growing into our lives. But eventually *we* carry *them*—they no longer carry us. As time, like the tide, smoothes their contours, we find a smaller, more comfortable place for them. Looking back, we can recognize the sea changes between then and now.

And the fire and the rose are one.
                    —T.S. Eliot, "Little Gidding"

Resources for Survivors
of Suicide

American Association of Suicidology
4201 Connecticut Avenue NW, Suite 310
Washington, DC 20008
(202) 237-2280

Founded in 1968 by Edwin Shneidman, the American Association of Suicidology seeks to understand and prevent suicide through research, public awareness, and education and training for mental health professionals and volunteers. The association includes many survivors among its members and offers the following resources:

- National directory of support groups for survivors, updated annually
- Newsletter, *Surviving Suicide*
- Annual conference for survivors of suicide
- Variety of activities in connection with the association's annual meeting (a preconference seminar for survivors, as well as workshops, panels, papers, and support groups)
- List of books and pamphlets on the aftermath of suicide

American Foundation for Suicide Prevention
120 Wall Street, 22nd floor
New York, NY 10005
(212) 363-3500
(888) 333-AFSP (for information on support groups)

The American Suicide Foundation works to prevent suicide through research and education, raising funds for research grants and sponsoring educational conferences and programs for survivors. From its inception in 1987, the foundation has been attuned to the role of survivors in its mission and also to their needs. Among the resources it offers survivors are the following:

- Support group referrals
- Training for leaders of support groups
- Newsletter
- National and regional conferences

The Compassionate Friends
TCF National Office
P.O. Box 3696
Oak Brook, IL 60522-3696
(630) 990-0010

The Compassionate Friends is an organization of parents whose children have died, whether from an illness, an accident, homicide, or suicide. Founded on a philosophy of mutual self-help, The Compassionate Friends offers bereaved parents and siblings friendship, understanding, education, and hope for the future. Approximately 600 local chapters hold regular meetings, publish newsletters, and maintain telephone support networks.

Friends of Survival, Inc.
P.O. Box 214463
Sacramento, CA 95821
(916) 392-0664
(800) 646-7322 (suicide loss help line)

Friends of Survival is a national outreach program for survivors of suicide that offers a range of services, including the suicide loss help line, a monthly newsletter, referrals, and conferences and retreats, as well as a program of community education about suicide.

The International THEOS Foundation
322 Boulevard of the Allies, Suite 105
Pittsburgh, PA 15222
(412) 471-7779

The THEOS Foundation helps widows and widowers cope with their grief. With more than one hundred chapters in the United States and Canada, THEOS sponsors self-help groups and an annual conference on bereavement. The organization also offers members an eight-month subscription to a magazine titled *The Survivor's Outreach* for $24.

Children's Grief Support Network
The Dougy Center
P.O. Box 86852
Portland, OR 97296
(503) 775-5683

Sponsored by The Dougy Center, the Children's Grief Support Network runs groups for bereaved children between the ages of three and eighteen. The network encompasses approximately sixty-eight centers throughout the United States and Canada that offer support groups led by mental health professionals and lay people, all trained at The Dougy Center. Some of the centers have formed separate groups for children whose parents have died by suicide. The Dougy Center also offers a range of publications dealing with children's grief, including *Helping Children and Teens After a Suicide* (available from the Dougy Center for $9.95).

Selected Bibliography

On the Aftermath of Suicide

Bolton, Iris. *My Son . . . My Son . . . A Guide to Healing After a Suicide in the Family*. Atlanta: Bolton Press, 1985. (Write to Bolton Press, 1325 Belmore Way N.E., Atlanta, GA 30338.)

Dunne, Edward, John McIntosh, and Karen Dunne-Maxim. *Suicide and Its Aftermath: Understanding and Counseling the Survivors*. New York: W.W. Norton, 1987.

Fine, Carla. *No Time to Say Goodbye: Surviving the Suicide of a Loved One*. New York: Doubleday, 1997.

Grollman, Earl A. *Suicide: Prevention, Intervention, Postvention*. Boston: Beacon Press, 1988.

Hewitt, John. *After Suicide*. New York: Westminster Press, 1980.

Lukas, Christopher, and Henry Seiden. *Silent Grief*. New York: Charles Scribner's Sons, 1988.

Rosenfeld, Linda, and Marilynne Prupas. *Left Alive After a Suicide Death in the Family*. Springfield, Ill.: Charles C. Thomas, 1984.

On Grief in General
and Survival After Other Losses

Epstein, Helen. *Children of the Holocaust*. New York: Bantam Books, 1981.

Grollman, Earl A. *Explaining Death to Children*. Boston: Beacon Press, 1967.

Kaplan, Barbara. "A Survivor's Story," *The Boston Globe Magazine*, March 6, 1983.

Kushner, Harold S. *When Bad Things Happen to Good People*. New York: Schocken Books, 1981.

Lewis, C.S. *A Grief Observed*. New York: Bantam Books, 1980.

On Suicide

Alvarez, A. *The Savage God: A Study of Suicide*. New York: Penguin Books, 1979.

Colt, George Howe. *The Enigma of Suicide*. New York: Summit Books, 1991.

Grollman, Earl A. *Suicide: Prevention, Intervention, Postvention*. Boston: Beacon Press, 1988.

Hendin, Herbert. *Suicide in America*. New York: W.W. Norton, 1982.

Mack, John E., and Holly Hickler. *Vivienne: The Life and Suicide of an Adolescent Girl*. New York: Mentor Books, 1981.

Styron, William. *Darkness Visible*. New York: Random House, 1990.

About the
Author

Victoria Alexander is cofounder of the organization After Suicide, which offers short-term support groups, consultation, and counseling for survivors. A member of the American Association of Suicidology, Alexander is the author of "Living Through My Mother's Suicide," in *Suicide and Its Aftermath: Understanding and Counseling the Survivors*. Formerly the editorial director at the Massachusetts Mental Health Center in Boston, Alexander is currently on the staff of the *New England Journal of Medicine*. She lives in Brookline, Massachusetts.